Teaching Exceptional Children and Youth
in the Regular Classroom

Teaching Exceptional Children and Youth in the Regular Classroom

TERRY CICCHELLI
CLAIRE ASHBY-DAVIS

SYRACUSE UNIVERSITY PRESS
1986

Terry Cicchelli is Assistant Professor of Education and Director of Elementary Pre-Service Programs at the Fordham Graduate School of Education, New York. She received her Ph.D. from Syracuse University in 1979. Claire Ashby-Davis is Associate Professor of Education and Director of Teacher Education Special Programs, Fordham Graduate School of Education. She received her Ph.D. from Fordham University in 1973. With the United Federation of Teachers and the New York City Board of Education, the authors were the recipients in 1982 of the Association of Teacher Educators award for a distinguished program in teacher education, for the pilot program which led to the present book.

The paper used in this publication meets the minimum requirements of American National Standard for Information Sciences—Permanence of Paper for Printed Library Materials, ANSI Z39.48-1984. ∞

Library of Congress Cataloging-in-Publication Data

Cicchelli, Terry.
    Teaching exceptional children and youth in the regular classroom.

    Bibliography: p.
    Includes index.
    1. Exceptional children—Education—United States.
2. Mainstreaming in education—United States.
I. Ashby-Davis, Claire. II. Title.
LC3981.C53 1986   371.96'0973   85-22210
ISBN 0-8156-2341-0
ISBN 0-8156-2342-9 (pbk.)

Manufactured in the United States of America

CONTENTS

LIST OF TABLES

LIST OF CHARTS

LIST OF FIGURES

FOREWORD

INNOVATION IN EDUCATION is often an evolutionary process. Legislative and judicial mandates, at times, place great pressures on that process. The Education for All Handicapped Children Act (PL 94–142) exemplifies the challenge of revolutionary change on an evolutionary system.

The following text is a result of a dynamic effort on the part of educators in response to the least restrictive environment mandate of PL 94–142. This response is based on the appropriateness of that issue, and as such is an endeavor to be in compliance with the spirit of the law that educational opportunity in the least restrictive, most appropriate environment is a human right. The goal of these efforts is to enhance the educational system so that eventually this issue will not be an issue.

In the fall of 1980, the directors of the United Federation of Teachers Mainstreaming Training Project met with the authors of this text at the Fordham University School of Education to discuss possible liaison activities. The goals of these activities would be influenced by their mutual concern for fulfilling the mandates of PL 94–142 in terms of the training of both preservice and inservice educators. To determine the specific goals of this liaison, both groups first conducted independent needs assessments and a pilot project. The staff of the Mainstreaming Training Project made an intensive analysis of a survey of the needs of New York City teachers conducted by the New York City Teacher Center Consortium. One of the major concerns of New York City teachers was found to be training in mainstreaming. They expressed a need for graduate and inservice courses in this area. Further, the staff of the Mainstreaming Training Project made an indepth search of the research literature in mainstreaming and in training teachers in knowledge, skills, attitudes, and habits to meet the needs of mainstreamed students. At Fordham, the authors developed a pilot project with preservice elementary and secondary school teachers preparing to teach in regular classes. This pilot project was unique in that it was planned by both the faculty of the Division of Curriculum and Teaching and the faculty of the Division of Psychological and Educational Services, especially those from the Unit on Special Education. A pre- and post-questionnaire instrument was given the student teachers. The treatment was a module in mainstreaming taught by five faculty members representing both regular and special education and evaluated by nine faculty members from both divisions.

The directors of the Mainstreaming Training Project and the authors of this text brought together their findings. A graduate course of study was designed which incorporated the issues identified by both groups. This course, Exceptional Children and Youth in the Regular Classroom, is taught by the staff of the Mainstreaming Training Project, the authors, and other Fordham faculty members.

Each term, in each section of the course, the instructors gather additional data through check list assessments which identify the perceived needs of that particular section of learners. The focus of course content thus varies for each section. This difference is to be expected. The principle of meeting individual student differences is the essence of PL 94–142. Its application to educators is equally appropriate.

The user of this text will gain or confirm an understanding of the practical application of educational strategies founded in theory and research which enhance classroom practices in educating the exceptional student in the least restrictive environment.

Mainstreaming Training Project   Howard Gollub
New York City Teacher Centers Consortium   *Director*
Spring 1985

PREFACE

Teachers who have or are about to welcome exceptional students into their classrooms without needed staff development are hampered in making this experience successful for themselves and their students. Working with more than 600 teachers since 1980 who were experiencing a change-over to a mainstreamed classroom, we gathered data on the needs of teachers in this special circumstance. The purpose of the needs assessments was to guide us in our selection of content and text organization for a book that would be a concise, highly concentrated resource for primarily busy teachers as they seek to develop their knowledge, skills, and attitudes in relation to mainstreaming. This text consists of a series of modules devised to meet the needs most frequently expressed by teachers in our sample. We hope the selected modules will help educators throughout the nation with similar experiences.

Analysis of the needs assessment data showed that the major areas of teacher concern were: their new role and responsibility in working alone as well as with interdisciplinary teams in understanding the nature of their performance and accountability in terms of federal, state, and local mandates and guidelines; the identification of exceptional students in the regular classroom with appropriate follow-up referrals; the structure and process of writing the Individualized Educational Program (IEP); the implementation of the IEP; the identification of several new ways of managing the classroom to improve education for students from widely different backgrounds including bilingual students; the development of new or modified instructional management strategies; and the identification of ways to bring about positive attitudes toward the exceptional person in mainstreamed classes, schools, and districts.

These identifications allowed us to synthesize related principles that support mainstreaming practices within the context of how an interdisciplinary team may share knowledge and coalesce into a "system" that becomes a decision-making resource relative to educating exceptional students in the regular class-room.

The modules that follow have been used and continually modified in graduate, preservice and inservice education courses, both at the university and on-site locations in the schools. They are presented in *minimum competency form.* This is to say, busy educators are offered basic introductory learnings with allusions to books, periodicals, resources and instructional materials for further research and use. Each module consists of one or more competency objectives, presented in terms of teacher behaviors; a rationale for the selection of the objective drawn from the needs assessments completed by the educators who have used the text; a series of enabling activities for achieving the stated objectives; one or more evaluation activities; enrichment activities; and a section called implications/applications.

Each implication/application section provides a variety of ways to put into operation the skills and knowledge gained from the module relative to the teaching of children and the working of an "interdisciplinary team." As far as possible, we wrote each module as a self-contained entity. This means that each module contains all the basic information to meet its stated objectives without necessarily having to refer to other modules. The purpose of this organizational feature is to enable the educator, workshop or institute leader, or the professor who will use the text to sequence instruction according to the stated needs of the group rather than the sequence of the text.

The text also includes a special bibliography which is keyed to the topics covered in the body of the work; a listing of selected resources and periodicals helpful to students, parents, teachers, support personnel and administrators; a selected listing of instructional materials; and a reference list of books and periodicals which show how art-related instruction may be used profitably in main-streaming.

We have found that the book can be used as either the major or supplemental text in graduate, preservice, or inservice education courses. Here it lends itself to various group dynamics approaches, with special emphasis on learning in small groups, pairs, or through individualized instruction. Thus, the educator participants have a chance to practice some of the classroom management strategies suggested in the text. The text can also be used by educators who are not attending formal courses. Since it is addressed directly to them, they may work alone or discuss questions and issues raised in less formal small groups that occur naturally at school.

Experience has shown that the best use of the book occurs when regular educators, special educators, and typical interdisciplinary team members are participants in a course, workshop, or institute. This fairly new interaction of these team members as they investigate together the dimensions of mainstreaming serves as a model for the successful collaboration which must accompany the process of referral, the writing and implementation of the IEP, and other processes needed for the better education of exceptional students. Growth in positive affect seems to occur as the course proceeds and then spills over into the real school setting.

One of the major foci of the modules is a challenge to educators to conduct self examinations of their attitudes and values in relation to exceptional students and their education. This private but continuing evaluation has enabled a number of them to change from stereotypical thinking to a more flexible response to mainstreaming.

Finally, educators have told us that after the course is ended they use the text as a handy desk-side compendium of knowledge and as a quick reference source to the variety of topics implied in mainstreaming.

ACKNOWLEDGMENTS

THE IDEAS, TECHNIQUES, AND ACTIVITIES presented in this text grew to their present form over a period of three years. The authors wish to thank the staff of the United Federation of Teachers Mainstreaming Project whose input in devising the course for which this text was originally intended, and whose collaborative input as adjuncts in the teaching of the numerous sections of the course, have been and continue to be a source of enthusiasm and encouragement.

First, we extend our thanks to Geraldine Flaherty and Howard Gollub, the original directors of the Mainstreaming Training Project, who gave us their dedicated support from the beginning. To the first field staff of the Mainstreaming Project — Myra Brahms, Frances Colletti, Joy Collins, Moses Dixon, Anthony Gallo, Harold Golubtchik, Joan Graburn, Rita Hirsch, Arnold Levine, Elaine Piesman, and Howard Rotterdam — a special thanks is in order for their participation and collaboration in planning and offering the course.

Also, we wish to thank those Fordham administrators and professors who have acted in consortium with the Mainstreaming Project. Our special gratitude is offered to former Dean Anthony Mottola who encouraged our project and first enabled us, along with the strong support of his associate deans, Anthony N. Baratta and Thomas G. Vinci, to engage in it. We thank Jay Sexter, associate vice president of academic affairs for his generosity in providing technical assistance. Further, for their hours of service on planning committees and participation in pilot projects, we thank

Mildred Lee, John Skalski, and Sayre Uhler (from the Division of Administration, Policy and Urban Education);

Carolyn Hedley, Gita Kedar-Voivodas, and Lillian Restaino-Bauman (from the Division of Curriculum and Teaching);

Dana Ardi, Rosa Hagin, John Hicks, John Houtz, Merrily Miller, Carolyn Nygren, and Sylvia Rosenfield (from the Division of Psychological and Educational Services)

Next, we are especially grateful to Barbara Herroder for her willingness to type and carefully prepare the manuscript and to Richard Baecher for his conscientious work as an editorial consultant.

Finally, we wish to thank Dean Max Weiner, current dean of the Fordham School of Education, who has consistently supported in every way our efforts in completing this text and in bringing courses in mainstreaming education to hundreds of educators in New York from both public and private schools.

Legislative and Historical Background for the Education of Exceptional Children and Youth

INTRODUCTION

M<small>AYNARD</small> R<small>EYNOLDS</small>, in writing the foreword to Corrigan and Howey's *Special education in transition: Concepts to guide the education of experienced teachers,*[1] advanced some important issues which are pertinent to this text. These issues are:

1. a period of rapid change in social and educational responses to Public Law 94-142 demands corresponding literature to assist those involved in effecting the changes;
2. the literature must be addressed to a sharing rather than a limited audience, i.e., administrators, supervisors, teachers, counselors, psychologists, and parents — anyone who must implement the law;
3. traditional textbooks are "too long and too formal" to be efficient and practical aids to the audience to be served.

The authors of this text are in complete agreement with Reynolds. We applaud the style of the Council for Exceptional Children Series, of which *Special Education in Transition* was the first number. Following in the tradition set by that series, the authors have devised a group of modules which have been honed over four years to meet the frequently stated needs of regular and special educators who have responded to needs assessment questionnaires and who have reaffirmed these needs in graduate inservice courses. These succinct learning modules lead the educator or parent to choose further activities to meet his or her special

---

1. Corrigan, D. and Howey, K. (1980). *Special education in transition: Concepts to guide the education of experienced teachers.* Reston, Virginia: Council for Exceptional Children. v–vi.

needs and to do deeper reading through a Topic Referenced Bibliography to be found on pages 232 to 262.

Module 1.0 is a response to three major questions asked by educators as they looked forward to welcoming exceptional children or youth into their schools or districts:

1. How did legislation concerning mainstreaming come into being? (See Module 1.1)

2. What precisely does Public Law 94-142 say I must do as a conscientious professional or parent to be of assistance to exceptional children or youth? (See Module 1.2)

3. What are the implications of current legislation and court decisions on the roles of school educators as individuals and as members of an interdisciplinary team? (See Module 1.3)

For further information concerning these related issues, see the Topic Referenced Bibliography on pages 232 to 262. Books and articles marked with the number *1* treat the history of educating exceptional children and youth in the United States of America; those marked *2* treat the legal aspects of such education; and those marked *3* develop the changing roles of regular and special educators (administrators, supervisors, counselors, psychologists, committees on the handicapped, regular teachers, special educators, resource room teachers, aides, nurses, therapists, parents, and students).

1.1 COURT DECISIONS AND LAWS

Minimum Competency Objectives

*1. You will be able to recognize the chief court decisions and laws which have affected the status of education of exceptional children and youth.

2. You will be able to summarize the chief results of recent court decisions and laws which affect your role in educating exceptional children and youth.

3. You will be able to translate these legal safeguards into a broader understanding of the teaching of exceptional students in today's schools.

*N.B. Modules are addressed to the teachers who take the course.

Rationale

Responses to needs assessments conducted with 600 teachers in the New York City area showed that they wished to know their legal responsibilities in working with exceptional children and youth. They wanted to learn the dimensions of their new roles in terms of some standards or guidelines. The information presented here is thus offered as a tool for developing a framework for teacher behaviors rather than an interesting set of background data. However, this tool takes on a special meaning when viewed in the context of the historical events that preceded the "first court case" as well as the climate of social change that prevailed during this era of litigation. This special meaning includes a broader understanding of the teaching of exceptional students.

Enabling Activities

1. Read the following outline of the chief court cases and laws concerning the education of exceptional children and youth and discuss the implications of each with your teacher and class, either as one large group or with some of your classmates in a small group.

2. As an aid to discussion, you may wish to assume the role of a parent of an exceptional child. In this case, each teacher should choose one type of handicapped child or youth. Develop with your colleagues the kind of educational climate which probably caused the court case or legislation to be enacted and your feeling within your role about the issues at stake in each instance.

TABLE 1.0

Court Cases and Laws Which Have Affected the Education of Exceptional Children and Youth in the United States of America

Date	Court Case or Law	Summary	Results
1. 1954	*Brown* v. *Board of Education of Topeka Kansas* (Supreme Court Decision)	Recognized the right of all children to have an equal opportunity to education. Landmark civil rights case.	Encouraged parents of exceptional children and youth to present their case as part of the larger civil rights movement. Exceptional children were being educated in isolated settings much like the "separate but equal"

TABLE 1.0 (Continued)

Date	Court Case or Law	Summary	Results
			facilities for minority students.
2a. 1958	PL 85-926 National Defense Education Act	Monies provided to assist teacher educators to train teachers of the mentally retarded.	2a–f. School systems set up special classes for exceptional students. These classes were in the same school house but often far from "regular classes." Special educators were educated in classes apart from regular teachers. They experienced the same isolation as their students during their training and teaching experience. In too many cases, youngsters considered to be "behavior problems" were referred to special classes. Since an inordinate number of students so referred were ethnic minorities, parents began to suspect a new segregation tactic.
2b. 1961	PL 87-276 Special Education Act	Monies provided to assist teacher educators to train teachers of the deaf.	
2c. 1963	PL 88-164 Mentally Retarded Facility and Community Center Construction Act	Monies provided to assist teacher educators to train teachers of other handicapped persons.	
2d. 1965	PL 89-10 The Elementary and Secondary Education Act	Monies provided for state and local district distribution to develop programs intended for exceptional persons and for the financially poor.	
2e. 1966	PL 89-313 Amendment to Title I of the Elementary and Secondary Education Act	Monies provided for state-supported programs for institutional and "other settings" for the handicapped.	
2f. 1969	PL 91-320 The Learning Disabilities Act	Monies provided for state programs for students with learning disabilities. Legally defined learning disabilities.	
3a. 1968	Hobson v. Hanson (Washington, D.C.)	The track system founded on the use of standardized tests for placement of special education students was declared unconstitutional because it dis-	3a–d. A number of court cases and laws represented criticism of the following in the education of exceptional children and youth: lack of due process; viola-

TABLE 1.0 (Continued)

Date	Court Case or Law	Summary	Results
		criminated against minority and financially poor students.	tion of civil rights; invasion of privacy; and racial prejudice.
3b. 1970	*Diana* v. *State Board of Education (California)*	Students cannot be assigned to special education classes on the basis of culturally biased tests or tests written in a language other than that spoken by the student.	
3c. 1971	*Pennsylvania Association for Retarded Citizens (PARC)* v. *the Commonwealth of Pennsylvania*	Landmark state court case. *All retarded children's* right to a free public education was established.	
3d. 1972	*Mill* v. *Board of Education of the District of Columbia*	Reiterated that every child has a right to education. School districts cannot claim lack of funds as a legitimate reason for not providing such education. Parents' rights to due process hearings in the case of right to education of their exceptional children were upheld.	
4a. 1973	*PL 93-112 Section 504 Rehabilitation Act*	Handicapped persons may not be excluded from federally funded programs solely because of their disability.	Special Education label extended to the gifted and talented.
4b. 1974	*PL 93-380 Education Amendments*	Monies provided for gifted and talented students through state and local districts. Upheld protection of rights of students and parents at placement hearings.	

TABLE 1.0 (Continued)

Date	Court Case or Law	Summary	Results
5a. 1974	*Lau* v. *Nichols* (Supreme Court Decision)	Court ordered that students be educated in a language they understand in order to guarantee equal participation in educational programs.	5a–d. Decisions and laws began to address problems of bilingual or multilingual children and youth whether in regular or special classes.
5b. 1974	*Aspira* v. *New York City Board of Education (U.S. Federal Court)*	Established bilingual education as a way to reduce educational inequality.	
5c. 1979	*Jose P.* v. *Ambach* (New York, U.S. Federal Court)	New York City Board of Education ruled as failing to evaluate and place exceptional children and youth. Ordered nondiscriminatory assessment. Recommended increase in bilingual personnel, resource rooms, development of non-categorical learning centers.	
5d. 1980	*Cyrcia S.* v. *Board of Education UCP* v. *New York City Board of Education* (U.S. Federal Court)	Court repeated provisions of 1979 *Jose P.* v. *Ambach.* See 5c. above.	
6a. 1975	*PL 94-142 Education for All Handicapped Children Act*	Mandated full free public education and due process rights for all exceptional children and youth.	Landmark federal legislation. (To be developed in greater detail in Module 1.2.)
6b. 1976	*New York State Education Law 1976 Chapter 853*	Mandated free full public education and due process rights for exceptional children and youth.	States were required to develop state plans to submit to the Bureau of Education for the Handicapped.
6c. 1978	*PL 95-561 Gifted and Talented Act*	Provided incentive monies for state and local educational agen-	Provided for the identification of the gifted and talented including

TABLE 1.0 (Continued)

Date	Court Case or Law	Summary	Results
		cies to develop programs.	those from disadvantaged backgrounds.
7a. 1979	*Reid* v. *New York City Board of Education*	Upheld provision of 30 days for pupil evaluation, 30 days for placement and free private placement if there is violation of the 60 day rule.	Upheld local district implementation of PL 94-142.
7b. 1979	*Lora* v. *New York City Board of Education* (U.S. Federal Court)	Court ordered school system-wide teacher training to reduce bias discovered in special education placements and to develop non-discriminatory procedures.	Teacher education was seen as one way to remedy racial and cultural bias in student placements. It was discovered, for example, that 95 percent of the school population of the special school for the emotionally handicapped came from minority groups.

Assessment

1. To check your knowledge of the court decrees and laws which have and are affecting the education of exceptional children and youth and your role as a teacher of these students as some of them begin to move into the regular classroom, fill in the blanks in the following chart. If at first you do not succeed, try, try again. (A simple example of mastery learning.)

Assessment table

Date	Court Case or Law	Summary	Results
1954		Recognized the right of all children to have an equal opportunity to education. Landmark civil rights case.	

Assessment table (Continued)

Date	Court Case or Law	Summary	Results
1961	*PL 87-276 Special Education Act*	Monies provided to assist teacher educators to train teachers of the deaf.	
1968	*Hobson* v. *Hansen* (Washington, D.C.)		
1972		Reiterated that every child has a right to education. School districts cannot claim lack of funds as a legitimate reason for not providing such education. Parents' rights to due process in the case of the right to education of their exceptional children upheld.	
1974	*Lau* v. *Nichols* (Supreme Court Decision)		Decisions and laws began to address problems of bilingual or multilingual children and youth whether in regular or special classes.
1975	*PL 94-142 Education for All Handicapped Children Act*		

2. From your class work and your study of the court cases and laws on the charts, develop an essay which summarizes the chronology of changes in American education policy for the education of exceptional children and youth. Present the essay to your instructor for evaluation. When it has been evaluated, place the text at the end of this module for future use. (You may wish to use the essay as the basis for a talk at a faculty meeting or a PTA meeting.)

Supportive Activities

Choose one or more of the following activities in conference with your instructor. This may be a week's assignment or a term project. Use the selected bibliography in the Appendix as a help in finding reference texts or periodical articles.

1. Using the table in this module, develop a broader discussion of the causes, dimensions and results of the court cases and laws listed. Add any court decisions or laws which you think have been omitted and which are important.

2. Trace the work of parent advocates, the Council for Exceptional Children, the Education Commission of the United States, and the U.S. Office of Education, Special Education Programs in the development of legislation to protect the rights of exceptional children and youth to an education.

Implications/Applications, Historical-Social Contexts

Unfortunately, prior to the nineteenth century, education as we know it was not intended for the exceptional youngster but was primarily reserved for "those who would best benefit from it." During this period of time, as one might expect, the form of "special education" that was provided was not concerned with a youngster's abilities, but rather with his or her disabilities. The following events in *Table 1.1* are interesting and do provide an historical context describing the form that special education took prior to and including the nineteenth century.

TABLE 1.1

Forms of Special Education

Dates	Events
Late 1500s	• The mentally retarded were diagnosed by asking individuals to measure a yard of cloth or name the days of the week. • Procedures for teaching the deaf were based on finger spelling. • Wax tablets were produced so the blind could "write" on them.
Late 1600s	• Attempts were made to distinguish between the mentally retarded person and the mentally ill person.

TABLE 1.1 (Continued)

Dates	Events
Mid–Late 1700s	• A "public" school for poor, deaf students was established in France. • Sensory methods were used to teach the "apparently retarded."
Early–Mid 1800s	• First special education program in the United States was organized by Thomas Hopkins Gallaudet. Presently called the American School for the Deaf. • Institute for the Blind was established. • Braille was developed. • Rhode Island passed the first state compulsory education law in 1840. • The first "special class" for retarded children was initiated in Germany. • Anne Sullivan worked with Helen Keller. • Public schools in Elizabeth, New Jersey started a multi-track system that grouped students according to learning rate. • Alexander Graham Bell's work led to hearing aids for the deaf.

From the early 1900s to the present, efforts to provide "special education" to exceptional students moved from placing the profoundly handicapped in state institutions to teaching the physically and mentally handicapped in separate classes and schools. Coincidentally, during this time frame the "tests and measurements" movement was actively underway. The seminal works of Edward Thorndike in 1900, Alfred Binet and Theodore Simon in 1910, Lewis Terman in 1916 and David Wechsler in 1939 have more than left their strong imprints on the assessment of exceptional students. In the late 1970s and early 1980s, the "discrimination" issues in testing have served to support and encourage the work in non-biased assessment that is being conducted by Thomas Oakland, Cecil Reynolds, Jonathan Sandoval and Daniel Reschly. No doubt this current focus on cultural bias in assessment is an outgrowth of PL 94-142.

But not to be overlooked on the progression and evolution of special education was the impact of the social-political context provided by the 1950s on to the late 1960s. During this period, the civil rights movement had entered public education, a prominent family, the Kennedys, took a personal as well as political interest in the handicapped, and the National Association for Retarded Citizens (NARC) was formed, proving to be a powerful political force in the fight for the rights of the handicapped.

As an activity, please test your special understanding of the Court Decisions and Laws with the reported historical and social context by discussing with a colleague the issues of:

1. the right to a free appropriate education;

2. nondiscriminatory testing;

3. due process;

4. individualized education program; and

5. placement in the least restrictive environment to the education of the following students in the present, in the year 1995 and in the year 2,010.

> a. Lila L, age 5 from Israel who speaks no English and may in fact be deaf.
>
> b. Jerry J, age 16 originally from Portugal who speaks little English, and is living in a foster home with an "uneducated" family.
>
> c. John D, age 16 from New York who writes novels that have been published but is not "achieving" in school.
>
> d. Nina N, age 10 originally from Puerto Rico who has moved back and forth from Puerto Rico to Chicago six times. She demonstrates limited proficiency in both Spanish and English.

1.2 PUBLIC LAW 94-142

Minimum Competency Objectives

1. You will be able to recall the chief regulatory provisions of PL 94-142.

2. You will be able to summarize these provisions.

3. You will be able to relate the implications of PL 94-142 to the concept of change in educational systems.

Rationale

Federal legislation has set national mandates for the education of the disabled. Since state and local plans must be in accord with federal law, it is necessary for educators to know the federal laws related to the education of exceptional children and youth. The most sweeping federal law concerning the education of the disabled is PL 94-142, the Education for All Handicapped Children Act, passed in November 1975. Its implications and applications may effect change in educational systems.

Enabling Activities

1. Read and study the following outline of the pertinent provisions of PL 94-142.

2. Discuss the implications of these provisions of PL 94-142 with your instructor and peers. You may wish to do so with the interdisciplinary team in your school.

3. If time permits, read the entire text of the law. See the Appendix to this text for the reference.

Major Provisions of PL 94-142

I.   Every state is required to offer a free public education to all handicapped persons, ages 5–21, no matter what the severity of the handicap. The foci of this regulation are:

    A.   Disabled persons, 5–21 years of age, who are not receiving an education.

    B.   Disabled persons, 5–21 years of age, who are most severely handicapped and who are receiving an inadequate education.

II.   Every state must guarantee due process to both persons with handicaps (5–21 years of age) and their parents. Due process consists of:

    A.   Parents shall have the right of prior notice.
Parents must be notified and give written approval before their children can be tested, evaluated, or given a placement.

    B.   Parents shall have the right of appeal.
Parents may appeal a placement decision to an impartial hearing examiner or to the courts.

    C.   Parents shall have the right of access to relevant records.
Parents may examine school records directly related to their children.

    D.   Parents shall have the right of independent evaluation.
Parents may arrange for an independent evaluation of their children in addition to the evaluation made by school personnel.

    E.   Parents shall have the right to re-evaluation.
Parents have the right to have their children re-evaluated each year.

III. Every state shall see to it that there is educational evaluation and prescription for each handicapped student.

    A.   Every Local Educational Agency (LEA) must set up a group to arrange for the testing, evaluation, and placement of handicapped students. The generic name for this group is the Committee on the Handicapped (COH). The group may have a different name, but it must consist of members from a variety of disciplines such as: regular education, special education, psychology, psychiatry, social work, guidance, and medicine, as well as representatives of parent groups. When a specific student is being discussed by the COH, the parents of that student are to be invited to the meeting.

B. Every state shall see to it that handicapped persons, ages 5–21, shall be tested and evaluated in a non-discriminatory mode.

    1. Tests/evaluations must be free of cultural or racial bias.

    2. No placement shall be on the basis of only one criterion, test, or discipline.

    3. Assessments shall be made through the use of the handicapped students' dominant language.

    4. Parents must be informed of the proceedings in their native language.

C. Every state shall see to it that handicapped persons, ages 5–21, shall be educated in the least restrictive environment.

    1. To the "maximum extent appropriate," handicapped students are to be educated with children who are not handicapped.

    2. "Special classes, separate schooling, or other removal from the regular educational environment" is to be permitted only when the nature or severity of the handicap is such that the education in regular classes with the use of supplementary aids and services cannot be achieved satisfactorily.

    3. The placement of disabled students in least restrictive environments is commonly referred to as "mainstreaming," but the federal law does *not* refer to this term.

D. For each handicapped student, an Individual Education Plan (IEP) shall be developed at the beginning of the year. The Plan shall include:

    1. involvement of parent, teacher and, when appropriate, the disabled person;

    2. details of present performance:

    3. long-term objectives for one semester or two semesters;

    4. short-term objectives for instruction:

    5. instructional plans for implementing the objectives, including specific educational services and extent of participation in regular classrooms;

    6. modes of evaluation;

    7. dates for periodic review of the IEP.

IV.   Funding

The law provides for a variety of ways to fund the implementation of its provisions. It should be remembered that Congress must appropriate the funds outlined in the law. The federal government has not yet appropriated the maximum amounts allowed by law.

Assessment

1. To check your knowledge of the provisions of PL 94-142 which have important implications for your role as an educator, fill in the blanks in the following passage and check Module 1.2 for the correct responses. Repeat the self-evaluation until you get 90% or 30 out of 33 correct.

Passage on PL 94-142

I.   Every state is required to offer a (1) _____ public education to all (2) _____ persons, ages (3) _____ to (4) _____, no matter what the degree severity of the handicap. The foci of this regulation are:

A.   (5) _____

B.   Disabled persons, 5–21 years of age, who are most severely handicapped and who are receiving an inadequate education.

.   Every state must guarantee due process to (6) _____ and _____. Due process shall consist of:

A.   Parents shall have the right of prior notice.
This shall consist of: (7) _____

B.   Parents shall have the right of appeal.
This shall consist of: (8) _____

Parents shall have the right to access to relevant records.

Parents shall have the right of independent evaluation.

Parents shall have the right to their children's re-evaluation. This shall consist of: (9) _____

;tate shall see to it that there is educational (10)_____
scription for each handicapped student.

ry (11) _____ must set up a group to arrange for the
ig, evaluation and (12) _____ of handicapped students.

Passage on PL 94-142 (Continued)

The generic name for this group is the (13) _____.
This group must consist of:

   1. members from a variety of disciplines such as
      (14) _____

   2. and representatives of (15) _____ groups.

B. Every state shall see to it that handicapped persons, ages 5–21, shall
be tested and evaluated in a (16) _____ mode.

   1. Tests/evaluations must be free of (17) _____ or
      (18) _____ bias.

   2. No placement shall be made on the basis of only one
      (19) _____, _____, _____.

   3. The language used in testing shall be (20) _____.

   4. Parents must be informed of the proceedings concerning test-
      ing and evaluation of their children in their (21) _____
      language.

C. Every state shall see to it that handicapped persons, ages 5–21, be
educated in the (22) _____ environment.

   1. To the "maximum extent appropriate," handicapped students
      are to be educated with (23) _____.

   2. Special classes, separate schooling, or other removal from the
      regular educational environment is to be permitted only when
      (24) _____
      _____.

D. For each handicapped student an (25) _____ will be developed at the beginning of the year. The Plan shall include:

   1. involvement of (26) _____, _____ and
      _____ when appropriate;

   2. (27) _____ objectives for a semester or two semesters;

   3. (28) _____ objectives for everyday instruction;

   4. (29) _____ plans, including specific educational ser-
      vices and the extent of participation in (30) _____
      classes;

   5. modes of evaluation, and

   6. dates for (31) _____ of the IEP.

IV. Funding
The law provides for a variety of types of funding. Congress must
(32) _____ these funds. Thus far, it has not done so up to the
(33) _____ allowed by law.

2. When you believe you have a fairly good grasp of the major provisions of PL 94-142, further review your understanding of the law by sharing this information with other educators in your school. You may wish to discuss the following topics:

1. name, date and foci of PL 94-142;
2. concept of due process;
3. nature and function of the COH;
4. nature of non-discriminatory assessment;
5. concept of the least restrictive environment;
6. concept of the structure of the IEP;
7. difficulties in funding PL 94-142.

Implications/Applications

Although PL 94-142 is a powerful force for potential change in the educational system, compliance with only the letter of the law, without its intent, cannot bring about positive change. In fact these are some reactions to the law which may even mitigate against educational systems moving toward incurring positive change. Table 1.2 provides a few examples of reactions to PL 94-142 and suggested remedies for positive change.

TABLE 1.2

Examples of Reactions to PL 94-142 and Suggested Remedies for Positive Change

Reactions	Remedies
1. The concept of "legislative learning" raises unrealistic expectations for the educational process. Historically, there is a limited research base to support its proposed effects.	Educational systems should seek to sponsor pilot or test sites, using appropriate research methodologies to test alternative approaches to educating the handicapped.
2. The financing of PL 94-142 is costly. The implementation of PL 94-142 has increased the handicapped population,	Educational systems should seek out creative, educationally sound ways of relieving the "financial burden" of

TABLE 1.2 (Continued)

Reactions	Remedies
which has resulted in an increase of staff to serve them.	PL 94-142. The following suggestions are offered:
	• Review the referral process in terms of its effectiveness as a decision-making tool.
	• The review may indicate too many casual referrals, as well as the inefficient use of administrators' and teachers' time.
	• Test the *bridging* of services between special education and regular placements.
	• Monitor the program on an ongoing basis to provide data to be used for continuous program allocation, cutting down on last minute budget requests.
3. The uneven acceptance of the principle of normalization by educators and parents may be due to their changed roles and responsibilities in the educational system.	The acceptance of the principle of normalization suggests that for handicapped students to be appropriately served in society, educational systems must serve them in "normal" settings that are common to both the handicapped and non-handicapped. In-service education focused on a common body of practices including the skills, knowledge and attitudes related to this principle must be provided on an ongoing basis to promote and put into operation this principle of normalization.

Specifically, the implications/applications of PL 94-142 with regard to the changing roles and functions of educators and parents are discussed in Module 1.3. Further, implications and applications of PL 94-142 run through every module in this text. These modules will provide educators and parents with a more complete understanding of PL 94-142 which may contribute to positive change in their respective educational systems.

1.3 IMPLICATIONS OF COURT DECISIONS AND LAWS FOR EDUCATORS

Minimum Competency Objectives

1. You will be able to draw up role expectation descriptions of the various persons involved in meeting new legislative and court mandates in educating the handicapped.

2. You will be able to describe the current understandings of the personnel in your school (school district, state) of their role expectations in terms of the new mandates for educating the handicapped.

3. You will describe the differences, if any, between ideal and real expectations for these roles and the possible consequences of these differences.

4. You will describe a new role for educators and parents as members of an interdisciplinary team.

Rationale

The implementation of PL 94-142 has not been rapid. Nevertheless, as the mechanisms for carrying out its mandates are better structured, the implications of the law will challenge all educators and parents. Understanding and carrying out new roles will be essential for educators and parents if they are to be successful in the education of both "regular" and exceptional children and youth. This module is dedicated to an examination of the possible new dimensions of educators' and parents' roles in terms of court decisions and laws related to the education of the handicapped. These are ideal changes. But educators and parents live in a real world which may not as yet have experienced role changes. Educators and parents need to know the differences between what should be and what is in terms of educating exceptional children and youth. A comparison of the ideal with the real serves to show how much has to be done in a given school or district to effectuate the ideal.

Enabling Activities

1. Together with your instructor and peers, fill in the Ideal Role Expectation Chart, basing your answers on what you now know about court and legal regulations concerning the education of the handicapped.

2. Using the Real Role Expectation Interview Guide, discover what your school staff and one or more parents in your school believe are their roles in relation to the education of the handicapped.

3. Compare the ideal with the real expectations of your school staff and parents in class discussion (large group, small groups, or in pairs).

4. Summarize your findings in a follow-up essay or chart which highlights role expectation differences and indicates possible areas of need for staff or parent development in terms of the education of exceptional children and youth.

CHART 1.3A

Ideal Role Expectations

Agent		Expectations for Behaviors Related to the Exceptional Student
I. Parents of Exceptional Student	A.	*Due Process Roles*
	B.	*Involvement with the IEP*
	C.	*Involvement with Special Educators*
	D.	*Involvement with Regular Educators*
	E.	*Involvement with Parents of Other Exceptional Children or Youth*
	F.	*Involvement with Parents of Children or Youth in the Regular Classroom*
	G.	*Involvement with School Administrators*
	H.	*Involvement with Support Personnel (Guidance Counselors, Social Workers, Therapists, etc.)*
II. School Administrator	A.	*Due Process Roles*
	B.	*Involvement with the IEP*
	C.	*Involvement with the COH*
	D.	*Involvement with the Least Restrictive Environment*
	E.	*Involvement with Staff Development*
	F.	*Involvement with Parents*
	G.	*Other*
III. Special Educator	A.	*Due Process Roles*
	B.	*Involvement with the COH*
	C.	*Involvement with the IEP*
	D.	*Involvement with Regular Educators*
	E.	*Involvement with Parents of Exceptional Students*
	F.	*Involvement with Parents of "Regular" Students*
	G.	*Involvement with School Administrators or Supervisors*
	H.	*Involvement with Other Support Personnel (Guidance Counselors, Social Workers, Therapists, etc.)*

CHART 1.3A (Continued)

Agent	Expectations for Behaviors Related to the Exceptional Student
IV. Regular Educators	A. *Due Process Roles*
	B. *Involvement with the COH*
	C. *Involvement with the IEP*
	D. *Involvement with Special Educators*
	E. *Involvement with Parents of the Exceptional Student*
	F. *Involvement with Parents of "Regular" Students*
	G. *Involvement with School Administrators or Supervisors*
	H. *Involvement with Other Support Personnel (Guidance Counselors, Therapists, Nurses, Social Workers, etc.)*

Continue with charts related to the role expectations for Support Personnel — Guidance Counselors, Social Workers, Therapists, School Nurses, School Psychologists, Psychiatrists, etc., as the population of the class and school dictates.

CHART 1.3B

Real Role Expectations Interview Guide

1. "Since the passage of PL 94-142 in 1975, would you say that your role (as a/an administrator, supervisor, regular teacher, special teacher, school psychologist, social worker, guidance counselor, therapist, psychiatrist, parent, etc.) has changed in any way?"
   Yes _____ No _____

2. If answer is YES, ask the person interviewed to describe these changes. Record the changes here.

3. If the answer is NO, ask the person interviewed to describe his or her role in relation to the exceptional student.

4. Ask the following questions after the description has been given. (Record "Yes" or "No" to appropriate questions.)
   a. "Are you part of a team that tests, evaluates, or places exceptional students?"
   b. "Is there such a team servicing your school?"
   c. "Are you involved with this team in any way?"
   d. "Have you ever been present when such a team was in session?"
   e. "Are IEPs written for exceptional students in your school?"

   f. "Do you make up the team that writes the IEP?"
   g. "Do you help to write the IEPs?"
   h. "Do you help to implement the IEPs?"

CHART 1.3B (Continued)

i. "Do you report student progress in an IEP to anyone?"

j. "Is the IEP reviewed during the semester, mid-semester, between semesters, at the end of the two semesters?"

k. "Are exceptional children and/or youth placed in settings other than special education classes in your school?"

l. "Do they go to resource rooms?"

m. "Do they go to the regular classroom?"

n. "Do they go elsewhere in school? Where?"

o. "Has there been any staff development to assist teachers, support personnel, and administrators to improve the education of exceptional children and/or youth?"

p. "Who conducted the training?"

q. "Who participated in the training?"

r. "Are you aware of the due process rights of parents of exceptional students?"

s. "With what school personnel do you work to educate exceptional children and/or youth?"

t. "With what parents do you work in trying to educate exceptional children and/or youth?"

Assessment

Comparing the Ideal with the Real

Analyze the Real Expectation Interview Guide. Compare your findings with the Ideal Expectation Chart findings. In an essay (or chart) state the major differences between the ideal and real roles of the persons in your school in relation to educating exceptional children or youth.

For Further Consideration

As you continue through this semester, try to determine causes for differences between ideal and real roles in educating exceptional children and youth. Is there ignorance of the implications of the law? Is there non-compliance with known law? What could be the causes of ignorance, non-compliance? What role does funding have in implementing the law? Is there a stated policy from the LEA? Is there sufficient staff training?

Implications/Applications

PL 94-142 is changing the roles and responsibilities of educators and parents. Many educators and parents may even be receptive to this challenge. In effect, they may use this opportunity to define new relationships with each other as well as with the exceptional students they work with. Since exceptional students require the services of various disciplines, a team that is representative of these disciplines may serve to define this new relationship. The interdisciplinary team provides a means of communication between educators and parents to better understand each others' changing roles in educating exceptional students. (See Module 7.1 on the IEP for a more complete discussion and examples of how an interdisciplinary team may function.) The overall value of the interdisciplinary team is its work as a system to provide a whole and not segments of an educational program for an exceptional student.

     Members of an interdisciplinary team may wish to work together to determine if their respective roles have changed with regard to educating exceptional students. Please respond "Yes" or "No" in terms of whether your role has changed in working with the following students.

CHART 1.3C

Changing Roles

Students	Current Position	
	Yes	No
1. Ada A, age 8, classified as mildly mentally handicapped.		
2. Bruce B, age 12, not classifed, perceived to be learning disabled.		
3. Carol C, age 17, classified as learning disabled.		
4. Dean D, age 6, not classified, perceived to be emotionally disturbed.		
5. Edna E, age 7, classified as educable mentally retarded.		
6. Frank F, age 11, not classified, perceived to be physically handicapped (hearing impaired).		
7. Gina G, age 6, classified as mildly emotionally disturbed.		
8. Harry H, age 13, classified as physically handicapped (visually impaired).		

The Least Restrictive Environment (LRE)

INTRODUCTION

THE FUNDAMENTAL PRINCIPLE enunciated in Public Law 94-142 is that exceptional children and youth will be educated in the least restrictive environment. Implementation of the law at the school or district level is dependent upon the mutual understanding by parents and educators of this principle. Experience in working with administrators, counselors, psychologists, teachers, and parents over four years has led the authors to see that misconceptions about this principle or lack of agreement about its implications can seriously threaten and even thwart the best intentioned mainstreaming efforts.

It is for this reason that Module 2.0 focuses on:

1. defining the least restrictive environment as it is outlined in Public Law 94-142;

2. outlining the consequent demands on a school system;

3. identifying the major misconception held by parents and educators concerning the least restrictive environment.

Theory is brought to practice in this module through the dissemination of questionnaires, one to fellow educators and parents, and one which is meant for the reader. The point of this distribution is to determine whether misconceptions concerning LRE are hindering mainstreaming efforts in your school or school district.

Further information on the topics of this module can be found in the Topic Referenced Bibliography on pages 232 to 262 under the numbers *2* (Laws) and *6* (Current Models for Planning Education of Exceptional Children and Youth).

2.1   OBTAINING A CLEAR CONCEPT
OF THE LEAST RESTRICTIVE ENVIRONMENT

Minimum Competency Objectives

1. You will be able to state in writing at least five major features which are true about the least restrictive environment for educating exceptional children and youth that have important implications for the school and/or school district in which you work.

2. You will be able to state in writing at least five misconceptions of the least restrictive environment.

3. You will be able to discern whether the objective features or the misconceptions of the least restrictive environment are more prevalent in your thinking and/or in the thinking of the educators in your school or school district.

Rationale

A major stumbling block to the implementation of PL 94-142 is the misunderstanding of the concept of the least restrictive environment as the mode for educating exceptional children and youth. You are invited to clarify your own thinking concerning the LRE and to discern whether the educators in your school or district hold the misconceptions noted in this module. This two-fold clarification should help you to proceed with some strategies for implementing the LRE.

Enabling Activities

Please read and discuss with your large group, small group or partner the following:

I.   Correct Concepts Concerning the Least Restrictive Environment for Educating Exceptional Children and Youth

   A.   Definition and philosophical basis
        Provision of a least restrictive environment means that school authorities are expected to enable exceptional pupils to take part in the everyday school life and activities as much and as independently as possible in support of the principle of normalization.

B.   Consequent demands on school personnel

School personnel must make appropriate diagnoses of students' strengths and needs; afford appropriate placements in one or more educational settings in terms of the diagnosed strengths and needs; offer individualized instruction in both special and regular education settings; provide access to the regular classroom with accompanying special services if needed in and/or out of the regular classroom.

C.   Consequences for exceptional students when the concept of LRE is correctly applied

1.   A search is mandated for locating exceptional children and youth who are not in school to make sure that they are not excluded from education.

2.   There are greater efforts to identify children and youth in the regular classroom who may be in need of special services available in the regular classroom, elsewhere in the school, or outside the school.

3.   Exceptional children or youth, frequently placed solely in special classes in a special part of the school, are diagnosed continuously and placed for all or part of their school day in a regular classroom with concomitant support services, if needed. This placement occurs only if and when the regular classroom is a place where the student can learn.

4.   Flexibility in placement from one set of learning circumstances to another is *dictated by the student's growth* in relation to his or her Individual Educational Plan. There are various models for providing such flexibility.

D.   Ideal consequences for special educators

1.   Some special educators will continue to work in special classes with exceptional children and youth who cannot benefit from being in a regular classroom for either all or part of a day.

2.   Some special educators will work with exceptional children and youth who spend part of the day in the regular classroom and part of the day with the special educator in a special education classroom, a resource room, or a regular classroom where the special educator will act as a consulting teacher.

3.   Many special educators will work as consultants and liaison persons for regular educators.

E.   Ideal consequences for regular educators

1.   They will gain increased knowledge about and use of diagnostic/prescriptive modes of instruction.

     2. They will gain increased knowledge about and use of individualized instruction for all children or youth in the classroom.

     3. They will gain increased collaboration with special educators, parents, and administrators in carrying out instruction.

F. Models for flexibility in placement

     1. The Cascade Model of Special Education Services was developed by Evelyn Deno. Level 1 of this model gives priority to the *prevention* of handicapping cognitive, affective, social and psychomotor behaviors. At Level 2, exceptional students are placed in regular classes. Some of these students will need supportive services; others will not. At Level 3, students attend regular classes, but have supplementary instructional services. Level 4 calls for student placement in part-time special classes. Students at Level 5 are in need of full-time special classes which are located in a regular public school. Level 6 placements are at "special stations," a term applied to special schools in a public school system. Level 7 refers to student placements at home where they are instructed by public school personnel. At Level 8, students are given instruction in a hospital, residential, or total care setting. Assignment of persons to Level 8 settings is governed by health, correctional, welfare, or other agencies. As a Cascade, the model suggests that students move toward placements at higher numerical levels only as far as necessary and return to lower numerical levels as quickly as feasible.

     2. Jerry Chaffin, in contrast to Evelyn Deno, describes a full service education model that emphasizes instruction for the mildly and moderately handicapped. Services are sequenced in a hierarchical order and include:

       a. *Indirect Services*
- consultation and observation
- formal and informal testing assistance
- supplying instructional materials

       b. *Direct Services*
- tutorial assistance in regular class (up to 2 weeks)
- resource room at random intervals
- tutorial assistance in regular class (1–6 weeks)
- contracted services
- resource room on a regular basis (6 weeks or more, 1–2 periods)
- resource room on a regular basis (6 weeks or more, 2–4 periods)
- other alternatives (e.g., special placement)

Chaffin intended his model primarily to provide institutional support and service for the teacher and the exceptional student in the regular classroom. In general, both models present a hierarchy of placement/services that start with the least restrictive environment and progress to the most restrictive.

II. Misconceptions Concerning the Least Restrictive Environment for Educating Exceptional Students

A. Mainstreaming is a popular term used to mean that exceptional students will be educated in the least restrictive environment. This term is often mistaken to mean that all children and youth in special education classes will be required to leave these classes and will be placed *en masse* in regular classes for an entire day.

This misconception may arise from two sources. The first is from semantic confusion concerning the term "mainstreaming." The term is based on an analogy. It suggests a fast rushing river in which all tributaries are mixed into the major course of flow. Unfortunately, the analogy also suggests indiscriminate and too rapid mixture of currents. PL 94-142 clearly indicates that placement in regular classrooms or special education classrooms depends on adequate diagnosis and parental consent. There is no mandate for the demise of special education. The second source of confusion over the term "mainstreaming" may be teacher fear that in a time of economic stress, cutbacks by school administrators may mean the firing of special educators with the consequent assignment of special education tasks to regular classroom teachers. The basis of this fear is quite real. In recent times, regular teachers have been asked, because of financial constraints, to take on the duties of school librarians, art teachers, physical education teachers, music teachers and reading teachers. It is not the intent of the law that regular educators replace special educators in this manner.

B. The concept of the least restrictive environment does not mean that educators are expected to change the exceptional student to somehow "fit" into an unmodified regular classroom. It is the regular classroom which must be changed to meet new populations which represent a greater mix of physical and mental abilities.

C. The least restrictive environment is not a regular classroom in which exceptional students are left without special materials or services.

D. Providing a least restrictive environment for exceptional students is NOT less expensive than educating these students in special education classes.

E.   There is no guarantee that providing a least restrictive environment will assure high quality education for exceptional students.

F.   Assessment of the least restrictive environment in any school system must not be based upon convenience, cost analysis, or ease of operation. Assessment must be based upon the mental, physical, emotional, social, and civic growth of students.

Administer the following questionnaire to a random sample of educators in your school or district. Be sure to include administrators, supervisors, regular and special educators, and support personnel. If time permits, ask parents to respond.

Questionnaire

Dear Colleague,

This is an anonymous questionnaire to determine what we know in this school (school district) about educating pupils in the least restrictive environment as mandated in Public Law 94-142.

     Please circle True or False for each statement. Answering the questionnaire should take five minutes at most.

1.   PL 94-142 demands that *all* exceptional students (students in special education classes) be placed immediately in regular classrooms.   TRUE   FALSE

2.   Mainstreaming means that we shall have to give exceptional students special training so that they can fit into the procedures of the regular classroom.   TRUE   FALSE

3.   Mainstreaming exceptional students into regular classrooms is an administrative ploy to discharge some or all special educators and to replace them with regular educators.   TRUE   FALSE

4.   When a school has mainstreamed exceptional students, there is a sizable reduction in costs per pupil.   TRUE   FALSE

5. Placing exceptional students in the regular
   classrooms is a guarantee that each will get a
   quality education.   TRUE   FALSE

6. Placing exceptional students in regular classrooms will take away the need for giving them
   special materials or services.   TRUE   FALSE

7. Our school model for mainstreaming should be
   evaluated solely in terms of its being cost efficient and easy to manage.   TRUE   FALSE

Assessment

---

1. Complete your own self-analysis. Check statements which you believe to
   be true on the list below. This analysis is meant to be private.

   _____ I honestly believe that the intent of the least restrictive environment concept as promulgated in PL 94-142 is to enable exceptional
   students *who are able to do so* to rejoin the community at school
   and in their local neighborhoods.

   _____ The real intent of the law is to end special education classes.

   _____ The regular teacher must now do the work of both regular and special educators, a process that saves money for the school system.

   _____ Continual diagnosis of exceptional students will result in student
   movement to appropriate school settings where learning can be
   improved.

   _____ Education in regular classrooms is a way to guarantee all pupils
   a high quality education.

   _____ Exceptional students in regular classrooms will not need special
   materials or services.

   _____ My school (district) will develop a mainstreaming model only if it
   is cost efficient and convenient to administer.

   _____ The major concern of my school in developing a mainstreaming
   model is to improve the physical, mental, social, and emotional
   welfare of all its students.

   _____ The LRE will be pushed in my school (district) as a way to increase
   job opportunities for special educators and/or support personnel.

As you proceed with the activities in this textbook, note if you experience any changes in your views.

2. Compile a summary of the responses you got to your LRE Questionnaire. Were they accurate? True? What can you do to clear up misconceptions concerning LRE in you school or district? What will happen if the misconceptions are not corrected?

3. Working with your peers, compare the responses to your questionnaire with theirs. How clear are educators in your schools about the concepts of LRE? What do these data reveal about the ease or difficulty of implementing the concept?

4. Using the descriptions of models by Evelyn Deno and Jerry Chaffin, develop a diagram which clearly indicates the use of one of these models. You may wish to use this diagram with your fellow educators at your school to demonstrate the flexibility of placements indicted by PL 94-142.

5. Prepare a written statement about the real concepts of the least restrictive environment alluding to at least five major aspects. You may wish to use this statement for a talk at a parent-teacher meeting or a faculty conference.

6. Prepare another statement of the misconceptions you have discovered concerning the least restrictive environment alluding to at least five major points. You may wish to use this statement in a talk to fellow faculty members.

Additional Activities *(if time permits)*

1. You may wish to do further reading on the issues raised in this module. Of special interest is Chapter Three of *Mainstreaming: A practical guide,* by Ann Turnbull and William M. Cruickshank (New York: Schocken Books, 1979); *Leadership and change in special education,* by Leonard C. Burrello and Daniel D. Sage (Englewood Cliffs, New Jersey: Prentice Hall, 1979; see especially pp. 75–80); *Handicapped children — strategies for improving services,* by Gary D. Brewer and James S. Kakalek (New York: McGraw Hill, 1979). This last book asks that all involved with educating the disabled enter into collaborative rather than rival processes to be of better service to all students.

2. An interesting class debate could follow from reading two articles in *Educational Leadership,* Volume 36, No. 5 (February 1979). These are: Rita S.

Dunn and Robert W. Cole, *"Inviting malpractice through mainstreaming,"* pp. 302–306, and Paul L. Tractenberg, "A response to Dunn and Cole," pp. 306–307. The first paper assumes that there will be little change in regular classrooms to meet the needs of special students with the consequent possibility of malpractice suits being initiated against regular teachers. The second paper calls for adequate training of regular educators with continual support to meet the needs of exceptional pupils and continual communication and coordination between regular and special educators.

3. For a helpful view of the philosophical bases of mainstreaming, see Mara Sapon-Shevin's views in "Another look at mainstreaming: Exceptionality, normality, and the nature of difference," in the *Phi Delta Kappan,* Vol. 60, No. 2 (October 1978), pp. 119–121. The author attacks the argument for mainstreaming exceptional children and youth which is based on the belief that "these children are the same as other children." Overemphasis on similarity may destroy the reality of individual differences between and among persons. It is not "good to be alike and bad to be different" (p. 119). Overemphasis on difference, on the other hand, destroys the concept of certain universal similarities we share as human beings—the rights to life, respect, and understanding for example. The author describes a collaborative model for instruction in the regular classroom which is worthy of study and imitation by regular educators.

Implications/Applications

The concept of least restrictive environment is not new since it was included in numerous state level special education statutes that were in effect prior to PL 94-142. Critical to this concept is the fact that the hierarchy of special services offered on a continuum must be fluid. That is, as student needs change, placement/service must change accordingly. In considering the LRE for an exceptional student, a basic question must be asked: "Does the suggested LRE provide for the most *productive* program possible?" For example, if a mildly handicapped, emotionally disturbed student is being considered for placement in the regular class with special resource services available, the answer to the question may be "yes." However, if a seriously physically handicapped student under heavy medication is being considered for placement in the regular class with special resource service, the answer might be "no."

Obviously, there are advantages and disadvantages to any program/service model. Table 2.1 shows the advantages and disadvantages of typical placement/service models offered in school settings.

TABLE 2.1

Advantages and Disadvantages of Placement/Service Models

Models	Advantages	Disadvantages
1. Regular class	Provides for optimal normalization experiences for exceptional students in their interactions with their non-handicapped peers. Labeling is not necessary.	Instructional management may not be differentiated enough to meet individual needs. Teacher requires training in working with exceptional students.
2. Regular class with support services itinerant persons, speech teacher, reading teacher, etc., and special educators available to provide services. Student would not be taken out of the regular class for any significant amount of time.	Provides assistance for diagnostic/prescriptive teaching relative to screening diagnosis and special instructional methods and materials.	Consultants or "special teachers" are sometimes viewed with suspect by the "regular teaching faculty." There exists the possibility of difficult coordination of assessment and teaching.
3. Resource room student is placed in regular class and taken out at regular intervals for remediation on an individual or small group basis.	Provides a way to mainstream a student. Separates the exceptional student for limited periods of time from his/her non-handicapped peers. May reduce labeling.	Often there are overenrollment and scheduling problems. Resource room teacher's role is often misunderstood relative to regular class and special class teachers' roles. There may be a lack of articulation between the students' regular program with the program provided in the resource room.
4. Self-contained special education class	This placement is the least restrictive environment for a *seriously* handicapped student who would have great difficulty in adapting to any mainstreaming activities.	Segregation and stigmatization are supported. The placement permits for limited interaction with non-handicapped peers.

As an exercise, you may wish to work with members of the interdisciplinary team. Place the following students in the LRE that would be most productive for their educational programs. Naturally, the student information provided is limited, but please make your best judgments based on the information offered. LREs include regular class, regular class with support and itinerant services, regular class and resource room, special class and resource room, and special class.

1. Sam is a 12-year-old sixth grade student who is often involved in fights with his peers. His relationship with adults is more aggressive than assertive. His academic achievement is approximately 2–3 years below grade level.

2. Alia, age 7½, repeated kindergarten because she was "not ready" for first grade. Currently, she is in the first grade, and her academic achievement is 2 years above grade level but she has no friends. When she is not involved in teacher-directed activities, she withdraws to the doll corner by herself and sometimes cries.

3. Don, age 8, doesn't seem to learn new skills very quickly. Instructions must be repeated several times and he has a great deal of difficulty working individually. However, over a period of time, he does learn what is required of him.

4. Ben, age 16, has been retained twice, however his assessment data indicates at least average ability. He has problems remembering material that is presented to him visually, and, in spite of help from the reading teacher, he still exhibits a great deal of difficulty in reading. His teacher believes that at this stage of the game he should be in a special education class with resource room services.

Identifying Exceptionality

INTRODUCTION

EDUCATING STUDENTS in a least restrictive environment implies a two-way movement for students. On the one hand, it means that regular educators and the interdisciplinary team can identify exceptional children or youth in the classrooms and can properly refer such students for appropriate assessment. On the other hand, it means that special educators working with the team can identify and help place exceptional students in regular classroom settings for all or part of the school day.

Module 3.1 is aimed at providing regular and special educators with insights into the pros and cons of labeling. Module 3.2 offers descriptions of the major categories of behavior which may lead regular and special educators to suggest a need for assessment relative to providing students with alternatives in classroom management and instructional strategies or settings.

See the Topic Referenced Bibliography on pages 232 to 262 for related information under the number 5.

3.1 WHY A LABEL?

Minimum Competency Objective

You will list the chief arguments for and against categorizing (labeling) exceptional students and you will take an initial stand on the issue which you will test again and again as you work through the modules in this text.

Rationale

Categorizing and providing labels for the identified categories are two important thinking skills. These cognitive acts are neither good nor bad in themselves. They merely serve as important bases for analysis of reality. When, however, one mistakenly categorizes or labels out of ignorance, prejudice, wish to deceive, or when one correctly categorizes or labels but others make improper use of these data, the processes become invalid in the former case, and frequently dangerous to the ethical and social fabric of society in the latter.

Semanticists tell us that the way society names and speaks about persons helps to frame our attitudes and values. It is important then to be aware of our understanding of the terms *exceptional, disabled* and *handicapped,* noting not only their denotation (dictionary definitions), but also their connotation (associated meanings which often carry an emotional response).

Examples of the Use of Labels

1. In a certain fruit and vegetable store, the owner put the following sign over the counter which contained apples, pears, cherries, oranges, nectarines, bananas, and plums:

FRUIT ON SALE

The items were categorized according to the principle of similarity, namely, the seed-bearing parts of a plant. The owner labeled this similarity, "fruit." The owner had reduced the price of the fruit from the amount he normally charged.

Critical Analysis: (1) The owner used a correct category; (2) the owner used a correct label.

2. In another store, the owner placed this sign over the fruit counter:

FRESH FRUIT ON SALE

A careful examination of the fruit showed that the fruit was not fresh.

Critical Analysis: (1) The owner developed a category of stale fruit; (2) the owner falsely labeled it "fresh fruit."

3. In another store, the owner placed the same sign over the fruit counter as in example 2, but an examination of his books showed that the fresh fruit were not sale priced.

Critical Analysis: (1) The owner developed a category of "fresh fruit";

(2) the owner correctly labeled it "fresh fruit"; (3) the owner incorrectly labeled it "on sale."

4. In a certain town, a business man bought a new store in an area where there were several grocery stores. He placed the sign:

FRESH FRUIT FOR SALE

over the counter of fresh fruit. The fruit prices were indeed lower than the usual amount he would have asked. Competing grocers saw this sale as an attempt to undersell them to attract customers away from them. They began a secret association to compete with the newcomer. They settled on a fixed reduced price for fruit sales which would always be under those of the new business man. Through this mode of labeling, they put the new man out of business.

Critical Analysis: (1) The new store owner correctly categorized the fruit; (2) the new store owner correctly labeled the fruit; (3) other store owners used these correct data to their own advantage.

5. The ABC Cat Food Company tried to compete in the market by use of labels in advertising. Since all the cat food produced by competitors was as nutritious and as cheaply priced, the ABC Cat Food Company began to claim that their dry cat food was "clean" or "neat" while their competitors' cat food was "messy."

Critical Analysis: (1) The ABC Cat Food Company correctly categorized the food as nutritious and economical. (2) The use of this food is easy and "clean" because the food is in dry form. (3) Other cat foods may seem less easy or "clean" to use because they are moist. (4) The label is questionable. The producer is appealing to the user's values.

These examples are intended to show the frequent uses of categorizing and labeling in everyday situations. Their use is neutral, in and of themselves, but the examples show how their use can result from error, wish to deceive, or other causes.

An Argument For the Category/Label: "Handicapped"

Federal, state and local funds for exceptional students are based on counting them as "handicapped." It is the label, not the services rendered, which establishes the count. See *A Practical Guide to Federal Special Education Law* by Philip R. Jones, published by Holt, Rinehart and Winston, 1981.

The regulations of Part B of the Education of the Handicapped Act, as published in the *Federal Register* (August 23, 1977), clearly state that a handicapped child may be counted only once, regardless of the number of programs or related services provided to him or her (pp. 27–28).

The law goes on to say that children with two disabilities will be labeled in a hyphenated mode, such as "deaf-blind." When a child has more than two disabilities, he or she is to be labeled "multihandicapped." (See the *Federal Register,* August 23, 1977.)

It is clear from these regulations that for a local education agency to attain funds from the Federal and State governments in accordance with PL 94-142, students MUST be labeled as handicapped, in a hyphenated mode, or as multihandicapped.

For Subcategories and Their Labels

It is educationally convenient to cluster exceptional children and youth in special education classes according to their labels, such as emotionally disturbed, mentally retarded, etc. Since this kind of grouping is so prevalent in our schools, we have also trained our teachers to instruct students according to these labels. Should we question our teacher training modes?

Argument Against the Category/Label: "Handicapped"

Since labels have serious consequences in the way society views exceptional students, it is important for educators to change the designations established by legislators who may not be as sensitive to the implications of their labels.

Further, legislative labels can be put to interesting uses, depending on the financial needs of the Local Education Agency or individual administrators.

Example

Many exceptional children and youth currently get services through other grant monies than those allocated through PL 94-142. Suppose that a high school is currently getting funds through Title I of the Elementary Secondary Act because the students in that school are labeled disadvantaged according to legal criteria. The other criterion for funds is that the students are in need of remediation in language and/or computation skills. The state and Local Education Agency do not have to match the funds given by the federal government. If the administrator changes the label of many of these students to "handicapped," the financial support of services becomes more expensive, since monies must come from the LEA and the state in addition to the federal government. (Since 1980, Congress has not appropriated the full amounts for educating exceptional children which were written into the law.)

Against Subcategories and Their Labels

The criterion of convenience should not be the ultimate value in education. Children with a single subcategory label may have several skills in need of remediation. Bringing together students with various exceptional labels according to their remedial needs or their talents makes educational sense. Further, teachers would be better trained to meet these needs as specialists rather than as generalists. To clarify, it would be *educationally* sound to train teachers as specialists in working to improve deficiencies and related reading/writing/computing skills, or to work with reading deficiencies and their causes among several categories of exceptional and "regular" students (e.g. crosscategories and multicategories).

Exceptional, Disabled, Handicapped: Denotation and Connotation

(1) The term "exceptional" appears to be more generic than "disabled" or "handicapped."

(2) The term "exceptional" is apt to have both negative and positive associations, depending on the context in which it is used.

(3) The term "disabled" causes the listener or reader to focus on lack of capability to be or do. A physical disability focuses on deviation from abilities to see, hear, smell, touch with sensation, or move. The term may have negative, positive, mixed, or neutral associations depending on the context or the educator's associations with the term.

(4) The term "handicapped" carries a stronger association with the negative. It may cause the listener to focus on the thought that a person with a disability is at a serious disadvantage in coping with life. This negative association can easily color the educator's behavior in working with exceptional children and youth. Taking a tone of pity or discouragement with the exceptional may cause the student to respond in negative ways.

The question to address is, "Why does this text attempt to more frequently use the term 'exceptional' rather than 'disabled' or 'handicapped,' even though these terms seem interchangeable in the literature?" To understand the reason, read the following two short poems (modified cinquains) to determine the attitudes revealed toward the subject of the poems.

New York
Mayor Koch, the Statue of Liberty
World Trade Buildings, Lincoln Center, Madison Square Garden,
Bustle, excitement, flair
New York.

Attitude toward New York? _____

New York
Drug addicts, muggers,
Slums, dirty subways, crowded streets
Fear, loneliness, anger
New York.

Attitude toward New York? _____

Assessment

Debate one or more of the following issues in class.

1. In order to get local, state, and federal funds appropriated in accordance with PL 94-142, school administrators must label students as handicapped or multihandicapped. This practice should continue as beneficial to exceptional students and their parents. (It may be helpful for participants in the debate to change sides after one half hour of discussion in order to understand their opponents' views.)

2. Labels are neutral. A rose by any other name would look like a rose. The practice of labeling exceptional students as handicapped or as a subcategory such as learning disabled, emotionally disturbed, or mentally retarded, should be continued in our schools as a convenient basis for grouping students for instruction in special classes and for identifying them for their teachers in the regular classroom when they are mainstreamed. (What does the subcategory label tell the teacher in the regular classroom about how to instruct the student?)

Implications/Applications

Social, political, and economic pressures have influenced the way that exceptional children and youth are described and categorized. No doubt, categorizing or labeling students has its supporters and opponents. The following pros and cons have been identified for your review.

TABLE 3.1

Categorization or Labeling

(terms will be used interchangeably)

Pros	Cons
1. Categorizing a "learning need" is a prerequisite to providing programming and services.	Programs should be based on needed services rather than type of handicap.
2. Categories can relate diagnosis to specific prescriptions.	A noncategorical approach, based on student's strengths and weaknesses may specify prescriptions.
3. Labels create visibility for funding purposes.	Categorization means exclusion.
4. Labeling allows educators to communicate on common terms, enabling them to classify and assess research findings.	Labels in schools have a permanency about them and may foster the self-fulfilling prophecy. A disproportionate number of minority students are labeled.
5. Special interest groups promote programs and special legislation.	Labels are a social stigma and have a negative effect relative to inadequacies or defects and may contribute to poor self-concept.

The following activity may be attempted by a class that is composed of regular and special educators.

1. Each member of the class will describe one academic and one social behavior of a student he or she comes in contact with.
2. The behavior will be listed on the board. They may include:
   Joe is a slow worker.
   Jane is easily distracted.
   Richard is a good citizen; he follows the rules.
3. Class members will identify themselves as regular educators or special educators.

4. Class members will quickly discern that the behaviors they have described are *common* behaviors to *both* regular and special settings.

5. The question to be discussed is, "Who is the exceptional student?"

3.2 CATEGORIES OF BEHAVIOR

Minimum Competency Objective

You will examine and be able to describe the major behaviors which would lead you to hypothesize that a child or youth may need referral for assessment which may result in providing alternative teaching strategies or settings.

Rationale

Parents and educators who are in continuous contact with children and youth should be sensitive and responsive to behavioral cues that suggest further assessment is appropriate.

The dangers concerning observation of behaviors also should be known.

1. "Deviant" behaviors defined by one parent or educator may not be so defined by others. Tolerance for, or ignorance of behavioral differences must be taken into consideration.

2. The criteria for each handicapping condition as defined by law usually contains the feature of "severe" or "marked" difference from the average. It is not an easy task to define these terms in exact ways, amenable to precise measurement.

3. Students may demonstrate one or more of the behaviors described and yet not need special help.

4. It is not the parents' or educators' role to discern the cause of behavior, but instead to help students to find appropriate assistance which will lead to the understanding of the causes of the exceptionality and effective remediation, if needed.

5. Knowing the behaviors and causes of a handicapping condition does not inform a parent or educator what specific instructional strategies to use with children and youth.

Enabling Activities

Examine individually or with members of an interdisciplinary team the following brief descriptions of exceptional behaviors which would lead a parents or educator to hypothesize that a student may need further assessment.

The following descriptions of exceptional behavior include a legal definition of a generic group of behaviors and an example containing some common clues which belong within that group.

Each description should be used with an awareness of the dangers listed in the *Rationale*.

I. Speech/Language Problems

    A. Legal definition: A speech impairment is a communication disorder, such as stuttering, impaired articulation, a language impairment, or a voice impairment, which adversely affects a child's educational performance. (PL 94-142, Section 121, a.5.)

    B. Example of common clues to speech problems: Irene, age 6, in the second grade, usually prefers to refrain from speaking and doesn't respond when initially addressed. But, when Irene is encouraged to respond, she prefers to use gestures rather than words. When she does speak, she rushes her words together, consistently mispronouncing them, and often repeats unnecessary words and phrases in an unusually low, loud nasal pitch. Additionally, when Irene struggles to speak, she stutters and uses strong facial gestures.

    C. Examples of common clues to langauge problems: Ira, age 10, in grade 5, uses an extremely limited vocabulary in speaking, reading, and writing for his age. He has great difficulty in trying to grasp the meaning of spoken and printed language as well as trying to structure communication in these forms. He sometimes uses grammar in quixotic fashion, and at other times his grammar is under-developed and inappropriate for his age. He cannot repeat a sequence of ideas.

II. Hearing Problems

    A. Legal definitions: Deafness: A hearing impairment which is so severe that the child is impaired in processing linguistic information through hearing, with or without amplification, which adversely affects educational performance. (PL 94-142, Section 121, a.5.)

        Hard of Hearing: A hearing impairment, whether permanent or fluctuating, which adversely affects a child's educational performance but which is not included under the definition of "deaf" in this section. (PL 94-142, Section 121, a.5.)

B.   Examples of common clues to hearing impairment: Beth, age 7, in the second grade, constantly says "What?" "Huh?" Pardon me." She speaks either too loudly or too softly, rushes her speech, and consistently mispronounces words. Beth does not respond to weak and distant sounds and frequently appears to be daydreaming or "lost in her self." She looks at the speaker's mouth and face with intense attention, straining to keep up with class activities. She has frequent earaches as well.

III.   Visual Problems

A.   Legal definition: A visual handicap is defined as a visual impairment which after correction adversely affects a child's educational performance. This term includes both partially seeing and blind children. (PL 94-142, Section 121, a.5.)

B.   Example of common clues to visual problems: Ed, age 8, in the third grade, is constantly squinting his red eyes in their swollen lids while losing his place in oral reading activities. When reading, he either holds the book too close or too far away and seems to tire easily. He has either sties or flaked eyelids and does not volunteer for tasks that demand keen vision. The physical education teacher has indicated that Ed has poor hand-eye coordination in playing games.

IV.   Physical Problems

A.   Legal definition: Orthopedically impaired — a severe orthopedic impairment which adversely affects a child's educational performance. The term includes impairments caused by congenital anomaly (e.g., clubfoot, absence of a limb, etc.), impairments caused by disease (e.g., poliomyelitis, bone tuberculosis, etc.), and impairments from other causes (e.g., cerebral palsy, amputations and fractures, or burns which cause contractions).

Other health-impaired — limited strength, vitality or alertness due to chronic or acute health problems such as a heart condition, tuberculosis, rheumatic fever, nephritis, asthma, sickle cell anemia, hemophilia, epilepsy, lead poisoning, leukemia, or diabetes that adversely affect a child's educational performance. (PL 94-142, Section 121, a.5.)

B.   Example of some common clues to physical impairments:
(obvious clues are not described)

Elsie, age 11, in the sixth grade, seems to be unusually awkward for her age. This past semester Elsie has broken both her legs in two separate accidents and complains about pains in her joints. Sometimes her lips look bluish and she often asks for a drink of water. Elsie seems to go to the girls' room frequently.

V. Perceptual–Motor Problems

A. Legal definition: Learning disability is a disorder in one or more of the basic psychological processes involved in understanding or in using language, spoken or written. This disorder may manifest itself in an imperfect ability to listen, think, speak, read, write, spell, or do mathematical calculations.

The term includes such conditions as perceptual handicaps, brain injury, minimal brain dysfunction, dyslexia and developmental aphasia.

The term does not include children who have learning problems which are primarily the result of visual, hearing or motor handicaps, of mental retardation, of emotional disturbance, or of environmental, cultural or economic disadvantages. (PL 94-142, Section 121, a.5.)

B. Example of common clues to learning disabilities: Joan, age 13, in the seventh grade, demonstrates above average scores on her standardized tests, however her academic achievement in her every day school work is quite low. There seems to be a serious discrepancy between her ability and her achievement. Joan is easily distracted, cannot concentrate for long periods of time, and appears to be "jumping out of her seat" all the time. She just can't seem to get herself "organized." She has difficulty in interpreting written directions and remembering what she has seen or read. Sometimes Joan has difficulty with directionality. The physical education teacher has commented on her limited athletic competence in group games. Joan becomes easily frustrated.

VI. Information Processing/Thinking/Memorizing Problems

A. Legal definition: Mental retardation is significantly subaverage general intellectual functioning existing concurrently with deficits in adaptive behavior and manifested during the developmental period, which adversely affects a child's educational performance. (PL 94-142, Section 121, a.5.)

B. Example of common clues to thinking/memory problems: Tony, age 7, in the second grade, is taking a long time to learn the alphabet. When it appears that he has learned the upper case letters, he seems to forget the lower case ones. Tony's attention span is very short, particularly if you ask him to perform a task that is not concrete. At times, he forgets to go to the bathroom and has an "accident" in the classroom.

VII. Social–Emotional Problems

A. Legal definition: Serious emotional disturbance is a condition exhibiting one or more of the following characteristics over a long period of time and to a marked degree, which adversely affects educational performance:

1. An inability to learn which cannot be explained by intellectual, sensory or health factors:

2. An inability to build or maintain satisfactory interpersonal relationships with peers and teachers;

3. Inappropriate types of behaviors or feelings under normal circumstances;

4. A general pervasive mood of unhappiness or depression; or

5. A tendency to develop physical symptoms or fears associated with personal or school problems.

The term includes children who are schizophrenic or autistic. The term does not include children who are socially maladjusted, unless it is determined that they are seriously emotionally disturbed. (PL 94-142, Section 121, a.5.)

B. Example of common clues to social–emotional problems: Bruce, age 12, in the sixth grade, is always talking too much, too loudly, and interrupting in group situations that result in bitter arguments with his friends and teachers. As a result, he becomes very angry, loses his self-control, and destroys any objects that are in his way. Then his mood might change dramatically, and he will withdraw from his friends or teachers and behave like a "loner."

VIII. Identifying the Gifted and Talented

A. Legal definition: Gifted and talented pupils are children and youth who are identified at the preschool, elementary and secondary level as possessing demonstrated or potential abilities that give evidence of high performance responsively in areas such as intellectual, creative, specific academic or leadership ability, or in the performing and visual arts, and by reason thereof require services or activities not ordinarily provided by the school. (PL 95-561, Title IX A, 1978)

B. Examples of common clues to identifying the gifted and talented: Marie, age 14, in the seventh grade, just won first prize in the annual all-county art show. She loves writing original plays and just recently directed one of them in the local playhouse. She is extremely popular and this past semester was voted president of her class.

Assessment

I. Debate one or both of the following issues in class:

    A. "Identification of the gifted has for too long been based on I.Q. scores. Children and youth may be gifted or talented in many ways other than intelligence."

    B. "Minority children and youth may score low on I.Q. examinations because of language problems, yet be highly intelligent or gifted."

II. Discuss the following issues with your colleagues noting whether you agree or disagree with the premises.

    A. Bias or prejudice

        1. Female teacher believes normal behaviors of boys or young adolescent males in class are "aggressive."

        2. Some educators associate certain behaviors with minority youth. They would accept or be tolerant of the same behaviors and not deem them negative if they witnessed them in nonminority youth.

        3. Marks, grades, and checklist scales are higher for students — or lower — depending upon the educator's attitude to the student's compliance with classroom or school rules, student's pleasant personality, student's playing up to the teacher.

    B. Error of "association" or "false correlation"

        1. Low scores on group I.Q. tests are thought by many educators to be predictive of low scores on reading tests. Since both tests demand reading, one is certainly predictive of the other.

        2. A student who has great difficulty in speech articulation is sometimes thought also to be suffering from comprehension problems.

    C. Error of using too few observations or using observations out of context

        1. Educator keeps no written records of what is observed trusting, unprofessionally, to memory.

        2. Failure to ask another professional to make observations of the child or youth in question in order to provide objectivity of observation.

    3.   Hasty generalizations of behavior without sufficient proof of a behavioral *pattern.*

III.   Discuss the implications of this statement:

"Educators easily identify the disruptive student and the bright student. They may fail to give adequate attention to the needs of the quiet, the shy, the loner, the inattentive."

Implications/Applications

Educating children and youth in the regular classroom or the mainstream suggests that students who differ on a continuum of functional ability are more alike than different. Exceptional students with a wide variety of handicapping conditions have participated successfully in well-developed programs that focus on the functional problems of students, rather than on the category of behavior assigned to them. Few educators would argue that categorizing students is necessary for instructional purposes. In fact, categories may provide information that is not relevant for instruction. The variation of skills and abilities within a given category may be greater than the variation or differences that exist between categories. As a result, the use of crosscategories and multicategories may be used to group students with common instructional needs.

Essentially, this text has focused on just this issue, or how to provide a professional response to exceptional student's needs in the mainstream.

Table 3.2 provides suggested ways that regular and special educators may respond to specific student needs.

TABLE 3.2

Student Needs with Responses from Regular and Special Educators

Student Needs	Responses from Regular and Special Educators
1. *Visual Needs* for Ed, age 8, in the third grade	a. Educators will acquire special learning aids (typewriters, Braille typewriters and books, tape recorders, large print materials).
	b. Educators will encourage the use and development of other senses (hearing, smelling, touching).
	c. Provide Ed with sufficient time to complete reading assignments.

TABLE 3.2 (Continued)

Student Needs	Responses from Regular and Special Educators
	d. Educators will seat Ed next to the window.
	e. Educators will encourage Ed to give oral reports, short speeches, serve as "master of ceremonies" for special activities.
2. *Hearing Needs* for Beth, age 7, in the second grade	a. Educators will seat Beth in a "favorable spot."
	b. Educators will provide Beth with extra assistance from a teaching assistant in speech instruction.
	c. Educators will encourage Beth to acquire a hearing aid and they may learn how the aid functions and how it is maintained (e.g., how do the batteries work).
	d. Educators may encourage Beth to use and develop other senses (seeing, touching, smelling).
	e. Educators will encourage Beth to use the computer and visual materials as learning tools.
	f. Educators will focus on the use of visual cues when speaking to and teaching Beth.
3. *Speech and Language Needs* for Irene, age 6, in the second grade and Ira, age 10, in the fifth grade	a. Educators will assist Irene and Ira to *hear* their speech and language by use of a tape recorder.
	b. Educators and peers will assist Irene and Ira in correctly pronouncing words by use of tape recorders.
	c. Educators will frequently encourage Irene and Ira to use correctly pronounced words.
	d. Educators will encourage Irene and Ira to practice their oral skills publicly (e.g., introducing a student to a teacher, short introduction to class skits, etc.).
	e. Educators will cue Irene and Ira that they will be called on.
	f. Educators will provide alternative activities that are not focused on speech and language.
4. *Learning Disability Needs* for Joan, age 13, in the seventh grade	a. Educators will observe Joan closely to determine her modality strengths.
	b. Educators will teach Joan in her modality strength including the use of manipulative materials at her *readiness* level (not her potential level).
	c. Educators will provide Joan with short, structured assignments that will lead to success.
	d. Educators will frequently review and assess Joan's understanding of her work.

TABLE 3.2 (Continued)

Student Needs	Responses from Regular and Special Educators
	e. Educators will provide Joan with enough time to respond to their questions and provide positive feedback.
5. *Thinking/Memory Needs* for Tony, age 7, in the second grade	a. Educators will identify a few critical relevant basic skills for initial instruction.
	b. Educators will provide Tony with very concrete activities that may be successfully mastered.
	c. Educators will provide Tony with instruction for *very short* periods of time, provide frequent feedback and review.
	d. Educators will provide Tony with simple step-by-step directions.
	e. Educators will provide Tony with many opportunities and practice to learn the same material.
6. *Social-Emotional Needs* for Bruce, age 12, in the sixth grade	a. Educators will explain to Bruce (in a kind manner) why others react the way they do to him.
	b. Educators will model or provide models for appropriate expressions of behavior for Bruce.
	c. Educators will "control" Bruce's inappropriate behavior so that it doesn't become totally unmanageable.
	d. Educators will provide Bruce with clear, firm behavioral expectations with the appropriate feedback (praise) and reinforcements.
	e. Educators will provide Bruce with a "time out corner" and/or "quiet corner" to work alone occasionally.
7. *Physical Needs* for Elsie, age 11, in the sixth grade	a. Educators will encourage Elsie to do as much as she can by herself.
	b. Educators will be sensitive to safety problems in the room and school.
	c. Educators will permit Elsie to have as many drinks and visits to the girls' room as needed.
	d. Educators will involve Elsie in some aspect of *every* physical activity undertaken by the class.
8. *Enrichment Needs* for Marie, age 14, in the seventh grade	a. Educators will encourage independent studies for Marie that will allow her to work as an "assistant" to a professional playwright.
	b. Educators will encourage Marie to identify, and *organize* special campaigns for selected issues in the school.

TABLE 3.2 (Continued)

Student Needs	Responses from Regular and Special Educators
	c. Educators will encourage Marie in a nondirect teaching style to pursue academic learning that is focused on analysis, synthesis, and evaluation of data.
	e. Educators will encourage Marie to engage in small research projects whereby she will use the skills identified in VIIIA.

In sum, educators may wish to exercise caution when hypothesizing that a student "belongs" in a special category.

Referral Matters

INTRODUCTION

WHEN TEACHERS IN THE REGULAR CLASSROOM believe that one or more students may be exceptional, they need to follow through on this belief with confirmatory processes. These processes are described in Module 4.0.

In Module 4.1, suggestions are given educators for alternative actions for use *prior* to referral for assessment. These actions are meant to satisfy the need for appropriate data gathering on student behaviors as well as their learning environment. The major processes discussed are: conferences with students and parents; the maintenance of records — anecdotal, duration time sampling, frequency recording, planned activity check, latency records, and checklists; the review of students' standardized test data and criterion-referenced tests; and the use of a consultant and the interdisciplinary team.

Module 4.2 examines the generic guidelines set forth in Public Law 94-142 for an appropriate referral process and requests that educators and parents examine the process in the local school or school district in relation to its fulfilling federal mandates. This module is an important data source for educators and parents because it reviews the law and clearly delineates the areas of responsibilities and rights of all concerned.

Further references to the referral process can be found in the Topic Referenced Bibliography on pages 232 to 262 under the numbers: *2* (Due Process, Hearings), *3* (New Roles for Educational Personnel and Parents), and *6* (Current Models for Planning Education for Exceptional Children and Youth).

4.1   TO REFER OR NOT TO REFER, THAT IS THE QUESTION

Note: The educator who refers believes, on the evidence of data gathered, that there is indication that the student may possibly need special services not available in the regular classroom and that the follow-up special assessment may reveal that *no* special services are needed or that the student may need special services. The educator must also face the reality that no services may be provided although needed.

Minimum Competency Objective

You will think about, discuss, and come to some opinion on the difficulties of defining where "regular" education and "special" education begin and end.

Rationale

Educators differ in their skills to assess "normal" student behaviors. Some student problems are blamed upon students when in reality the problems may stem from improper, inadequate, irrelevant instructional strategies, or poor classroom management. Before educators rush to refer students to special education settings, several alternative actions should be considered including the systematic examination of the learning environment that considers the nature and quality of instruction provided. The purpose of this module is to give you a chance to think about these alternatives. You may think of others and are urged to do so.

Enabling Activities

I.   With at least one member of an interdisciplinary team, discuss the following suggestions for action before referral of students to possible special education settings.

    A.   The team members will ask themselves whether they used proper data-gathering techniques to conclude that the student needs referral. Some data-gathering approaches and instruments could be:

        1.   *Conference/interview with student*: Interviews with students provide them with the opportunity to present a description of, and discussion about their behaviors.

        2.   *Conference/interview with parents*: Educator verifies whether school behaviors match student behaviors at home or in the community.

3. *Anecdotal Records*: Written records without teacher evaluation or interpretation of student's behaviors immediately or as soon after the event as possible which include:

   a. a brief statement of the setting
   b. a concise and correct description of what the student did
   c. a notation as to whether this was a representative or unusual example of the student's everyday behavior.

4. *Duration Records*: Student's behavior is recorded over a number of days by using a stopwatch during a predetermined interval each day. For example, 20 minutes a day for 5 days, Jimmy's actual attention to the book he is silently reading is recorded. Then an average time for on-task attention to silent reading is recorded.

5. *Time Sampling Records*: For students who evidence high incidence of a certain behavior, the observer decides on an observation interval, divides the interval into equal parts, and records student behavior *only at the end of the interval division.* This kind of recording helps to avoid the statement that Johnny is "always" doing something. The last statement may be based on the educator's memory only of the disruptive behavior rather than the times Johnny was behaving in acceptable ways.

6. *Frequency Recording (sometimes called Event Recording)*: When a student's behavior seems fairly frequent to an educator, he or she may check this assumption by keeping a record through the use of tally marks on a piece of paper or the use of a counter discreetly used during a portion of the school day.

7. *Planned Activity Check* (often called PLACHECK and described by Thomas Risley in 1971): This is a record keeping strategy for groups rather than individuals. At predetermined intervals, the educator counts the number of pupils engaged in the assigned activity and makes a record of this number. The educator also records the total number of students present in the educational setting at that time. By assigning the total engaged as a numerator of a fraction and the total number of students present as a denominator of a fraction, a percent of those engaged in the task may be obtained. For example, eight of ten students were on task at 9:00 a.m. or 80 percent; nine of ten students were on task at 9:10 a.m. or 90 percent; seven of fourteen were on task at 9:20 a.m. (Students returned from reading instruction) or 50 percent; fourteen of fourteen were on task at 9:30 a.m. or 100 percent; nine of ten were on task at 9:40 a.m. (Students were taken away from class for reading

instruction) or 90 percent. Adding the percents and dividing by the number of intervals recorded gives the average time the group remains on task 22 percent. (T.R. Risley (1972) "Spontaneous language and the preschool," in J.C. Stanley (ed.), *Preschool Programs for the Disadvantaged*. Baltimore: Johns Hopkins University Press.

8. *Latency Records*: A timed record of interval, usually recorded in minutes, between the educator's direction to do or not to do something and the student's compliance. For example, the educator tells the class, "Open your books to page 53." Tommy takes eight minutes to do so, while the rest of the class is on task, reading and doing the activities required.

9. *Attendance Records*: How often a student is absent is directly related to how much exposure a student has to the curriculum, which may result in how much time a student spends on task.

10. *Standardized Achievement Tests*: Student's achievement data may permit educators to compare student's performance with peers.

11. *Criterion-Referenced Tests*: The data from these tests may determine if the student has or has not learned what he/she was taught (See Module 9.3 on Mastery Learning).

12. *Checklists*: Many types are possible. The focus of this checklist is based on a setting that identifies student and teacher classroom management behaviors (See Modules 8.1 and 8.2).

CLASSROOM MANAGEMENT CHECKLIST

		Yes	No
a.	Students sometimes work in large groups.	___	___
b.	Students always work in large groups.	___	___
c.	Students sometimes work in small groups.	___	___
d.	Students always work in small groups.	___	___
e.	Students sometimes do individualized work.	___	___
f.	Students always do individualized work.	___	___
g.	The room has places for students to:		
	• blow off steam	___	___
	• rest	___	___
	• quietly read	___	___
h.	Seating, tables, desks are movable.	___	___
i.	There is adequate lighting.	___	___
j.	Street noises are at a minimum.	___	___

B.   Educators thinking of making referral will ask themselves if they have had sufficient contact with parents or guardians to ascertain their similarities (differences) of observation of the student in school, home, community.

C. Educators thinking of referral will ask themselves whether they have been as objective as they can be. To make sure, they will ask another educator in the building to verify their observations in the classroom setting. This professional may be an administrator, supervisor, special educator, guidance counselor, school nurse, school psychologist, reading specialist, etc. Sometimes a personal bias may affect objectivity.

D. The regular educator may ask for and receive services of a consulting special educator or school psychologist who will work with the regular educator in observing the student's behaviors within a designated period of time, using more frequent checks on progress in academic, social, and/or physical skills. *The regular educator will follow recommendations for changes in classroom management or instructional strategies to see whether these changes have positive effects.* Further, the consultant may suggest the use of other services in the existing program or the change of a student to another grade or another class within the same grade. The following are samples of suggestions often made by consultants and interdisciplinary teams to assist students:

1. change the level of readability of materials concerning the same content focus;
2. change verbal learning focus in class to a multisensory approach;
3. change highly abstract approach to a more concrete approach to teaching concepts;
4. give shorter assignments;
5. sequence instruction in smaller steps;
6. provide immediate feedback on short step assignments; reward for academic, physical, social success;
7. try another teacher or teachers if student is in a departmental setting;
8. set up an individual contract with the student with reasonable levels of achievement within reasonable intervals of time;
9. assign an interested peer to tutor the student;
10. ask for a paraprofessional or volunteer parent to tutor the student;
11. increase your liaison with the parents/guardians of the child in order to enlist their cooperation in checking progress;

12. check additional professional services in school which may give the needed assistance (librarian, mathematics and reading specialists, bilingual program teachers, gifted and talented program teachers);
13. ask principal, assistant principal, chairperson, etc., for a change in the student's daily schedule, classroom, or grade.

Assessment

1. With the interdisciplinary team try to define where regular education and special education begin and end.

2. On the basis of your readings and discussion in this module, with one team member write the steps you would take in gathering data and in verifying its objectivity before you would refer a student for diagnosis (assessment) to determine whether that child or youth needs special education.

Additional Activities

Choose one or more of the data-gathering instruments described in this module and try it/them with your class. Note the difficulties of recording, ways to simplify the technique for yourself, and the rewards of gathering the data.

Implications/Applications

"To refer or not to refer" has serious implications for a student. Current research in special education suggests there must be a systematic examination of the learning environment and the nature and quality of the instruction provided the student *prior* to any attempt to diagnose a disorder. Only after deficiencies in the learning environment have been ruled out by documentation and the student fails to learn under reasonable alternative approaches should the student be exposed to the risks of stigma and misclassification inherent in referrals and individual assessment.[1] This examination and documentation of the teaching/learning environment may best be conducted by an interdisciplinary team.

1. Messick, Samuel. (1984). Assessment in context: Appraising student performance in relation to instructional quality. *Educational Researcher* 13, pp. 3–8.

Table 4.1 provides examples of factors in the learning/teaching environment that interdisciplinary team members may examine and document their effects on student academic and social behaviors. Documentation is conducted by interdisciplinary team members relative to their typical job functions.

Collecting and analyzing data on the teaching/learning environment in relation to student academic and social behavior provide the interdisciplinary team with documented information that may be used to identify a student's learning difficulty. As a result of this identification, appropriate alternative instructional management modes, instructional strategies, teaching styles, and curriculum materials are provided to the student for program modification. The alternatives which are selected as most appropriate depend on the availability of resources and services as well as the knowledge and competence of the teachers who may work with the student. In addition, parents should be informed of the use of these alternatives in program modification.

There is much to be gained by examining and documenting the degree to which a student learns or fails to learn in a variety of classroom arrangements with appropriately defined instructional/management tools before classifying or labeling that student.

TABLE 4.1

Factors in the Learning/Teaching Environment
and Team Members' Documentation

Factors in the Learning/Teaching Environment	Team Member(s) in Documentation
1. Identify frequency of use and effects of classroom organization modes on student behavior: • individualized instruction • independent study • peer tutoring • pair tutoring • small group • large group	a. Observational data on the frequency of use of classroom organization mode may be collected by regular and special teachers, educational evaluators, school administrators, and supervisors. b. Observational data (see Enabling Activities) on student's social behavior may be collected by regular and special education teachers, school psychologist, educational evaluators, and supervisors. c. Academic performance data on student may be collected by teachers and educational evaluators with criterion-referenced tests, teacher-made tests, and evidence of student's work. d. The relationship of these modes to student academic and social behaviors may be determined by school psychologist,

TABLE 4.1 (Continued)

Factors in the Learning/Teaching Environment	Team Member(s) in Documentation
	educational evaluator, and regular and special education teachers. *Example*: Independent study is the most frequently used mode and based on observation data, the student's social behavior is often inappropriate.
2. Identify frequency of use and effects of instructional tools/materials on student behavior: • programmed instruction • computers/CAI • contracts • workbooks • Individually Prescribed Instruction • A.V. materials (tape recorders, television, etc.) • games	a. Observational data on the frequency of use of instructional tools and materials may be collected by regular and special education teachers, supervisors, administrators. b. Observational data (see Enabling Activities) may be collected on student social behavior by school psychologist, educational evaluator, supervisors, regular and special education teachers. c. Academic performance data may be collected by teacher aides, regular and special education teachers with criterion-referenced tests, evidence of student's work, and results of CAI packages. d. The relationship between instructional tools/materials and student academic and social behaviors may be determined by school psychologist, educational evaluator, regular and special education teachers. *Example*: Contracts and games are the most frequently used tools and materials and based on teacher-made tests, the student's average performance is at the 50% level of accuracy.
3. Identify frequency of use and effects of instructional strategies and teaching styles on student behavior: • mastery learning • task analysis • use of objectives • teacher direct instruction • indirect instruction	a. Observational data on the frequency of use of instructional strategies and teaching styles may be collected by regular and special education teachers, educational evaluators, and school psychologist. b. Observational data (see Enabling Activities) on student's social behavior may be collected by regular and special education teachers, school psychologist, educational evaluators, and supervisors. c. Academic performance data may be collected by regular and special education teachers, educational evaluator, and

TABLE 4.1 (Continued)

Factors in the Learning/Teaching Environment	Team Member(s) in Documentation
	school psychologist with criterion-referenced tests.
	d. The relationship of instructional strategies and teaching styles to student academic and social behaviors may be determined by school psychologist, educational evaluator, and regular and special education teachers. *Example*: Mastery learning taught in a direct teaching style is the most frequently used instructional strategy and student achievement on criterion-referenced tests is comparable to that of peers.
4. Identify availability and frequency of curriculum materials and program: • Does the material/program reflect the needs of different ethnic, linguistic, and socio-economic groups? • Are the curriculum materials *current* and *useful*? • Are the curriculum materials available in different levels (beginning to more advanced)? • Are social skills programs in operation? • Are alternative learning programs used?	The curriculum coordinator and regular and special education teachers will determine through observational data how often a student is exposed to a particular curriculum material and program. School psychologist, educational evaluator, and regular and special education teachers will use standardized achievement tests and criterion-referenced tests to assess student performance.
5. Determine the absentee records of the school population as a whole as well as the student's individual attendance record. Identify the reasons why the student is absent.	School administrators will determine the absentee records of the school population as a whole as well as for individual students. School social worker will identify the reasons the student is absent.

4.2 THE REFERRAL PROCESS

Minimum Competency Objective

You will take a close-up view of the referral process in your school and base your observations on the guidelines offered in this module. You will thus know what happens to your referrals when local guidelines correspond with federal and state legislative guidelines.

Rationale

The educator who has tested and documented reasonable alternatives in the teaching/learning environment of a student may still have to refer the student for formal assessment with the possible outcome that this student will be offered special education of some type. Now it is time for all the educators in the school to follow the provisions of PL 94-142. State regulations typically define referral and assessment procedures, placement and review operations, specific timelines for each phase in the placement process, appropriate caseload for special education teachers and related personnel, and general principles (such as due process) which must be observed in providing special services. This module provides information with the recommendation that educators do research in their own schools or school districts to discover what specific forms and procedures are used to implement PL 94-142.

Enabling Activities

Read the following materials and discuss the processes of referral with your large group, small group, or partner, noting deviations from the general referral process in your school or school district. Compare various forms and procedures within the schools or school districts represented by educators in your class.

I. The General Referral Sequence

    A. The school has a printed referral form. In some school districts, this form is standardized for all schools. Get a copy of this form and discuss its parts and implications for gathering data and making referrals.

    B. The school has a promulgated standardized procedure for sending this completed form to a specific person who is then responsible for recording the reception of the referral, the number of referrals made by this teacher, and the steps taken concerning the referral. This person may be the school administrator or a person designated by him or her. A designee may be the chairperson of the school's IEP team. When referrals are fairly numerous, the school administrator may find it necessary to ask one or more faculty members to take a referral load to see that all needed forms are handed in and complete, that the referral is processed in a speedy manner, the student's parents are informed of the referral, and the necessary follow-up meetings are called. A record of these steps must be made and kept as a permanent record in a school file. (Who is designated to do this work in your school? Where are permanent files kept which contain records of referral procedures?)

C. Ideally, the first step after the teacher referral reaches the designated person responsible for checking, recording and following through on the referral process, is to follow the procedures discussed in Module 4.1. After that, a resource room teacher or another team member may go over the referral with the regular educator. Classroom observations and other pertinent data may be collected on the student by the resource room teacher and other team members who may or may not recommend follow-up assessment. If no assessment is recommended, the teacher may be given assistance by the resource room teacher or other team members in devising new classroom management or instructional techniques. (Is this step present in your school?)

D. If assessment is recommended, parents must be notified immediately and their consent obtained. Parents must be notified in their first language that a meeting will be held by the school district team (federal law calls this team the Committee on the Handicapped) which may be called the COH or any other name so long as it keeps within the guidelines of the federal law and the specific state plan sent to Washington for implementation of the federal law. In some places, this group is called the Child Study Team. Parents also must be told the modes of assessment the team will use and the due process regulations provided them and their children under the law.

E. To protect the student from poor decision making on the part of school personnel or parents, a due process hearing may be held under the following circumstances:

1. The school district initiates a due process hearing when:

   a. parent/parents/guardians refuse permission to have the assessment team evaluate the referred student;

   b. parent/parents/guardians refuse permission to place the student in a special education setting after assessment has been made.

2. The parent/parents/guardians initiate a due process hearing when:

    a.   a referred student is not given assessment;

    b.   assessment is deemed inadequate by parent/parents/ guardians;

    c.   parent/parents/guardians disagree with the special education placement after referral and assessment;

    d.   the school district does not provide a special education placement after referral and assessment and the parents do not agree with this outcome.

II.   The Due Process Sequence (Generic Procedures)
(Check with your school district to compare their procedures with the generic procedures listed here.)

A.   Parents/parent/guardians make a formal request for a due process hearing. This is done in writing to the school district superintendent. This letter should contain the following:

    1.   a description of the problem;

    2.   a request for a due process hearing date;

    3.   a request for the appointment of a due process hearing officer.

B.   The superintendent tries to resolve the problem by negotiating informally.

C.   If step two above fails, the superintendent asks the state education department agency involved with due process hearing to appoint a hearing officer.

D.   A due process hearing date is set which is convenient for all concerned persons.

E.   Present at the hearing are the hearing officer, legal counsel for the school district, school district personnel who have information about the issues of the case, the parent/parents/guardian, their legal counsel if they so wish, or a parent surrogate. Parents may demand the presence of certain school personnel if they are not present. A verbatim record of the hearing is kept by a court stenographer or by means of a tape recorder.

F.   The hearing officer may give an immediate recommendation or ask for more information. The gathering of information has a deadline which differs from state to state.

G.   The recommendation is binding if neither the school district nor the parent/parents/guardians make a formal response to the recommendation.

H.   Formal response is a written appeal to the state education department.

I.   In the case of a formal appeal, a state level panel or hearing officer examines the local proceedings, and may ask for more information.

The panel makes its recommendation to the chief state school officer who, in turn, makes a formal recommendation that is binding.

J.   If either the school district or the parent/parents/guardians do not agree with this recommendation, the case must go on to a law court.

Assessment

1. Outline the specific guidelines for referral used in your school or school district. Place this outline and the forms you have collected from your school, your school district, and other schools or districts during this module at the end of this lesson for easy reference when you need them.

2. Write in one paragraph the implications for prior record keeping by educators who may be called to a due process hearing.

Additional Activities

1. Discuss the implications for the involvement of parents of poor or minority children or youth in the due process sequence. What procedures are used in the case of students with limited English proficiency?

2. Since the due process sequence assumes an adversary stance for both the parent and school district personnel, draw up an alternative model for helping the school district and parents to *collaborate*.

Implications/Applications

No doubt, the referral form represents a statement about a student's learning difficulty. Most school districts use standard forms that range from simple to complex. Simple forms usually require brief statements about the learning problem and complex forms may require descriptions of student performance. In either case, the referral should include information that is precise, specific, descriptive and documented. For example:

1. If Jane, age 12, in the sixth grade, is having a "reading problem," it is appropriate to report that Jane's reading achievement scores on the ABC Standardized Reading Test dropped 20 percentile points in the past academic year, even though her language skills, measured by a criterion-referenced test increased by 18 points from 70% to 88%. In contrast, it is not appropriate to report that Jane is having reading problems and her academic achievement is low.

2. Saying that Jane is "hyperactive" does not describe her actual behavior, but saying that "Jane does not sit at her desk for more than 3 minutes within a 20-minute class period, always tries to be first in line, and, without being recognized, yells out answers on the average of ten times during a 40-minute class period," provides behavioral descriptions of Jane's actions in the classroom.

Further information on the referral form should include documentation of the learning problem, test scores, baseline performance data and a description of the alternative instructional strategies and materials that were tried.

An important aspect of the referral process is the actual filling out of the referral form by two or more members of a school-based interdisciplinary team since it allows team members to check the adequacy and validity of the information. Making a referral together is a way of establishing a collaborative relationship with a peer who will provide a second opinion as well as assistance. Upon completion of the referral form, it is necessary for the interdisciplinary school-based team to review and analyze the referral and respond to the referring persons. Essentially, conducting the referral analysis permits the school-based team to make a determination as to when the student's case should be reviewed by the assessment team for possible special services. If assessment is recommended, parents must be notified as to its purpose, the tests and procedures used, and the right to receive an explanation of the procedural safeguards available to them under PL 94-142.

Due process provides a procedural safeguard on the rights of students and parents. However, there are critics who claim that due process procedures are quite costly, add to the already existing mountain of paper work, and are especially time consuming, particularly when a due process hearing is involved. Regardless, the procedures are important since they call for parent involvement in important decision making. The school-based interdisciplinary team should make every effort to provide a personalized approach to informing parents of the legal involvement in the referral process. The following hints may help encourage a personalized approach to explaining procedures and obtaining parent consent to the referral. *Make every effort* to set up a conference *in person* in order to:

a. *review* referral procedures and obtain consent;
b. *encourage* parent or parent advocate to ask questions concerning the procedures;
c. *suggest* advocacy assistance if necessary to aid parents in pursuing due process procedures;
d. *provide* written information, perhaps in pamphlet form, entitled "Guide For Parents in Due Process Procedures";
e. *inform* parents of their rights; it may *reduce* the number of due process hearings.

Assessment of Exceptional Children and Youth

INTRODUCTION

According to Public Law 94-142, the placement of a child or youth in special education and/or a mainstreamed classroom is a function of the COH. This module takes a close look at the general structure of the committee as outlined by federal law and then challenges you to find out how the law has been implemented in your school district (Module 5.1).

As an educator, you may be called upon to serve on or with such a committee. You will be better able to do so if you review some of the underlying philosophies of, and approaches to assessment which currently govern decision making on such teams. Module 5.2 addresses this issue.

Module 5.3 asks you to take a close look at present modes of assessing student achievements and behaviors. You are asked to look with the sharpest scrutiny at standardized tests, including the newer criteria-referenced tests. This module is meant to remind you of the danger of placing too much trust in one or a few diagnostic tools. For example, deaf readers across the nation on the average never achieve beyond the fourth grade level on standardized reading tests! Teacher experience with the students and their comprehension levels suggests that the tests rather than the students are at fault. A recent research study by Carolyn Ewoldt of Gallaudet College proffers a logical reason for the poor test results.[1] The deaf students she studied read selections ranging in difficulty from fifth grade through twelfth grade with comprehension comparable to a similar group of students with hearing. What was changed through her study were the test modes. The deaf and hearing students were given whole, meaningful, longer, interesting, and predictable stories to read, rather than the snippets offered in

---

1. Ewoldt, Carolyn. (1981). A psycholinguistic description of selected deaf children reading in sign language. *Reading Research Quarterly,* 27, 58–114.

most standardized tests. They were then tested through Goodman's analysis of errors, retelling of the stories, and the filling in of blanks in passages to test for comprehension. Familiarity with the deaf would indicate that these test modes enabled the students to use all the language skills available to them to show what they comprehended. Restriction to written responses on most standardized reading tests denies deaf students the freedom to indicate the fullness of their reading comprehension skills.

Additional references to the Committee on the Handicapped, testing procedures, and the overall assessment of exceptional children and youth can be found on pages 232 to 262 in the Topic Referenced Bibliography. Books and articles related to these issues are marked with the numbers 6 and 8.1.

5.1 THE STRUCTURE OF THE ASSESSMENT TEAM

Minimum Competency Objective

You will review the legislative guidelines of PL 94-142 and your state plan related to these guidelines concerning the structure of the assessment team (COH) responsible for testing and placement of students in special education programs. You will compare these guidelines for the structure of the COH with the actual structure of the COH in your school or school district.

Rationale

In the life of any child or youth referred for special education, the assessment team is an extremely important decision-making group. It is no less important to special and regular educators who must implement the decisions of this group. It is therefore important that educators know the make-up of the local teams, particularly to note whether there is sufficient representation of special and regular educators from local schools on the team.

Enabling Activities

Working in a large group, small groups, or pairs, conduct the following research:

1. Review the federal guidelines for the assessment team, known as the COH. (See Module series 1.0 in this text or refer to the text of PL 94-142.)

2. Look up the approved plan of your state which was accepted by the federal government on the grounds that it met federal guidelines in PL 94-142.

3. Research the mandated structure of the COH for your school/school district.

4. When these data have been gathered, compare the structure of the local COH with federal and state guidelines.

Assessment

1. Draw up an ideal structure for the COH in your district, taking into account:

    a. frequency of referral of students;
    b. nature of the exceptionalities usually referred;
    c. difficulty of assessing referred children/youth;
    d. financial considerations;
    e. efficiency factors;
    f. the federal and state guidelines.

2. Compare your model with the following model:

TABLE 5.0

"Ideal" Committee on the Handicapped Members for a School District

Local School *Permanent* Members	Local School *Ad Hoc* Members	Assessment Specialists Appointed to Serve the School District on an Ad Hoc Basis
1. Local School Principal 2. Local School Administrator of Special Education 3. Representative of Special and Regular Education	1. Parent or Parent Advocate of Referred Student 2. Referring Teacher 3. Referred Student	1. Audiologist 2. Curriculum Specialist 3. Guidance Counselor 4. Occupational Therapist 5. Opthalmologist 6. Optometrist 7. Physical Education Teacher 8. Physical Therapist 9. Physician (Generalist/ Specialist) 10. Psychiatrist 11. School Nurse 12. School Psychologist 13. Social Worker 14. Speech Pathologist 15. Vocational Rehabilitation Counselor 16. Other — as needed

3. Compare your model with the actual model in your district.

Additional Activity

What overall recommendation would you offer for the structure of your school district's COH based upon your research and comparisons in this module?

Implication/Applications

In using a team, it is assumed that a group decision may provide a safeguard against the error that an individual may make while assuring greater adherence to due process requirements. A range of expertise contributes to the assessment, planning, and evaluation activities of the team. Table 5.1 provides a relationship of typical team members of a COH to their particular contributions.

TABLE 5.1

Relationship of Typical COH Team Members to Their Particular Contributions

Team Members	Contribution
1. Teachers (Regular and Special)	May provide information on many aspects of student behavior, but are particularly expert on student's *current* academic and social performance that includes and compares student's social skills with peers, performance on informal and criterion-referenced tests, and responses to different instructional management modes.
2. Educational Evaluator	May provide assessment data from various standardized instruments on student preformance in basic skills and general academic achievement. Data will be interpreted to define appropriate instructional strategies and curricular materials.
3. School Psychologist	May provide more formal assessment data on the cognitive, social, and adaptive behaviors of a student and is usually responsible for administering the assessment instrument and *interpreting* the data, particularly in terms of its psychological consequences. In combination with the data presented by

TABLE 5.1 (Continued)

Team Members	Contribution
	teachers and the educational evaluator, the data provided by the school psychologist allows the team to compare a student's *actual* performance with some indication of his or her *possible* performance.
4. School Social Worker	May provide critical information on the family including students' background and general home life. The school social worker may assist parents and the child in identifying goals, strategies and resources for positive action in the home and in the community.
5. Guidance Counselor	May provide data on academic and behavioral history of the student as well as additional information on the family. This kind of information is useful in making decisions regarding student placement and the use of appropriate instructional management tools.
6. Speech/ Language Teacher	May provide assessment data on student's communication skills as well as instructional assistance in working with students with speech/language disabilities
7. Medical Personnel (including school nurse)	May provide a biomedical history including information on vision and hearing, and information about drug therapy particularly related to physical and emotional functioning.
8. Personnel for Motor Development (including the physical education teacher, physical therapist, and occupational therapist)	May provide information about student's fine and gross motor abilities.
9. Parents/Parent Advocate and Student	May provide historical and developmental information on all aspects of the student's behavior. Student has an opportunity to express attitudes and feelings. May contribute to the support of the program in which the student will become involved.
10. School Administrators (including the principal, director of special services, and supervisors)	May provide information on the administrative options and their participation should increase the likelihood that the program will be supported.

The professional expertise offered by a team provides a broad data base for decision making that puts legal definitions into operation.

5.2   EDUCATIONAL PHILOSOPHIES AND APPROACHES TO THE ASSESSMENT OF LEARNING PROBLEMS AND THEIR IMPLICATIONS FOR TEACHERS AND STUDENTS

Minimum Competency Objectives

1. You will study the two major philosophical approaches to assessment related to learning problems and some of the assessment instruments related to these philosophies. You will develop a critical approach to assessment.
2. You will describe additional approaches of assessment that may be used in combination with the assessment instruments discussed in Objective 1.

Rationale

The types of follow-up instructions recommended for students with learning problems who are given special education placements often depends on the mode of assessment used. The mode of assessment, in turn, depends upon the educational philosophies and preferred approaches of the assessors. It is important for educators to know the major philosophies and approaches concerning assessment of learning problems, to be aware of their weaknesses and strengths, and to be sensitive to the implications for follow-up instruction related to assessment.

Enabling Activities

Read the following text, discussing its implications with members of an interdisciplinary team. Make every attempt to include a school psychologist and educational evaluator in your group.

Assessment strategies for special education screening and placement of students who have learning problems may be divided into these major groups: the Differential-Diagnosis-Prescriptive Teaching Approach (DD-PT), the Skill Training Approach, and Alternative approaches.

1. *The Differential-Diagnosis-Prescriptive Teaching Approach (DD-PT)* This is essentially a process model of assessment and instruction.

Here, assessment is based upon investigation of what are termed *underlying abilities*. These underlying abilities are assumed to be sensory-perceptual, motor-perceptual and/or psycholinguistic skills which, if deficient, are said to be the causes of the students' learning problems. It is also assumed that follow-up remedial instruction will be directed to helping the student build up weak underlying abilities. The result of this build-up is said to be increased learning.

The assessment instruments and follow-up instructional methods suggested by the proponents of DD-PT assume that sensory-perceptual, motor-perceptual, and psycholinguistic skills needed for learning may be *differentiated* into subskills. Some proponents assume that these differentiated subskills should be arranged and taught in that sequence.

The major proponents of the DD-PT Philosophy are:

a. Marianne Frostig (See M. Frostig, D. Lefever, and J. Whittlesey. *The Marianne Frostig Developmental Test of Visual Perception.* (1964). Palo Alto, California: Consulting Psychology Press.)

b. Newell Kephart (See E. F. Roach and N. C. Kephart. (1966). *The Purdue Perceptual Motor Survey.* Columbus, Ohio: Charles Merrill.)

c. Samuel Kirk (See S.A. Kirk, L. McCarthy and E.D. Kirk (1968). *Illinois Test of Psycholinguistic Abilities,* rev. ed. Urbana, Illinois: University of Illinois Press.)

2. *The Skill Training Approach (A Task Analysis Model)*
Here, proponents believe that students have not learned the prior, small steps necessary to attainment of a more complex skill. Their learning deficit is their problem — not some underlying cause founded in visual, motor or psycholinguistic perception.

Proponents believe that attention to finding underlying sensory, motor or psycholinguistic skills wastes time at least and is invalid at most. Analysis of student learning problems would thus be an attempt to discover at what step in attaining a complex skill a student failed to achieve partial or full mastery. Follow-up instructions would give the student ample time to master the skill now known and to proceed along a sequence of skills until the complex skill is mastered. The instructional methodology related to this philosophy requires the educator to make a task analysis of the complex skill, to provide time for the student to practice each of the identified subskills, often in a variety of ways, and to give quick feedback to the student on his or her success or failure in mastering the small steps.

Skill training programs (assessment and follow-up instruction) are of several different types. Some of these are: mastery teaching, applied behavior analysis, precision teaching, behavior modification, and direct teaching. For fuller explanations of these types, see Module 10.0 in this text.

Assessments used to determine learning problems are usually of two types: *general screening* tests and *special diagnostic* tests.

Samples of generic screening tests are:

a. Jastak, J. and Jastak, S.R. (1965). *Wide Range Achievement Test (WRAT)*. Wilmington, Delaware: Guidance Associates.

b. Durost, W.N. et al. (1971). *Metropolitan Achievement Test (MAT)*. New York: Harcourt Brace Jovanovich.

c. Dunn, L.M. and Markwardt, F.C. (1970, 1979). *Peabody Individual Achievement Test (PIAT)*. Circle Pines, Minnesota: American Guidance Service.

Samples of specific diagnostic tests are:

a. *Language Arts Skill Center*. (1970). New York: Random House. (Comprehension, vocabulary, spelling, punctuation. Grades 7–9, in a criterion-referenced form.)

b. Lee, L.L. (1970). *Northwestern Syntax Screening Test*. Evanston, Illinois: Northwestern University Press.

c. Clymer, T. (1969). *Reading 360*. Boston: Ginn and Company. (Criterion-referenced for Grades 1–12.)

d. *Individual Pupil Monitoring System*, rev. ed. (1971). Boston: Houghton-Mifflin. (Mathematics skills, criterion-referenced.)

e. Connelly, A.J., Natchman, W., Pritchett, E.M. (1971). *Key Math: Diagnostic Arithmetic Test*. Circle Pines, Minnesota: American Guidance Service. (Criterion-referenced, Grades K–9.)

I. Take a close-up view of *Some Assessment Instruments Used by DD-PT Proponents* to understand the nature of the assessments used in Table 5.2.

TABLE 5.2

Some Assessment Instruments Used by DD-PT Proponents

Name of Test	Intended Audience	Subtests	Modes of Reporting Scores
Developmental Test of Visual Perception (DTVP)	Children, 3–9 years of age	1. Eye-motor coordination 2. Figure-ground discrimination 3. Form constancy	Perceptual quotients

TABLE 5.2 (Continued)

Name of Test	Intended Audience	Subtests	Modes of Reporting Scores
		4. Shape relationships	
		5. Spatial relationships	
Purdue Perceptual Motor Survey (PPMS)	Children, 6–10 years of age	1. Balance 2. Posture 3. Body image 4. Perceptual-motor match 5. Ocular control 6. Form perception	Scaled scores
Illinois Test of Psycholinguistic Abilities (ITPA)	Children, 2–10 years of age	1. Auditory reception 2. Visual reception 3. Auditory association 4. Visual association 5. Verbal expression 6. Manual expression 7. Visual closure 8. Auditory closure 9. Grammatic closure 10. Sound blending 11. Auditory-sequential memory 12. Visual-sequential memory	Scaled scores Psycholinguistic ages Psycholinguistic quotients

II.   Take a close-up view of *Some Assessment Instruments Used by Those Advocating Skill Training* to understand the nature of the instruments used.

TABLE 5.2A

Some Assessment Instruments Used by Those Advocating Skill Training

Name of Test	Intended Audience	Subtests	Modes of Reporting Scores
Wide Range Achievement Test (WRAT)	Level I: Children 5–11 Level II: Persons from 12–64 years	1. Reading 2. Spelling 3. Arithmetic	Grade Ratings Percentiles Standard Scores

TABLE 5.2A (Continued)

Name of Test	Intended Audience	Subtests	Modes of Reporting Scores
Peabody Individualized Achievement Test (PIAT)	For students in grades K–12	1. Mathematics 2. Reading recognition 3. Reading comprehension 4. Spelling 5. General Information	Grade Equivalents Age Equivalents Percentiles Standard Scores

Criterion Test of Basic Skills (CTBS)	Children 6–10 years of age	1. Reading
		2. Arithmetic
			For items tested, student's scores are interpreted as:
			90% correct—
			    Mastery Level
			50–89% correct—
			    Instructional Level
			0–49% correct—
			    Frustration Level*

*Frustration level is defined as "Student is not yet ready for the objective tested."

III.   Your reading of the text thus far may have led you to make some positive or negative criticisms of the philosophies or instruments used to test students. What follows is meant to acquaint you with the critiques of these tests which have been offered by experts in testing and curriculum development. Discuss the implications of their remarks.

  A.   Critiques of DD-PT Tests and/or Instruction

   1.   DTVP (Developmental Test of Visual Perception)

     a.   Current research shows that the five subtests of the DTVP really test only two skills.

     b.   The success of follow-up efforts to improve visual perception skills/weaknesses identified through the DTVP has not been supported by research.

     c.   The success of follow-up efforts to improve academic learning by trying to strengthen visual perception skills identified on the DTVP has not been supported by research.

          For fuller discussions of these critiques, see: D.D. Hammill and J.L. Wiederholt. (1973). Review of the *Frostig Visual Perception Test* and the Related Training Program. In L. Mann and D.A. Sabatino (Eds.). (1972). *The first review of special education,* Vol. 1. Philadelphia: J.S.E. Press.

    Are the COH teams in your local school district useing the DTVP? What are the implications for the students? for you?

2. PPMS (Purdue Perceptual Motor Survey)

    a. The sample used to establish norms for this test is too small.

    b. The validity of the scale, based on the statistics used, is questionable.

        For a fuller discussion of these critiques, see: J. Salvia and J. Ysseldyke. (1978). *Assessment in special and remedial education.* Boston: Houghton-Mifflin. The authors state that the scores on this test should never be used in making diagnostic decisions.

    c. Motor-perceptual follow-up training has not been shown by research to improve significantly academic learning.

        For a fuller discussion of this critique, see: L. Goodman and D. Hammill. (1973). The effectiveness of the Kephart-Getman activities in developing perceptual-motor cognitive skills, *Focus on Exceptional Children,* 9, 1–9.

        Is the PPMS used by the COH in your school district? If so, what are the implications for your students? for you?

3. ITPA (Illinois Test of Psycholinguistic Abilities)

    a. Research does not support the assumption that the 12 subskills of this test are discrete psycholinguistic processes.

        For a fuller discussion of this critique, see: D.D. Hammill and S.C. Larsen. (1974). "The Effectiveness of Psycholinguistic Training," *Exceptional Children,* 41 (1974): 5–14.

    b. In 70 percent of research studies reviewed, 11 of the 12 subskills did not improve significantly when students were given direct focused instruction in those skills. The exception was *verbal expression.*

        For a fuller discussion of this critique, see: R.A. Sedlak and P. Wiener. (1973). Review of research on the *Illinois Test of Psycholinguistics Abilities.* In L. Mann and D.A. Sabatino (Eds.). (1972). *The first review of special education, Vol. I.* Philadelphia: JSE Press.

        Are there members of the COH in your school district using the ITPA? What are the implications for your students? for you?

B.   Critiques of Tests Used by Skill Training Proponents
1.   WRAT (Wide Range Achievement Test)
   a.   Reading as defined in this test is "saying words in isolation." In other words, comprehension is not measured.
   b.   Spelling in this test is defined as "writing words correctly from oral dictation." There is no effort to check spelling in continuous written text.
   c.   Arithmetic in this test is defined as "a series of skills ranging from counting to reading numerals, and solving orally presented and written problems."
   d.   The narrow focus of this test leads one to question its use as a screening test rather than as a specific diagnostic test of just a few skills, one of which is certainly not "reading."

   This test is in wide use in the field. Does your COH use it? What would be the implications for your students? for you?

2.   PIAT (Peabody Individual Achievement Test)

   The age-grade range is so wide that the test can provide only some very general guidelines for placement.

   Is the PIAT used by your COH? What are the implications for your students? for you?

3.   CTBS (Criterion Test of Basic Skills)
   a.   Since this is a criterion-referenced test, it is limited — as are all such tests — to the range of the objectives tested.
   b.   Like the WRAT, this test does not assess comprehension. It tests letter recognition, lower case letters, capital letters, letter discrimination, vowel and consonant sounding, blending, and sequence of sounds.
   c.   The number of test items used to assess a skill is sometimes so limited that only one error would indicate frustration level.

   For a fuller discussion of these issues: see T. and A. Mahon. (1981). *Assessing children with special needs.* New York: Holt, Rinehart and Winston.

   Is the CTBS used by members of the COH in your school district? What are the implications for your students? for you?

Assessment for DD-PT and Skill Training Approaches

Fill in the appropriate answers which represent your current thinking about choice of DD-PT and Skill Training assessment instruments by the members of the COH.

	True	False
1. Because members of the COH are competent professionals, they will agree about the proper assessment instruments to use in order to diagnose and place referred students.	____	____
2. Sensory-perceptual, motor-perceptual, and/or psycholinguistic underlying abilities have been shown through research to be the causes of learning problems.	____	____
3. DD-TP follow-up instruction has been shown by research to improve academic learning.	____	____
4. DD-TP follow-up instruction has been shown by research to improve the weakness in the underlying ability detected through assessment of that ability.	____	____
5. Despite serious negative criticisms of DD-TP tests and follow-up instruction, these tests are still in general use.	____	____
6. Proponents of the Skill Training Approach believe that a learning deficit rather than an underlying sensory or motor perception deficit is the student's problem.	____	____
7. In analyzing tests usually used to determine specific learning problems, educators should take a close look at the subtests, noting whether the definitions of the sections match their definitions. (Example: Is "reading" as defined on this test your definition of reading?)	____	____
8. In analyzing tests used by the COH, educators should examine the tests for their applicability to follow-up instruction and placement rather than placement alone.	____	____
9. Criterion-referenced test scores can be unfair when too few items are used to test a skill.	____	____
10. This module has shown me that I must be more critical of the nature and value of the tests used to diagnose and place students who have been referred to the COH.	____	____

C.   Additional Approaches To Assessment

In addition to the basic assessment approaches of DD-TP and Skill Training, a comprehensive assessment battery may include the following approaches as well.

1. An orientation involving direct measurement of learning is provided by Feuerestein in the Learning Potential Assessment Device (LPAD). LPAD may be a promising approach to assess "what a student is capable of learning." LPAD is a "test-train-test" model where the test giver becomes a "teacher" and tries to create and promote an optimal learning and motivational environment for the student. The tests begin with simple tasks and progress through more complex reasoning processes. This dynamic model involves testing in the art of learning and assessing the process of learning, thus specifying differences in thinking or cognitive strategies and style. This information may be applied to what should be taught and how it should be taught.

2. The Adaptive Measure Scales are another assessment approach that describe behavior, rather broadly, and define it as the degree to which the student meets established criteria of personal independence and social responsibility expected for his or her age or cultural group. These scales do not imply intelligence testing, but rather focus on assessing adaptive behavior. The Adaptive Behavior Scale, by Lambert, Windmille, Cole, and Figueroa (1975), is completed by the teacher and focuses on ten areas of personal and social competence and twelve areas of maladaptive behavior as evidenced in school settings. Mercer's *Adaptive Behavior Inventory for Children* (1979) is completed by the mother and concentrates on practical skills and social behaviors. Adaptive behavior scores provide data to be used in the design of programs focused on improving practical skills and social behaviors.

3. An approach that focuses on the use of biomedical measures should be used to determine indications of students' health that may be related to their learning problem. A unique assessment approach may combine the traditional biomedical measures (e.g. hearing, vision, neurological exams, etc.) with Mercer's *System of Multicultural Pluralistic Assessment* (SOMPA). SOMPA includes measures of physical dexterity, sensory acuity, perceptual motor development and health history, to screen for physical and biological problems that might affect an intelligence test score.

D. Issues Related to the Selection and Evaluation of Assessment Measures

In selecting tests for an assessment battery, members of an interdisciplinary team may wish to consider the following factors relative to whether the test is assessing the students' *functional* need.

1. Does the test provide the information that answers your specific assessment questions?

2. Is the test appropriate for the age and/or grade level of the student?

3. Is the student "able to take the test?" Specifically, can the student "attend to the test" relative to time requirements, or is an individual, untimed test more appropriate than a group test? Does the test match the student's mode of communication? Is it nondiscriminatory relative to ethnic group, sex, and handicapping conditions?

4. Is the test of good quality? These four critical characteristics are noted in evaluation of test quality:

   a. Standardized sample is important because the results of a test *compare* a student's performance to that of others in the *sample*. The sample should reflect the characteristics of the student who is taking the test. You may wish to examine sampling in terms of size, age, and sex of persons in sample, representativeness by geographic region, socioeconomic status, race, handicapping conditions, and languages spoken by persons in sample. Further, the date of test standardization is important as well since it reflects the group used to establish the norms at that time. Over a period of time, it is possible that group characteristics change, therefore the norms would change accordingly.

   b. *Reliability* refers to the consistency of the test scores. If the test were to be given several times to the same person, test results should be stable and more similar than dissimilar.

   c. *Validity* refers to whether a test measures what it is supposed to. Test content, or content validity, should be noted relative to the appropriateness of the types of test items, completeness of the sample of test items, and the way in which the test items assess the content.

   d. *Measurement error* refers to the error in the "theoretical" true score. If it were possible to administer a reliable and valid test to the same student more than once under the same conditions, the two scores obtained would most likely be different. The single score reported actually represents a range of scores, depending on the standard error of measurement (which should be reported in the administrator's manual for the test). Let us suppose that Marie scored 70 on an I.Q. test and the Standard Error of Measurement on that test was three points. Then the score represents 70 *plus* or *minus* three points, or a range of 67 to 73. After translating the score properly, we could say according to the information given in the manual, chances are 68 times out of 100 that her true score would be between 67 and 73. It would also be accurate that her true score would be 70 plus or minus 6 points. In this case the chances are 95 out of 100 that her score would be between 61 and 76. In view of these facts, rigid adherence to a single score as the absolute cut-off point for special education placement is both illogical and unfair. Check your state plan to see whether a single test score on one or more I.Q. tests is used for placement of students in special education settings.

5. Arguments against the use of intelligence tests in assessing minorities have raised the issue of the fairness and accuracy of assessment. Presently, it appears that a nondiscriminatory measure is one that results in similar performance across cultures, relative to differences in language, values, and learning strategies. Tests that attempt to establish the primary language of student have been developed, including the *Language Assessment Scales* (DeAvila and Ducan, 1977), and a Spanish/English *Flexibility Language Dominance Test,* (Keller, 1974). Tests free of cultural bias also have been devised and include the *Black Intelligence Test of Cultural Homogeneity* (BITCH — Williams, 1971) and *REFER* (Kunzelmann and Koenig, 1980) used for preschool and kindergarten screening.

6. Interdisciplinary teams should not hesitate to evaluate assessment measures that they are currently using. Excellent sources are available for team members' use so that they can become knowledgeable consumers of assessment approaches, measures, and related issues. They are:

   a. The American Psychological Association has prepared *Standards for Educational and Psychological Tests.*

   b. *Mental Measurements Yearbook.* Buros, O. K. Highland Park, N.J.: Gryphon Press, 1978.

   c. *Journal of Educational Measurement in Education* 1230 17th Street, N. W. Washington, D.C. 20006

   d. *Journal of Educational Research* 4000 Albemarle Street, N. W. Washington, D.C. 20016

e. *Journal of Learning Disabilities*
101 East Ontario Street
Chicago, Illinois 60611

f. *Journal of Special Education*
3515 Woodhaven Road
Philadelphia, PA 19154

g. *Learning Disabilities Quarterly*
University of Kansas Medical Center
Department of Special Education
39th and Rainbow Boulevard
Kansas City, KS 66103

Additional Activities

For many years, the individually administered I.Q. examination has been the only instrument used to determine mental retardation. It is also used to compare students' academic achievement with their mental ability. PL 94-142 has forbidden the use of only one test as a criterion for student placement in special education. It is necessary for educators to understand the reasons for this decision, and to note the weaknesses of I.Q. testing.

Read and discuss the issues concerning I.Q. tests stated below:

a. Test scores on I.Q. tests neither tell where a student should be placed nor what he or she should be taught.

b. The school psychologist, usually responsible for administering this test, often has no further voice in instructional planning.

c. If the test is used as the sole criterion for determining mental retardation, the use is in violation of both federal and state guidelines.

d. Different states have different cut-off points on the *same* I.Q. tests to determine mental retardation.

e. The language or dialect on the test may be totally or partially different from the language or dialect of the students taking the test. PL 94-142 demands that children and youth be tested in their own language. Is this law being obeyed in your school district?

f. The items on many I.Q. tests are not free of cultural bias. Often they represent what the children or youth of a certain ethnic or socioeconomic class would know concerning everyday life or have been taught in school. For example, a student may be asked on an I.Q. test to identify by name the objects presented in pictures. A child from a poor urban background could easily fail to identify by name a microwave oven for reasons cited above.

g. Scores on I.Q. tests are quite sensitive. Thus students may score lower than their actual mental ability for such reasons as:

- fear of test taking in general;
- fear of the formal setting in which an adult tests a child or youth in an individual oral mode;
- fatigue during the test;
- illness before or during the test;
- general health conditions;
- boredom with taking tests (Many children are wary of the endless battery of tests which are given them with no seeming results.)

Assessment

Discuss these issues with your school psychologist. Find out the policy of your COH concerning I.Q. testing.

Implications/Applications

Multiple information gathered by various assessment approaches provides a data base for the interdisciplinary team when making decisions relative to the program planning and placement of students. School psychologists and educational evaluation by virtue of their roles and functions may serve as "consultants" to the team in analyzing, interpreting, and applying the assessment data in the following ways:

1. They may identify the appropriate assessment approaches and measures that will provide information that is functional to the educational program of a student.

2. They may interpret assessment data in educational terminology, rather than psychological terms, so that the information may be translated into instructional/management activities for the student.

3. They may collaborate closely and participate with guidance counselors in counseling activities and in developing behavior modification programs.

4. They may work closely with school administrators in modifying the student's schedule.

5. They may work closely with the parents and the student in interpreting the data, particularly as in relation to the student's schooling.

However, it should be mentioned that assessment must be viewed with caution and in no way perceived as a one-time measure of a student's learning. Rather, assessment must be viewed within the context of the ongoing team decision making that is related to the educating of all students.

5.3   THE JUDICIOUS USE OF NORM-REFERENCED AND CRITERION-REFERENCED TESTS BY THE COMMITTEE ON THE HANDICAPPED

Minimum Competency Objectives

1. Using your knowledge of the strengths and weaknesses of norm-referenced tests and criterion-referenced tests, you will examine one example of each used by your COH and evaluate it for its judicious use in your school district.

2. You may at some time apply the information from Objective 1 to a case study in your school.

Rationale

As Module 5.2 has shown, assessment approaches for special education placement include norm-referenced or criterion-referenced tests. It is important for educators to understand the strengths and weaknesses of such measures to choose among them wisely according to their structural quality, and to use them only for appropriate goals. It is also important for educators who have referred students or who have students placed in their classes to know which sort of measures were used for placement and whether the measures used can be of assistance in planning classroom instruction.

Enabling Activities

I.   Review with your large group, small group, or partner the usual structure of norm-referenced and criterion-referenced tests. Use the tables below to help you.

TABLE 5.3A

Ideal Standardized (Norm-Referenced) Tests: Achievement Tests

1. Author/Authors	One or more persons considered to be expert in the area to be tested.
2. Content	Content items are devised as the result of examination of curricula in several schools with a wide geographical distribution or with widely differing school populations. Content items are then chosen to be representative of these curricula. As a result, the number of items used to test any given academic area would be fewer than the number used by a classroom teacher to test for that area after instruction. The range of items may be related to one or more grade levels.
3. Piloting the test	The test is given to several children or youth. Test items are revised over and over for clarity, efficiency, and appropriateness.
4. Format of the test items	Most often in multiple choice form, students usually use pencils to fill in blank squares, rectangles or circles to note their answers.
5. Test/Retest	The test is brought out with equivalent forms so that students may be given pretests and posttests of achievement related to classroom instruction.
6. Hierarchy of test items	Often the test is divided into sections, each a subtest of the major achievement area to be tested.
7. Method of reporting scores	• Often the companies which publish the tests machine score them and send several reports to the school and/or school district. • Sometimes teachers are expected to hand score the tests and send reports to the school principal or other administrator.
8. Mode of reporting scores	a. raw scores (actual number of items correct) b. translation of raw scores into: 　• standard scores 　• grade equivalents 　• percentile ranks
9. Uses of the tests	They are used to *compare* students with the group used as the norm (standard) for the test. They also measure increase/decrease in areas of achievement over a period of time in relation to the usual growth of the norm group over the same period.

TABLE 5.3A (Continued)

	They check a teacher's capabilities to offer instruction.
10. Norm group	This is usually a large sample such as a national random sample, a regional sample, a sample drawn from special school types (public, private), a sample of just urban schools or just suburban schools, etc.
11. Test qualities	Reliability is high.* Validity is high.**

*A standardized (norm-referenced) test is said to be reliable if the following are true:

1. Students would get nearly the same scores if they took an equivalent form of the test.
2. Students would get nearly the same scores if they took the test at two different times (with no related intervening instruction).
3. Test scores are stable over time.

**A standardized (norm-referenced) test is said to be valid when it is a test of what it is designed to test. This means that the test authors have included test items which sample the major knowledges and skills which are taught in the school systems where the test was normed. This statement assumes that the authors have studied the *domain* of the content areas offered in the schools which formed the norm group and have selected appropriate test items which represent by their frequency of occurrence the *importance* of these skills in the curricula examined.

TABLE 5.3B

Ideal Criterion-Referenced Tests

1.	Author/Authors	One or more persons considered to be experts in the area to be tested.
2.	Content	The domain of a content area is spelled out by authors in terms of major objectives to be attained. Major objectives are subdivided into smaller steps, usually sequenced from least difficult to more difficult. Test questions, in relation to these small steps of knowledge/skills, form the body of the test. A number of questions are used to determine the student's mastery or non-mastery of the small steps.

TABLE 5.3B (Continued)

3. Piloting the test	The test is given to many children/youth. Test items are revised over and over for clarity, efficiency and appropriateness.
4. Format of the items	May be multiple choice form, or student may have to write in answers, showing or not showing work done to arrive at the answer.
5. Test/Retest	If the test is to be given as a pretest or posttest, equivalent forms may be available.
6. Hierarchy of the test items	See 2 above in this chart.
7. Method of reporting scores	After machine scoring test, company that publishes the test reports scores to the school or school district. Teacher reports hand corrected scores to administrative official.

8. Modes of reporting scores	In percents of mastery. Samples:
	  90% of items testing a skill are correct.
	    (Mastery or Independent Level)
	  50–89% correct (Instructional Level)
	  0–49% (Frustration Level—Student is not
	    ready for skills assessed)
	Tests also may be evaluated as successful/not successful (Pass/Fail)

9. Uses of Criterion-referenced tests	They determine specifically the knowledges and/or skills a student has or does not have in relation to a group of curriculum objectives which are tested on the criterion-referenced test. They place students in an instructional setting which matches skills/abilities known/not known. They also are used to check growth over a period of time in the student's learning of specific skills.

TABLE 5.3C

A Global Comparison of Norm-Referenced Tests and Criterion-Referenced Measures

Norm-referenced	Criterion-referenced
1. Measures individual performance in comparison to a group.	Measures individual performance relative to a fixed standard or criterion.

TABLE 5.3C (Continued)

Norm-referenced	Criterion-referenced
2. Measures are often used to describe students "at grade level" and so on.	Measures are not concerned with describing grade level.
3. Often unrelated to the instructional content.	Content is specified.
4. Not concerned with defining mastery or success.	Concerned with operationally defining mastery and success.
5. The standardization aspect supports objectivity.	Lack of standardization decreases objectivity.
6. Can easily reveal individual differences among students.	Does not focus on revealing individual differences among students.
7. Test items are measured in reference to students.	Test items are measured in reference to instructional objectives.

A. Review with your large group, small group, or partner the chief differences between norm-referenced and criterion-referenced tests in relationship to their appropriate uses.

B. Norm-referenced tests are comparisons between the assessed person's performance on the test with the performance of others in the norm group on the same test.

C. Criterion-referenced tests tell the assessors which knowledges/skills the tested student has attained and which skills are weak or absent in relation to the range of skills found on the specific criterion-referenced test given.

D. In view of these differences which would be the better type test for placement in instructional settings?

II. Review weaknesses of norm-referenced tests. See Module 5.2, *Additional Activities*. Weaknesses on the I.Q. standardized tests cited under 5.2 are the same weaknesses of all norm-referenced tests.

III. Review the weaknesses of criterion-referenced tests.

A. There is the possibility that the test does not have content validity in terms of what this student has learned or what this teacher has taught. (Sample: Teacher A has taught formal grammar in class. A certain criterion-referenced test assesses knowledge and use of correct English, but does not demand the labeling of parts of speech. Or Teacher B has taught percentages, taxation, etc., and the test is focused on algebraic sets.)

B.   Since several of these are scored by percentages representing mastery, instructional, and frustration levels, sufficient test items must be assigned to each small step. The test must be analyzed for its validity not only from the nature of the content tested, but also the frequency of test items related to each small step probe.

C.   The educator should note whether he or she agrees with the author's definition of subtests. A test author, for example, may define reading as word recognition reported in oral or written settings. The educator who uses the test may define reading as comprehension of whole text in a silent reading setting.

D.   The educator who analyzes for content validity must also remember that the test authors may have assumed that they have discovered all the small steps necessary for the attainment of the complex skill which is being probed. Further, some test authors assume that the sequence in which they write the test is the sequence in which the complex skill is learned and should therefore be taught. Test authors may vary with regard to the number and sequence of simple skills necessary to attain a complex skill.

E.   There often is the assumption on the part of criterion-referenced test authors that it is important to determine student competency at each small step leading to a complex skill. As Donald McClelland points out, adequate performance may not demand mastery of each small step which makes up a complex skill. McClelland holds that assessment should be in terms of clustered steps rather than individual specific steps. For example, a student may recognize 90 percent of the words in a passage without being able to name the letters of the words, spell the words, or identify whether letter combinations are blends. For a fuller discussion of this issue, see D. McClelland. (1973). "Testing for competence rather than for 'intelligence'," *American Psychologist*, 228, pp. 1–14.

Assessment

Determine whether your Committee on the Handicapped tends to use norm-referenced or criterion-referenced tests to assess and place students. Identify one of these tests and review it in terms of the information presented in this module. What are the implications of what you find in terms of your students' instruction?

Additional Activities

1. Read pertinent sections of B.S. Bloom, J.T. Hastings, and G.F. Madaus. (1971). *Handbook on formative and summative evaluation of student learning.* New York: McGraw-Hill Book Publishing Company.

2. For the relationship of criterion-referenced tests to follow-up individualized instruction, see J.L. Housden and L. Le Gear. (1974). An emerging model: Criterion-referenced evaluation, William Georgiades and D.C. Clark (Eds.). (1974). *Models for Individualized Instruction.* New York: MSS Information Corporation, and W.J. Popham and R.S. Ray. (1969). Implications of criterion-referenced measurement, *Journal of Educational Measurement,* 6, 1–9.

Implications/Applications

In reality, tests can only measure "samples" of skills, abilities, etc., but educators need them to make decisions to design instructional management and provide appropriate placement. Both norm-referenced and criterion-referenced measures have unique roles to play, since they contribute in different ways to the understanding of a student's learning abilities. Criterion-referenced procedures lend themselves to behavioral objectives based on task and behavioral analysis, whereas norm referenced procedures measure a student's position in relation to others, thereby identifying individual differences. Both tests can provide useful information. Which is more appropriate depends on the nature of the information sought.

Read the following case study on Lori and indicate what useful information is needed.

Case Study on Lori

Lori, a 10-year-old fifth grader, was referred for assessment. Throughout the primary grades, she struggled to get promoted, but this year she may be retained. Her teacher feels that she can memorize very well but has no reasoning ability. In fact, her teacher suspects that Lori may even be "a little retarded." No doubt, the teacher is looking for some explanation for Lori's pattern of learning and perhaps these explanations might provide her with some ideas as to how to work with Lori to decrease some of the frustration she is manifesting in trying to learn. Regardless, Lori is in a precarious position where she may be retained and/or classified.

In evaluating this case, consider the following:

1. It is necessary to determine *if* Lori is retarded.
2. It is necessary to determine Lori's pattern of strengths and weaknesses in learning.
3. It is necessary to determine Lori's skill proficiency level for completing fifth grade work.
4. It is necessary to determine which assessment approaches will give you answers to questions 1, 2, and 3.

Question 1—might be answered by information provided by a criterion-referenced test.

Question 2—might be answered by information provided by process analysis.

Question 3—might be answered by information provided by content-related validity and task analysis.

Lori was administered the WISC-R, a norm-referenced, process-oriented instrument (see Module 5.3). The results follow:

Verbal I.Q.	91	(25th percentile)
Performance I.Q.	99	(45th percentile)
Full-Scale I.Q.	92	(30th percentile)

A view of these scores may suggest that Lori's mental abilities were developing a bit more slowly than average, but she is not retarded. Other analysis of scores indicate that Lori's visual-spatial and immediate auditory recall activities were above average, and her verbal expression and comprehension were below average. Lori's attention was focused when the task was highly structured and involved direct stimulation. A criterion-referenced measure established the following data:

1. Lori can orally define less than 50 percent of the words identified as appropriate fifth grade vocabulary.
2. On a word identification test, Lori can correctly pronounce 50 percent of the words taken from her fifth grade tests.
3. Lori can perform arithmetical computations with 85 percent accuracy on fifth grade text book examples, but she performs with 10 percent accuracy on fifth grade mathematical word problems.

In addition, during the testing period, Lori had some difficulty getting organized when she was given more than one activity to complete.

Based on the information that the assessment approaches provided, what kind of an educational program would you suggest for Lori? With a member from an interdisciplinary team discuss the following questions:

1. Would Lori benefit from a direct instruction pattern? (See Module 9.4)

2. Would the use of visual pattern exercises, multisensory associations in word learning, and phonetic analysis with color coding assist Lori in word recognition skills?

3. Would memorizing very long lists of vocabulary words assist Lori in word comprehension?

4. Would very short problem solving riddles not focused on mathematics provide Lori with an opportunity to identify the *steps* in solving the riddle?

5. Would monitoring Lori's daily performance provide you with some measure of her success?

Placement of Exceptional Children and Youth

INTRODUCTION

IT IS THE TASK of the committee on the handicapped to place exceptional children and youth in a least restrictive environment. The definition of this environment and this placement must be an ongoing process rather than a once for all step. Placement is thus closely related to a repeating sequence of diagnosis-instruction-evaluation events which dictate the next set of events and related placements. Module 6.0 focuses on student placement of this type.

Module 6.1 asks you to examine the recording of assessments of exceptional students in your school and district in relation to the requirements of the law. Then it requests that you critique the current forms in use. Module 6.2 asks you to contrast placement as a one-time event with placement as an ongoing process particularly with the use of ecological assessment procedures.

Further information on assessment of exceptional students can be found on pages 232 to 262 in the Topic Referenced Bibliography under the numbers *2* (Due Process, Hearings) and *8.1* (Assessment Procedures).

6.1 RECORDING ASSESSMENTS IN RELATIONSHIP TO PLACEMENT OF EXCEPTIONAL CHILDREN AND YOUTH

Minimum Competency Objective

By applying criteria for the appropriate recording of assessments related to determining placements in special education, you will determine the strengths and weaknesses of various planning forms (and, in particular, the planning form used by your COH).

Rationale

The assessment conducted for possible placement of referred students must be recorded and kept in a permanent file. This record is kept confidential. Access to the records is given by law to the parents of the child or youth and to the appropriate educational professionals who must make the assessment. An analysis of a blank form for such a planning process of your COH will give you a fairly accurate idea of what the COH members think is important to assessment.

Enabling Activities

With a member(s) of an interdisciplinary team, read and discuss the following criteria for developing assessment plans. You will apply what you learn (and agree upon) to some model assessment forms (and, if possible, the assessment form used by your COH).

PL 94-142 demands adequate and non-discriminatory assessment of students referred to the COH. Some of the implications of these mandates are:

1. The student must be viewed as a whole person, having a home, community, and school history.
2. The student's native language or dialect must be taken into consideration.
3. The student's health should be noted in terms of its past and present state.
4. The past and present classroom settings for this student should be reviewed in terms of the teaching/learning environment.
5. Student's progress in using communication skills should be analyzed.
6. It may be necessary to review the student's functioning in social settings.
7. Analysis of student's use of motor skills may be needed.
8. Student's emotional responses to self and others may be in need of analysis.
9. Specific cognitive, affective, sensory, motor, psycholinguistic ability strengths and/or weaknesses should be diagnosed as necessary.
10. The plan must be given to parents for their signed approval.
11. Parents must be told their rights and the rights of their children.
12. Parents must be told the date for a meeting to discuss the results of assessment.
13. Dates for completion of parts of the assessment are to be specified.

Review the following plans for assessment by a COH in terms of the criteria cited in this module and any further criteria you may have agreed upon with members of the interdisciplinary team.

TABLE 6.1A

**General Assessment Plan of the COH for School District #5
Everywhere City, United States**

Plan prepared for _____ who is a student in
Student's Name

_____ who has been referred
Grade   Class   School

by _____.
Name of Teacher(s)   Grade   Class
Other

Plan Development as of _____
Date

Reason for Referral

Description of Current Teaching/   Person(s) Responsible
Learning Environment   for the Assessment

Check (√) areas to be assessed

School Environment History	Assessment Instrument or Other Techniques Used	Person Responsible for the Assessment
Review of school records in permanent file		
Review of current report card		
Health Records: Past Current		
Language Dominance		
Skill Strengths/Weaknesses in:		
Basic academic areas: Mathematics Reading Spelling Other		
Cognitive Assessment		
Adaptive Assessment Behavior		
Sensory/Motor Assessment		
Use of oral language		
Development of communication skills		
Social interaction with others		
Emotional responses to self, others		

This plan cannot be initiated until the signature of a parent/guardian is given below.

I give my permission for the assessment described above. Due process assures that the results of these assessments will be kept confidential and that I (we) shall be asked to a meeting to go over the results.

Parent/Guardian	Please Print

Parent/Guardian's Signature	Date

Review Assessment Plan #2 in the same way.

TABLE 6.1B

Assessment Plan of the COH for School District #24
Circlevilleton, Arizona

Information	Assessors	Assessment Instrument	Date
Environmental:			
Family History			
Structure of Family			
Resources/Strengths			
Stresses			
Economic conditions			
Parents' expectations for student			
Developmental:			
Physical growth			
Psychological growth			
Academic growth			
Medical:			
General medical state			
Visual problems			
Hearing problems			
Physical disabilities			
Seizures			
Other			

I hereby give permission for the assessment outlined above to take place. I understand that I must be notified of a meeting to discuss the results of the assessment. No assessment of my child can be made without my signature. No placement of my child can be made without my consent.

_____

Parent/Guardian's Signature   Date

Assessment

Evaluation of these forms will differ according to criteria which you have developed in addition to those offered in this module. If you can obtain a copy of the assessment form used by your COH, evaluate it as you did the plans in this module.

Implications/Applications

The recording of assessment on a form provides a data based profile of a student from which some important decisions will be made by the interdisciplinary team. Consequently, the team must exercise care and caution in reporting the relevancy of the data so that it will serve the functional needs of a student. Relevancy may be adhered to by using the following guidelines:

1. Report facts and dates accurately and simply.
2. State specific sources of data.
3. Mention the absence of critical data.
4. Address discrepancies between the data and present some possible explanations.
5. Report test administration errors and description of any conditions that may have affected the validity of the testing.

The student's profile will be interpreted by the interdisciplinary team to determine whether there is a school performance problem, if it is related to a handicapping condition, and its educational implications relative to need and/or services.

Since the assessment is critical to educational planning, the student's functional needs must be clearly defined. The team must engage in analysis, synthesis and evaluation of these data to determine appropriate recommendations. At all times, validation should occur between and among the assessment measures as well as with observation data, interview information, etc., especially when a range of assessment techniques have been used. Essentially, the evaluation of these data by the team should provide a clear and full description of the student's learning problem and a clarification of the problem relative to existing instructional management processes in a regular classroom.

6.2 PLACEMENT AS AN ONGOING PROCESS

Minimum Competency Objective

You will review one placement process. This is a process which is based on the philosophy that assessment is ongoing, an activity which involves continual hypothesis making about what is to be tested. Assessment is thought to be the conceptualization of relationships between data gathered and specific goals. It includes the ecological assessment of the exceptional student's current environment. This approach is in direct contrast to the concept that assessment is a process which continues until the truth concerning a student is completely known. This latter approach assumes that assessment is meant to come to conclusions about the student.

Rationale

Educators and parents should understand that assessment, especially assessment by a Committee on the Handicapped, should not be an absolute statement of the physical, mental, emotional, adaptive, behavioral, or academic status of the referred child or youth. It is but a beginning statement about the child/youth's needs which necessitates much more information from several more sources over time, in which changes are noted and followed up. PL 94-142 demands the constant review of the Individual Educational Plan for referred students so that ongoing assessment and placement can take place. A critical aspect related to the review of the Individualized Educational Plan is ecological assessment; this can be experienced by exceptional students as they adapt to new placements, especially if they are placed in a regular classroom.

Enabling Activities

Read the following text and discuss its implications with a member(s) of the interdisciplinary team in your school.

Placement Procedure in Terms of Assessment Is an Ongoing Process

1. The COH reports to school officials and to the referred student's parents on the assessment data gathered and conclusions reached that the student seems to be in need of special education services.

2. Parents/guardians give their consent.

3. If consent is not given, due process hearings take place. The student remains in the regular classroom until a hearing takes place and a decision is handed down.

4. If consent is given, the local school IEP team is alerted to the student's needs.

5. The IEP team devises an instructional plan to meet the needs of the student.

6. Suggestions for placement are based on the IEP.

7. Parents must approve the placement and plan.

8. If approval is not given, due process hearings take place. The student remains in the regular classroom until a hearing takes place and a decision is handed down.

9. If approval is given, the instruction and placement must be reviewed at least once a year.

10. The IEP team is asked to follow the following guidelines insofar as they are best for the student: Place student in his or her local school and in the regular classroom in as many instances as possible.

Ecological Assessment as Related to Placement in the Regular Classroom

One reason for the failure of some placement decisions is that exceptional students experience problems in leaving their current environment and adapting to their new placement. No doubt, the differences in the two environments, such as class size, class rules and regulations, and grouping practices are real and may present serious adjustment problems to the exceptional student. One way of assisting the student to adapt to the new environment is to conduct an ecological assessment of the student's current placement and the recommended placement. In general, ecological assessment permits teachers to do the following:

1. objectively describe and compare the differences in the two environments;
2. using the information from (1) above, minimize the discrepancies between the two environments;
3. assist the exceptional student to adapt to his/her new environment.

More specifically, the following suggestions are offered as a basis for effective ecological assessment:

1. Regular and special education teachers will jointly identify and describe the necessary behaviors for student success in their current placement and recommended placement.

2. If there are marked differences in expectations for student behavior, regular and special education teachers will jointly determine the modifications to be made in either the regular classroom environment or in the student's academic or social behavior.

3. Ecological assessment as related to placement is ongoing in order to maximize exceptional student adaptation to new environments.

Assessment

1. Examine the process described in this module to determine the basic philosophy of assessment that is used.

2. Critique with a member(s) of the interdisciplinary team in your school the value of ecological assessment as an element to be included in the basic philosophy of placement as an ongoing process.

Additional Activities

Discuss the following issues:

1. To what degree should students be evaluated during the assessment period while the COH carries on investigation? Several states have issued guidelines or mandates which provide for assessment in relationship to the degree of complexity/severity of the suspected handicap.

2. C. Blankenship and M. Stephen Lilly believe that there has been a tendency on the part of the COH to "overdo the evaluation process for students with mild learning and behavior problems." (*Mainstreaming Students with Learning and Behavior Problems,* New York: Holt, Rinehart and Winston, 1981.) How much assessment of such children or youth would you consider to be excessive? Why?

Implications/Applications

At present, placement is broadly defined to mean the locating of students in settings that provide them with a least restrictive environment. Placement in the least restrictive environment means applying the principle of normalization or arranging ecological variables so that exceptional students have an opportunity to participate in class and school activities as much as possible. The following figure identifies typical placement options, all equally valuable as a least restrictive environment for a particular exceptional student with special needs.

FIGURE 6.2

Typical Placement Options

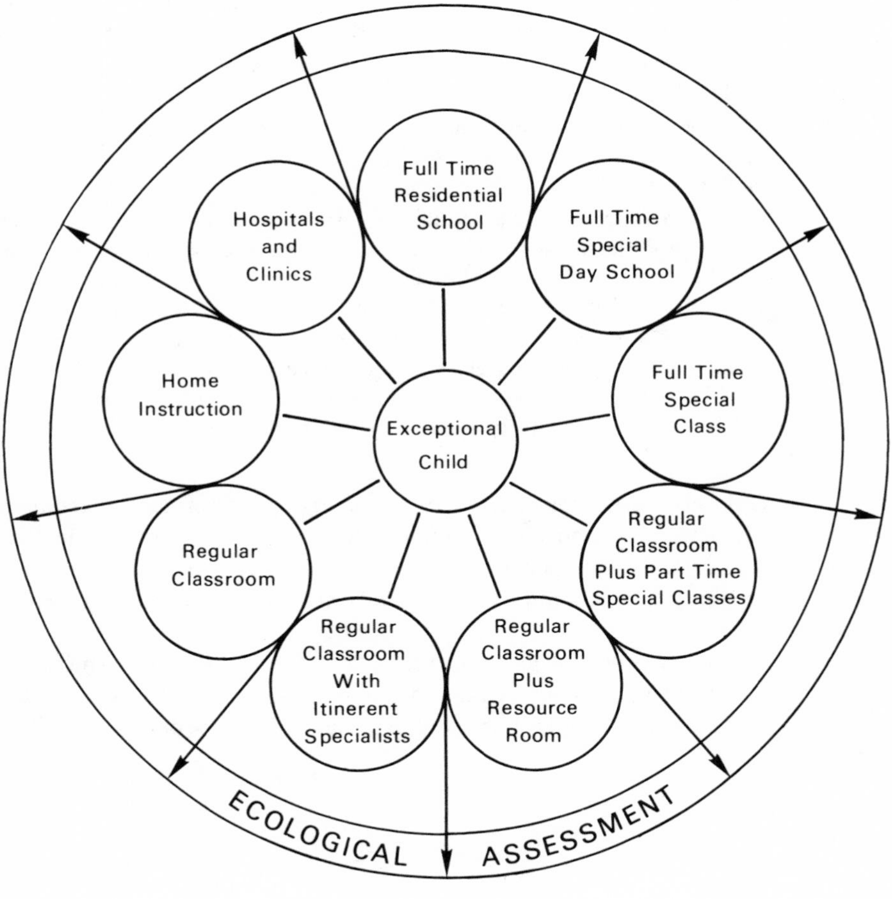

The diagram shows that ongoing assessment should be used to detect changes in exceptional students' needs and related placements in environments which are enabling and supportive of the principle of normalization. The use of ecological assessment as a tool may assist in creating such environments. The following steps may be used in the ecological assessment of the differences between a regular class and a special education class:

1. The special educator and regular educator jointly decide on who is most likely to succeed if placed in a regular classroom.
2. The special education teacher visits the regular teacher's classroom to observe and note the student behaviors that are appropriate and necessary to succeed in that environment.
   Examples: Students raise hands to be recognized.
   Students complete unfinished homework after school.
3. The regular education teacher visits the special education class to observe and note the behaviors to succeed in that class.
4. The regular education teacher will observe the exceptional student who will be placed in her/his class.
5. Both teachers (regular and special) note where there are discrepancies between the expectations for students in the regular class and the behaviors of the exceptional student.
6. Both teachers (regular and special) discuss the discrepancies to determine whether modifications are to be made in the regular classroom environment or in the behavior of the exceptional student. At times, the discrepancies may be minor and therefore no modifications will be made.
7. If modifications are to be made in the behavior of the exceptional student, he/she must be taught or trained in these behaviors *prior* to placement, to minimize the discrepancies between the two environments and increase the student's ability to adapt to the new environment.

Table 6.2A provides an example of an ecological assessment instrument to be used by a team composed of a regular teacher and a special education teacher to identify the difference in the two environments for the possible placement of Jane Smith, age 9, a mildly emotionally disturbed student, in a regular classroom.

Table 6.2B is provided as an example of an ecological assessment instrument to be used by the regular and special education team to identify differences in Jane Smith's behavior and the expected behaviors in a special education class.

TABLE 6.2A

Ecological Assessment Form I

Miss Brown's Class (Third Grade)   *Ms. Jones's Class (Special Education)*

+ = Behavior is expected
− = Behavior is *not* expected
V = Presence of discrepancy

Ecological Factors		Regular Education Classroom	Special Education Classroom
1. A place for students to "take time out" is used by students	V	−	+
2. Some work is completed individually at student's own pace		+	+
3. Some work is completed in small groups		+	+
4. Students are expected to work in large groups at times		+	+
5. Students are expected to raise their hands to recite	V	+	−
6. Students are expected to settle disagreements verbally		+	+
7. Students receive reinforcers (social and tangible)	V	−	+
8. Students are required to complete daily homework	V	+	−

TABLE 6.2B

Ecological Assessment Form II

Ms. Jones's Special Education Class   *Jane Smith's Behavior*

+ = Student acts as expected
− = Student does *not* act as expected
V = Discrepancy

Ecological Factors		Jane Smith's Behavior
1. Students are expected to solve disagreements verbally	V	−
2. Independent seat work is to be done quietly	V	−

TABLE 6.2B (Continued)

Ecological Factors		Jane Smith's Behavior
3. Homework assignments are begun with teacher assistance in class time		+
4. Homework not completed in class time must be completed at home	V	−
5. Some work is *completed* in small groups	V	−
6. Students are expected to pay attention to the teacher in a large group when necessary	V	−
7. Students receive reinforcers (social and tangible) when appropriate		+
8. Students may use the "time out" corner if necessary		+

An Ideal Individualized Educational Program (IEP)

INTRODUCTION

M ODULE 7.0 focuses on the Individualized Educational Program (IEP), which is mandated by Public Law 94-142 for each exceptional student who is given one or more placements in a school setting in order to provide learning in a least restrictive environment. This custom-tailored program, set up in terms of identified student needs, provides for short-term and terminal performance goals within specified amounts of time.

This mode of instruction, familiar to special educators as an ordinary mode of instruction, is often unfamiliar to regular educators. The cooperation between regular and special educators and interdisciplinary team members needed to write the IEP for students sent to the regular classroom should increase the sharing of the use of this kind of planning, instruction, and evaluation.

This module takes a close look at the kind of planning and operating guidelines that are appropriate to the IEP, especially as related to team decision making. Then it examines the federal guidelines for the content of the IEP. Finally, you are asked to use the guidelines to prepare an IEP in collaboration with one or more educators or the interdisciplinary team in your school. The focus of the IEP will be one student in your class (who may or may not have been mainstreamed).

Further information on writing the IEP can be found in the Topic Referenced Bibliography on pages 232 to 262 under the number *8* (Writing the IEP).

7.1 THE IEP: DESIGN, DEVELOP, AND IMPLEMENT

Minimum Competency Objective

1. You will be able to recall the notions and operating guidelines related to instructional planning for an IEP.

2. You will be able to demonstrate an understanding of the IEP content requirements vis-à-vis PL 94-142 by designing an ideal IEP form.

3. You will be able to complete an IEP given your own ideal sample form.

4. You will perform as a contributing member of an interdisciplinary team to implement an IEP.

Rationale

With the advent of PL 94-142, instructional planning or an Individualized Educational Program must be developed and implemented for students with handicapping conditions. Moreover, the contents of the IEP are mandated by law and the regulations require that evaluation and placement procedures be made by an interdisciplinary team. The use of a team in making a group decision may provide safeguards against individual errors in judgment and support greater accuracy and validity in evaluation, classification, and placement decisions. In fact, the interdisciplinary approach to the design, development, and implementation of the IEP has a powerful potential to provide a legitimate arena for: voicing differing values and points of view; sharing and interpreting assessment data, planning, and programming across disciplines; articulating the assessment process with the treatment process; identifying the resources provided by team members for operating the IEP efficiently and effectively; and most importantly, providing professional support for team members in a collaborative setting. Consequently, a well-structured IEP is based on input from an interdisciplinary team which provides a broad data base needed to create a custom-tailored educational program to accommodate specific student needs.

Enabling Activities

1. Read and discuss the content section of this module.

2. With a member of the interdisciplinary team in your building, review the IEP forms used in your school district.

3. With a member of the interdisciplinary team in your district, critique a selected number of IEP forms from urban, suburban, and rural communities within your own state or from other states.

4. Interview regular education teachers, special education teachers, specialists, administrators, parents, and students about their opinions and experiences regarding the design, development, and implementation of IEPs.

Planning: A Process

Since exceptional children are being mainstreamed into the regular classroom, educators must be made aware of the skills necessary to handle the complex instructional planning required to meet the needs of these "new clients" in the regular class.

Naturally, no single set of instructional plans applies to all settings or all students. However, a systematically designed, sequenced planning process may have broad implications in terms of increasing more effective instruction appropriate to individual needs.

Perhaps the following notions may assist you in this kind of instructional planning. The IEP will enable you to:

1. make use of data gathered on learner characteristics (academic/social) and available resources in order to determine an optimal instructional program for each child;
2. establish realistic specific short-term objectives that support long-term goals. Remember that short-term objectives are sub-components of a long range plan;
3. include provision for collecting data on student performance on an ongoing basis to be used for cumulative, formative evaluation;
4. use all information as a data base to be used for making decisions regarding individual student programming.

Operating Guidelines

The general planning process that was described may be better implemented with the inclusion of some guidelines.

Specifics:

Precision in planning is necessary to accommodate learner problems. Be concerned with:

- reliability and validity of data regarding student entry characteristics
- student learning style
- use of appropriate materials
- teaching styles
- monitoring and evaluating student programs
- desired student outcome

Systems:

Be aware of the systems that operate within the school community; that is to say, the decision-making structure as well as school system ecological variables that may affect the way a school as a system operates. Chief among these may be class/grade organization, curriculum organization, teacher attitudes, teacher competence, resource availability, interpersonal relations with teachers, peers and others, and, in general, school climate.

Sequence:

Use the information from the "specifics" and "systems" sections to establish *written* long range goals and short term objectives in a sequenced, logical and meaningful way. The sequence of goals/objectives may move from general areas to specific goals. Priority should be given to the academic/social problems that led to the referral. The sequence should include the scheduled arrangements for implementation of appropriate services needed to support the goals/objectives.

IEP Content

PL 94-142 is specific in describing the content of an individualized education program. (Federal Register, August 23, 1977.)

Sec. 121a.346 Content of Individualized Eucation Program

The individualized education program for each child should include:
1. a statement of the child's present levels of educational performance;
2. a statement of annual goals, including short-term instructional objectives;
3. a statement of the specific special education and related services to be provided to the child, and the extent to which the child will be able to participate in regular educational programs;
4. the projected dates for initiation of services and the anticipated duration of the services; and
5. appropriate objective criteria and evaluation procedures and schedules for determining, on at least an annual basis, whether the short-term instructional objectives are being achieved.

It should be noted that the notions discussed in the *Operating Guidelines* section must be considered in detail when utilizing the IEP as a vehicle for quality education. Devising the IEP should not be just a paper exercise that satisfies a legal mandate.

Suggested Steps for Developing and Implementing the IEP

After completing an analysis of the referral data, student instructional history, assessment data and available resources, the team is ready to develop a comprehensive document, integrating all known data into a workable program. The major concern of this program should include criteria that integrate the data into annual goals and short-term objectives.

I. Goals and Objectives: Functions
   A. Prioritize and establish the critical skills that need attention in terms of student's needs.
   B. Provide accountability by specifying what is to be learned within the determined time period.
   C. Provide the team with a target that may be measured, monitored, and evaluated.
   D. Improve communication with the instruction team. When the IEP is written in a team setting, all members share information and direct it toward a common concern.

Most importantly, once the annual goal is determined, the next step is to identify and specifically describe several short-term objectives for each goal, keeping in mind the sequence of steps necessary to complete the goal.

II. Delivery of Services
   Identifying, organizing, and delivering appropriate educational and related services are needed to support annual goals and short-term objectives. Attention should be directed to the following:
   A. A written statement should describe all services necessary to support goals and objectives.
   B. Specified dates and lengths of time when services will be in operation should be stated.
   C. Materials for teacher and student that are necessary to complement and implement goals and objectives should be noted.
   D. Time schedules (dates, length) related to student participation in regular education and special education classes must be included.
   E. Extent of student participation in regular education or special education classes should conform with the concept of the least restrictive environment and requires documentation.
   F. Documentation includes a description of the extent of student participation in special/regular education classes as well as justification for the placement.
   G. Monitoring of services should include information on short- and long-term services by specialists and assignments to a particular setting (e.g. resource rooms).

III. Evaluation
   In order to provide optimal benefits to a student, every IEP should con-

tain an evaluation component. Systematic collection on student progress as well as careful analysis of the data will enable the team to monitor and modify determined goals and objectives accordingly. Data may be collected from the following:

A. standardized tests;

B. criterion-referenced tests;

C. teacher-made tests;

D. student's daily work;

E. teacher observation;

F. determination of time necessary for learning (learning rate);

G. accuracy of student's work.

In addition to educators, the evaluation team should include parents and the student in making decisions related to determining the usefulness of the IEP. Feedback to parents and students may include the following information:

A. quality of communication among educators/parents/students;

B. receptivity of students and parents to the proposed and operating IEP;

C. any concerns that may impinge upon the implementation of the IEP.

The successful implementation of an IEP involves commitment, cooperation, and communication among the COH team and the IEP implementers, as well as the parents/guardians and the students — in other words, an interdisciplinary team.

Assessment

1. Design a sample IEP form that includes the components of an ideal IEP as specified by the Federal Register August 23, 1977 guidelines.

2. Consider the use of your IEP form for one of your students. Think in terms of eligibility information and placement options.

3. Complete your sample IEP form for one student. Include the following:

- Student Entry Characteristics
  - strengths
  - weaknesses
  - learning style
- Goals

- Objectives
- Special/Regular Services
    - indicate persons responsible for providing a specific service
- Materials
- Teaching Style (optional)
- Teaching Strategies (optional)
- Schedule of Services
- Documentation/Monitoring Procedure
- Evaluation Procedures

You are encouraged to complete your IEP with the assistance of COH team members, suggested implementers, and others in a team setting in order to utilize your resources/expertise in the decision-making process.

4. If possible, implement your IEP for a specified period of time. Collect appropriate data as to its functioning. Is your IEP working? Why? Why not? Have you made modifications in the plan? Is it an appropriate and useful plan for your student? Have you used the resources of your team?

5. What are your opinions regarding the design, development, and implementation of your IEP? What problems did you run into? How did you resolve them? What were your successes? How valuable was the team approach to decision making?

6. Given a choice, will you try another IEP? Why? Why not? Would you rather work alone or with a team?

Implications/Applications

While the interdisciplinary team approach to the design and development of the IEP has the potential to facilitate greater accuracy in the decision-making process, it has operated with some limitations. In training teachers in actual mainstreaming practice, the regular classroom teacher is often the least involved in the team decision-making process. In fact, regular classroom teachers are seldom asked to offer a contribution to the IEP beyond what is included in the original referral form and often perceive the recommendations made by the COH team members to be inappropriate or lacking in usefulness for everyday teaching of mainstreamed youngsters. Similarly, parents find themselves relatively uninvolved during the planning process, except for their legally required presence at the COH meeting.

Certainly, the success of any IEP is enhanced by the input and active involvement of the regular classroom teacher and parents, the persons who have the most contact with youngsters on a daily basis and who are directly responsible for managing their academic and social behaviors.

Suggestions for Increasing the Effectiveness of the Interdisciplinary Team in Producing the IEP

A necessary condition for team building is the parity of team members in collaborative decision making. This parity means that the interdisciplinary team members share their responsibilities while acting in a non-hierarchical and flexible manner. The team spirit grows as members acknowledge mutual benefits from their collaboration and openly communicate differences. The parity, as described, results in a productive interdependence essential to the IEP decision-making process.

1. Focus on shared responsibility among team members. Even though team members may need to feel that their functions are distinct and unique, the deliberate involvement of two or more members in a specific task increases the validity of the decision that they make.

> *Example*: The regular and special education teachers, after the diagnostic data have been interpreted by the assessment team, will design the annual goals and the specific short term objectives for the IEP.

2. Provide continuous consulting support for each team member during the operation of the IEP. Regular classroom teachers in particular need to be supported in their everyday workings with the mainstreamed youngster.

> *Example*: Regular and special education teachers may team teach in each others classes — always a learning experience for both.

3. Deliberately increase the active involvement of the regular classroom teacher and the parent in the decision-making process. By providing substitute teachers for the regular classroom teacher and baby-sitting services at school for parents, principals may assist both parties to take on equal roles on the team.

> *Example*: Regular teachers can provide the team with progress reports on student academic and social behavior, and parents can report on home or community conditions which help or hinder the student's progress.

4. Clarify the roles and responsibilities of team members, not only at the onset of team development, but also as the team process continues. Team members need to continually identify changing resources and to be reminded that their efforts are mutually reinforcing.

Example: At first, the principal and the special education teacher may identify the materials to be used in teaching the mainstreamed youngster. Eventually, the regular classroom teacher and even students themselves may be involved in materials selection.

5. Plan for ongoing program evaluation by all team members. This assessment should identify which programs are most effective for specific students. It also should seek out reasons for success.

Example: Feedback from all team members may be used by regular and special education teachers to modify long-term goals which may not be appropriate, by developing new short-term behavioral objectives that are easier to evaluate and modify.

Interdisciplinary team members may contribute, in varying degrees depending on their expertise, to the planning, implementation, and evalution of the IEP. The team approach can serve to improve the decision making, which is necessary to produce a more effective educational management plan for teaching exceptional children and youth in the regular classroom.

Table 7.1 is offered as an example of an IEP in terms of its typical components including descriptions, examples, and suggested interdisciplinary team member functions.

TABLE 7.1

Typical Components of an IEP and the Interdisciplinary Team

IEP Components	Descriptions	Examples	Team Member(s)	Function
A. Present level of student's educational functioning	Data that give actual skills and levels at which a youngster is functioning. Data obtained from: 1. formal testing—norm-referenced 2. formal testing—criterion-referenced 3. informal testing (ex. Informal Reading Inventory) 4. Learning Style Inventory	Mary can add two single or double digit numbers from 1 to 20 with 100% accuracy	1. school psychologist/educational evaluation 2. regular and special education teachers 3. regular and special education teacher and reading teachers 4. regular and special education, classroom teachers and school psychologist/educational evaluator	To gather data and then to analyze and share responses to the data, each team member using personal expertise and/or experience in working with the student.
B. Annual Goals	Based on data from present level of educational functioning a "hunch" as to how far a youngster can progress during a school semester or year.	Mary can add 3 digit numbers (one addend without regrouping) with 90% accuracy.	1. regular and special education teachers 2. assessment team 3. Mary 4. Mary's parents	Using data base and shared discussion in A., above, to agree upon hypothetically appropriate terminal academic/social goals.
C. Short-term instructional objectives	An objective written in behavioral terms (see Module 9.1). List the *specific* intermediate steps between present-level functioning and the annual goal.	Mary will be able to add zero as addends with 90% accuracy.	1. regular and special education teachers 2. Mary 3. Mary's parents	To agree upon small-step behavioral (overt) objectives which lead to the accomplishment of the terminal goals in terms of the academic/social abilities of the students.
D. Materials	All materials that are appropriate to carrying out	Mary will use the CAI package on a terminal	1. regular and special education teachers	To agree about the choice of instructional

TABLE 7.1 (Continued)

IEP Components	Descriptions	Examples	Team Member(s)	Function
	annual goals based on assessment data. Materials may include skill-focused worksheets, texts, computer games, puzzles, etc.	to practice Section I—number concepts and horizontal addition.	2. principal 3. Mary 4. Mary's parents	materials which best assist the student to complete the small-step behavioral objectives.
E. Teaching Style	The instructional management style based on *teacher* behavior.	Mary will be taught by the direct instructional teaching pattern (see Module 9.4).	1. regular and special educators 2. school psychologist	To agree on the choice of method(s) which will assist the student in completing the small-step behavioral objectives.
F. Schedule of Services	Projected dates for the starting and duration of immediate services and anticipated services of any type youngster will receive.	January, 19__ to June, 19__ Mary will be evaluated every 6 weeks. Services may include speech therapy, resource room, etc.	all interdisciplinary team members	To determine the services needed by the student and scheduling of the services.
G. Documentation/Monitoring Services	Statements of criteria and evaluation procedures for the completion of short-term behavioral instructional objectives.	Mary's work will be monitored by criterion checklists, teacher-made tests, and her progress with CAI.	all interdisciplinary team members including Mary and parents	To prepare or identify appropriate modes for evaluating the student's work.
H. Evaluation Process	IEP must be reviewed at least annually to determine whether short-term objectives and annual goals have been met.	On June 1, 19__, Mary's IEP will be evaluated.	all interdisciplinary team members including Mary and parents	To use identified modes of evaluation to check the student's progress in achieving terminal goals.

Classroom Organization and Instructional Strategies Appropriate for Exceptional Children and Youth

INTRODUCTION

E<small>DUCATORS</small> who welcome exceptional children and youth into the regular classroom need to reexamine their classroom organization to see whether it will need modification to meet the learning, emotional, physical, and social requirements of these students. Module 8.1 asks you to analyze your current modes of classroom management strategies through a questionnaire which is meant to offer you overt proof of your organizational style. You are then asked to critique the results in terms of the functional needs of the exceptional students you will be working with.

Module 8.2 offers you a closer look at the advantages and disadvantages of using large group, small group and/or one-to-one instructional modes.

For further information on classroom organization, look at the Topic Referenced Bibliography on pages 232 to 262 under the number 9 (Classroom Management).

8.1 AN ANALYSIS OF CLASSROOM ORGANIZATION AND INSTRUCTIONAL STRATEGIES

Minimum Competency Objectives

1. You will examine various modes of grouping, classroom arrangements, and instructional strategies in this module and Module 8.2 which you may use to assist both regular and exceptional students to perform up to their potential in your classroom.

2. You may cooperate with curriculum coordinators, school psychologists, teacher aides, and volunteers in facilitating various classroom organizations and instructional strategies for exceptional students.

3. For this portion of the module you will analyze your current modes of grouping, classroom arrangements, and instructional strategies to detect their strengths and possible weaknesses in terms of helping incoming mainstreamed children or youth.

Rationale

Many teachers already use classroom management, grouping, and instructional strategies which can be beneficial for working with exceptional students. There is no one way that best meets all students needs. However, in view of the possibility of a wider range of cognitive, affective, motor perceptual, and social-emotional skills of the students you will teach in mainstreamed circumstances, you may wish to use some of the following:

1. Individualized instruction
2. Independent study
3. Peer tutoring
4. Pair learning
5. Small group instruction

At present, you need to reevaluate your knowledge and use of these modes of instruction: arrangement of classroom furniture, modes of maintaining classroom order, team teaching, and your current preferred modes of overall instruction.

Enabling Activities

Read the following questionnaire and fill in the blanks. Compare your answers with the *Analysis* at the end of the questionnaire. Use this information as a data bank for reading, discussing, and practicing the strategies suggested in Module 8.2.

QUESTIONNAIRE

1. I arrange my classroom with student desks in vertical lines with the teacher's desk at the front of the classroom for the following percentage of time each week:

    80% to 100% _____
    50% to 70% _____
    20% to 40% _____
     0% to 10% _____

2. I arrange my class in one large circle. I sit anywhere I wish as part of that circle for the following percentage of time each week:

    80% to 100% _____
    50% to 70% _____
    20% to 40% _____
     0% to 10% _____

3. I arrange my class in small circles or in small areas (learning centers). I move from group to group. I do this for the following percentage of the week:

    80% to 100% _____
    50% to 70% _____
    20% to 40% _____
     0% to 10% _____

4. I arrange my class in small groups (circles, centers, etc.). I remain at my desk, monitoring all the behavior. Students have to come to me either individually or in small groups for instruction. I do this for the following percentage of the week:

    80% to 100% _____
    50% to 70% _____
    20% to 40% _____
     0% to 10% _____

5. I arrange my class so that I work with one fairly large group while students go to smaller centers in the classroom where they either work alone or with paraprofessionals or other aides. I do this for the following percentage of the week:

    80% to 100% _____
    50% to 70% _____
    20% to 40% _____
     0% to 10% _____

6. I have a class arrangement that is not described here. (Fill in description.) I use this arrangement for the following percentage of the week:

   80% to 100% _____
   50% to 70% _____
   20% to 40% _____
    0% to 10% _____

7. I prepare lessons for the large group. The entire class is expected to follow the same textbook, workbook, literature text. All are expected to do the same assignments.   Yes _____   No _____

8. I prepare lessons for the large group. While the students begin with the same text, workbook, or handout, they are encouraged to do other work for the assignment, this work being related to the students' varying abilities. Yes _____   No _____

9. I prepare lessons for small groups in the class. I relate these lessons to the interest/abilities of the small groups.   Yes _____   No _____

10. I prepare lessons for small groups. In addition, I prepare lessons for individual students in the groups who may or may not be able to do the work of the group. These lessons are related to the interest and ability of the individual student.   Yes _____   No _____

11. I ask my students to pair up from time to time in order to learn what I have taught.   Yes _____   No _____

12. I select tutors within the class to help other students who may not be doing so well.   Yes _____   No _____

13. I use the help of parents, aides, or paraprofessionals.
    Yes _____   No _____

14. I use the assistance of a resource teacher in the classroom.
    Yes _____   No _____

15. At times, my students leave the classroom for special help, such as reading, mathematics, therapy, etc.   Yes _____   No _____

16. I use the help of a school librarian either in the classroom or in special library classes in that room.   Yes _____   No _____

17. Of all of the above modes of preparing lessons, I prefer the following:

    _____ .

18. I make use of the following most often:

    workbooks _____
    textbooks _____
    my own handouts _____
    published handouts _____
    students take notes in their own books _____
    students use the library in the classroom _____
    students use the library in the school _____
    typewriters _____
    art materials _____
    other _____

19. I make use of the following most often:

    film slides _____
    8 mm. film _____
    16 mm. film _____
    overhead projector _____
    opaque projector _____
    radio _____
    television _____
    audio tape recorder _____
    record player _____
    video tape recorder _____
    other _____

20. Movement in my class consists primarily of the following:

    Teacher moves about the room _____
    Students move about the room _____
    Teacher and students move about the room _____
    Students stay at their places _____
    Teacher stays at the desk _____

Assessment

Analysis of Questionnaire

1. If you judge that you use large group teaching most of the week, you will have to consider how to enable:

- gifted and talented children and youth to engage in activities that go beyond the average;
- slower students to rehearse, remediate;
- students with special needs to work with a partner;
- students to be seated for safety, sight needs, hearing needs, and movement needs.

2. If you use small group teaching for the most part, you will need to consider how to arrange these groups to assist the student who is gifted, slower, partially deaf, partially sighted, mildly retarded, etc. in these groups.

3. If you use individualized instruction, you will need to consider how to use grouping, pairs, tutoring, learning centers, paraprofessional services, resource teachers, and parent volunteers.

4. Looking at your major teaching styles, which will have to be altered to meet the needs of mainstreamed students?

5. Have you already decided what style or combination of styles would best help in the mainstreamed class?

6. How do you plan to implement your analysis of your teaching style?

Implications/Applications

Teachers should be encouraged to provide a classroom environment that facilitates the needs of exceptional students by testing various ways of organizing classrooms and using a variety of instructional strategies. Regular and special education teachers who consciously provide different physical arrangements in the classroom, use a variety of grouping modes, select diversified materials, and utilize a range of instructional strategies are responding to the individual academic, physical, and social differences of exceptional children. Table 8.1 provides you with an example of how grouping modes, classroom physical arrangements, materials, and instructional strategies may be coordinated to provide a learning focus for exceptional students.

The effective use of the information provided in Table 8.1A may require the skills of a team composed of regular and special education teachers, a curriculum coordinator, and a school psychologist to review and interpret the assessment data on the exceptional student and the academic and social history of the student including the student's successes and failures. The information in Table 8.1A may be applied to Tom Quick, an eight-year-old learning disabled student as shown in Table 8.1B.

8.2 GROUPING MODES: TO MEET NEEDS OF EXCEPTIONAL STUDENTS

Minimum Competency Objectives

1. You will be able to describe the major advantages of the large group, small group and one-to-one instructional modes.

2. You will review Module 3.2 and be able to identify the eight major groupings of exceptional conditions in students.

3. You will be able to select and defend an appropriate instructional mode for exceptional students by working with some interdisciplinary team members in your school.

Rationale

Recent research on grouping modes suggests that there is no single best grouping arrangement or mode for all students in terms of student learning. The many outcomes that are generated by the interaction between student characteristics and grouping modes need to be determined and analyzed in terms of optimal student effects in cognitive and affective domains. Hence, prior to the use of a grouping mode, teachers in collaboration with some interdisciplinary team members may wish to consider the following variables that may impact on social and academic student outcomes.

Enabling Activities

1. Read and discuss the sections on grouping modes and handicapping conditions as a large group (perhaps with a portion of the faculty of your school).

2. With a small group (or members of the interdisciplinary team in your school), make a list of the pros and cons of each instructional mode.

3. With one peer, apply the findings from your list (Question #2) to youngsters in the eight groupings of handicapping conditions (see Module 3.3).

I. Large Group Mode

The large group mode of classroom organization is appropriate when used for student outcomes related to whole class academic and social behaviors.

TABLE 8.1A

Coordination of Grouping Modes, Classroom Organization, Materials, and Instructional Strategies for a Learning Focus

Grouping Mode	Classroom Physical Organization	Materials	Instructional Strategy	Learning Focus
• Individual	• tutoring center • learning station • study carrels • quiet study corner • office/private booths	• computers • CAI packages on terminals • programmed instruction • tape recorder • record player • typewriters (e.g. Braille and primary typewriter) • slide/tape filmstrips • games • drill and practice materials • television	• individualized instruction • independent study • peer tutoring • pair tutoring • child directed/ teacher monitored • teacher directed/ teacher monitored	• student intensive skill development • student assessment • student enrichment • student remediation • student attention to task • student establishes rapport with peers • student establishes rapport with teacher and other adults, (e.g. aides, teaching assistants, volunteers)
• small group	• learning centers • small circles • interest corners • special project centers	• games • manipulative materials • texts (basal and supplemental) • worksheets • drill and practice materials • tape recorder • slide/tape filmstrips • television	• student directed • teacher directed • class committee • polar group (students who are opposites in some way) • peer tutoring • pairs	• grouping by achievement level • grouping for academic skills (i.e. strengths and weaknesses) • grouping for socialization • grouping for cooperation and collaboration • grouping by mental age for learning comfort • grouping for reinforcement • grouping for enrichment • grouping for special purposes

TABLE 8.1A (Continued)

Grouping Mode	Classroom Physical Organization	Materials	Instructional Strategy	Learning Focus
• large group	• student desks in vertical lines with teacher's desk at the front • student desks in large circle — teacher's desk is part of circle • student desks in clusters — teacher's desk in corner • student desks in "U" formation — teacher's desk part of the "U"	• television • text books and supplemental materials • magazines/workbooks • manipulated materials • opaque projector • blackboard • overhead projector • films • tape recorder • filmstrips • computers/terminals in a computer laboratory	• teacher-directed teaching style • teacher demonstrates • student role playing • student simulations	• teacher in charge • class spirit building • teacher imparting general information/directions efficiently • class sharing of ideas and concerns that affect the whole group • teacher monitoring of student on task engagement • teacher proximity to all students may be supportive • teacher introducing new material • teacher stimulates discussion abilities of students

TABLE 8.1B

A Program for Tom Quick In A Regular Class

Grouping Mode	Classroom Physical Organization With Rationale	Materials	Instructional Strategy	Learning Focus
• Individual —Tom by himself	• office/booth to limit distractions that seem to affect Tom's ability to concentrate	• colorful pictures • printed materials • filmstrips without sound • flashcards for drill and practice • computers and CAI packages • programmed instructional materials	• teacher directed/ teacher monitored (teacher will give directions in short, simple, direct sentences; teacher will *write out* expected assignments)	• Tom's skills will be remediated • Tom's frustration will be controlled
• Tom with peer	• learning station that is focused on academic skill development for Tom	• written short skill lessons sequenced by difficulty • computer with CAI material	• peer tutoring (peer may introduce Tom to computer terminal; peer and Tom may jointly complete software package; peer can test Tom *slowly* on skill lessons)	• Tom's skill development will be intensified • Tom will establish rapport with a peer
• Tom with teacher/ teacher aide or volunteer	• tutoring corner that is a small space partitioned off from the large classroom, allowing Tom to control	• short game focused on visual inputs and visual outputs should be used for a controlled period of time	• pair tutoring—adult tutoring will limit the number of times the game will be played	• Tom will establish rapport with teacher, teacher aid, or volunteer • Tom will control frustration and distractability

TABLE 8.1B (Continued)

Grouping Mode	Classroom Physical Organization With Rationale	Materials	Instructional Strategy	Learning Focus
	his physical environment			
• Tom in a small group	• special projects center focused on use of visual materials	• short filmstrip to be used as a model for students to develop their own filmstrip or comic strips	• polar groups made up of students who manifest other modality strengths— Tom's visual sense can contribute to the group project by providing visual details and a vivid imagination	• Tom will increase his socialization skills • Tom will increase his cooperation/collaboration behaviors with peer's • Tom's skills will be enriched
• Tom in a large group	• a large circle. Tom is to be seated next to the teacher in order to support the interpersonal relationship that is important for Tom's success	• blackboard that is used to *write out* series of events (agenda) for the day, as well as the daily and homework assignments • textbooks and related print materials	• teacher-directed teaching style (Tom will know what to do, how to do it and when to do it. Tom's on-task work will be monitored by teacher. Reinforcement will be provided. Short handout will be provided to review instructional objectives of an activity.	• Tom will establish rapport with his teacher • Tom's on-task work will be monitored • Tom's classroom behavior will be controlled

More specifically, when the teacher is working with the large group in a teacher-directed teaching style, student behavior is more easily observable and therefore may be monitored accordingly. It has been stated that teacher monitoring supports student academic engagement on task. This monitoring results in positive student achievement. In addition, this monitoring behavior (walking around the room, checking on students), takes on a "teacher in-charge" climate that may assist in better classroom management. The large group arrangement also may be an efficient mode for imparting knowledge or general information/directions, developing whole class interaction, class spirit building, and a general sharing of ideas and concerns affecting the whole group.

II. Small Group Mode

It is important to discuss why the small group mode of classroom organization may be of benefit to students in terms of learning. In a small group setting, instruction may be specifically geared to the common skill needs of the group. Furthermore, this type of grouping may accommodate different rates of learning, general aptitudes, interests, and similar student academic and social entry behaviors. Additionally, the small group mode is appropriate for supporting more active student participation. Students may feel more comfortable asking questions of the teacher and one another, and this interaction may be especially beneficial for shy and less able youngsters.

However, a word of caution is in order when using student activity groups in the small group mode. Students should be provided with clear assignments as well as an accountability system that has immediate implications (for example, due dates on group projects, group reports). If group work is not discussed or reacted to by the teacher, students will perceive activity groups as time fillers with little real value.

III. One Student with Teacher Mode: One-to-One

It would appear that the grouping of one student working with a teacher has some advantages. If we accept the fact that the one-to-one instructional mode has benefits, it is important to discuss why this mode may make a difference in student cognitive and affective outcomes. From an academic perspective, students and teachers may benefit from one-to-one instruction because it allows for intensive instruction, especially when used in small time segments. One-to-one instruction has been used successfully to assist students with learning problems to acquire new skills. Under the direct supervision of a teacher, the student's attention to task may be monitored easily and teacher pacing of instruction may be modified accordingly.

Additionally, the benefits from one-to-one instruction may have positive social ramifications. The rapport that develops between a teacher and one student contributes to a relationship that supports a sense of security on the part of a youngster. This relationship may provide some relief from the student's sense of frustration that sometimes occurs in a larger group instructional mode.

Assessment

1. With a peer, answer the following question. Use the diagrams to visualize the classroom.

In a large group instructional mode, where would you seat the students in Plan X and in Plan Y who have:

a. speech and language problems
b. hearing problems
c. visual problems
d. physical problems
e. perceptual math problems
f. information processing/thinking/memory problems
g. social-emotional problems
h. gifted and talented performance

FIGURE 8.2

Seating Plans

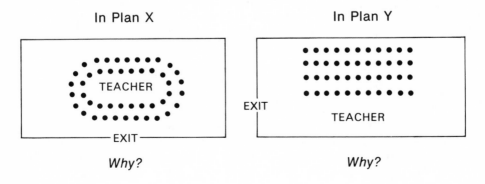

In Plan X   In Plan Y

Why?   Why?

2. Design an ideal small group made up of exceptional and regular students. Describe the students. Why did you select these students? How does this small group setting meet the special cognitive and affective needs of the students you described?

3. Work out a one-to-one instructional mode with a student in your class for a one week period, planning on 15 minutes of intensive instruction daily. Gather data on student attention to task and teacher pacing of instruction by filling in the following chart.

CHART 8.2

Student Attention and Teacher Pacing

	Day 1	Day 2	Day 3	Day 4	Day 5
Student Attention to Task (Approximate time in minutes)					
Pace of Instructor (slow, moderate, fast)					

With your instructor, analyze your data in terms of trends that might indicate an interaction between student attention to task and teacher pacing of instruction.

Additional Activities

Students may be paired for instruction, research, review of instruction, or evaluation of instruction. In pairing situations, the students may be similar or different in academic achievement, emotional response, use of senses, or physical abilities. Analyze a series of weekly lesson plans you wish to give, noting where paired groups would facilitate learning, review, and/or testing. Note in particular how you could pair students of dissimilar abilities. How does pairing of students of dissimilar academic talents assist the education of the more capable student? Do you need to offer special instruction when pairing?

Implications/Applications

To meet the varied physical, academic, and social needs of exceptional students, teachers may wish to experiment with various grouping modes. The physical design of grouping modes in classrooms can influence behaviors in desirable ways. Careful analysis of individual student performance can help regular and special education teachers, acting with the school psychologist, to determine the advantages of a particular grouping mode in relation to a student's academic/social needs. Additionally, since students learn at varying temporal rates, different modes of grouping may be used to accommodate these rates. Table 8.2A briefly describes grouping modes and their instructional advantages to categories of exceptional students.

TABLE 8.2A

Grouping Modes and Their Instructional Advantages to Categories of Exceptional Students

Grouping Mode	Instructional Advantages	Categories of Exceptional Students
One student alone and one-to-one	Tutoring, programmed instruction, individual prescribed instruction (IPI), independent study, computers/CAI, and "contracts" are basically instructional methods that produce low error rates. This is to say, student responses are usually reinforced during progression through instruction. As a result, students acquire appropriate behaviors in relation to facts, concepts, and/or social skills through immediate feedback. For example, tutors make comments, identify errors, clarify, or suggest; thus students usually arrive at the correct answer. Tutors also may provide observational	a. All categories including: • speech and language problems • hearing problems • visual problems • physical problems • perceptual math problems • information processing/thinking/memory problems • social/emotional problems • gifted and talented performances

TABLE 8.2A (Continued)

Grouping Mode	Instructional Advantages	Categories of Exceptional Students
	learning by serving as models for exceptional students. Another advantage includes the use of appropriate learning materials (content by interest, skill, or level) based on individual student assessment data. The long range goal of this instructional mode is more independent learning at the student's own rate.	b. Peer/pair tutoring may be arranged in various combinations. Examples: • gifted and talented student with speech and language problem • teacher aide with socially-emotionally disturbed student • visually impaired student with teacher • physically handicapped student with non-handicapped student
Small group	Small groups in particular allow for exceptional students to more easily contribute to and participate in group activities. (One small group may be given a structured activity to which each member must make a unique contribution. The contribution should support the exceptional student's strengths and should be separate and different from the contributions of other group members.) In addition, small groups encourage students to listen and observe, both important elements in "vicarious learning" (observing and sympathetically participating in the experiences of another group member). The rate of learning of the individual may be controlled, depending on the purpose of the group.	All categories of exceptional students and varying combinations of students in small groups may occur for different purposes (See Module 8.1).
Large group	Large group instruction that is teacher directed has advantages in improving the learning of exceptional students (See Module 9.4). The direct instruction pattern is characterized by teacher behaviors that include instructional organization and	All categories of exceptional students may learn in a large group setting. Seating arrangements relative to the exceptional cate-

TABLE 8.2A (Continued)

Grouping Mode	Instructional Advantages	Categories of Exceptional Students
	management in which the teacher is the center of attention in response to pupils and in organizing and presenting materials. A strong advantage of the direct instruction pattern is that the teacher can monitor and maintain appropriate students' academic and social behaviors. The rate of learning of the individual student is not easily controlled.	gory are obvious. Examples: • Visually impaired student will sit close to blackboard. • Physically handicapped student will sit next to exit. • Socially-emotionally disturbed student will sit next to teacher.

More specifically, the following examples in Table 8.2B may further clarify the advantages of the various grouping modes matched to the appropriate needs of the categories of exceptional students.

TABLE 8.2B

Advantages of Various Grouping Modes to Needs of Categories of Exceptional Students

Category of Exceptional Student	Grouping Mode	Advantages
I. Mildly mentally retarded students (Alice A.)	One-to-one	Alice may establish rapport with tutor/teacher because of greater tutor/teacher contact and supervision. The use of individualized behavior modification techniques on a one-to-one ratio may increase the support for appropriate behaviors. Instruction techniques may be organized in small steps. Material selection may be at an appropriately low reading level but still high in interest level. Alice will learn at her own rate.

TABLE 8.2B (Continued)

Category of Exceptional Student	Grouping Mode	Advantages
II. Socially-emotionally disturbed students (Jack J.)	One-to-one	All of the above are advantages for Jack, but an emphasis should be placed on developing socialization and communication skills using the creative arts. Jack will learn at his own rate.
III. Students who have specified information processing problems (Dawn D.)	One-to-one	All of the above are advantages for Dawn. Add a focus on circumventing the disability and use the appropriate modality channels with an emphasis on the task-training approach (See Module 5.2). Dawn will learn at her own rate.
IV. Students who have a speech and hearing problem (Don Q.) V. Students who have perceptual math problems (Sam P.) VI. Students who have an information processing problem but have auditory strength in learning. (Donna L.) VII. Non-handicapped students who have the same mental age (MA) as Don, and Donna. (Beth B. and Sara V.)	Small group organized by mental age (MA) for math skills, using computers/CAI, hand calculators, soundless filmstrip, skill work sheets, and puzzles.	From categories IV–VII, Don, Sam, Donna, Beth and Sara will be taught a new skill at approximately the same learning rate. This small group mode for mental age grouping will support new skill acquisition, retention of the skill, and the transfer of the skill from one situation to another, with practice.

TABLE 8.2B (Continued)

Category of Exceptional Student	Grouping Mode	Advantages
VIII. Students with gifted and talented performance (Gail G.)	A large group that has some "main-streamed" students.	The large group supports the principle of normalization and encourages class interaction, spirit building, and a general sharing of ideas and concerns of all students. Large groups composed of exceptional and non-handicapped students reflect society. Since the learning rates of society are not easy to control, instruction must be varied and diversified.
IX. Students with visual problems (Vera V.)		
X. Students with physical problems (Alex A.)		
XI. Non-handicapped students who demonstrate diversity in knowledge, skills, and attitudes	A large group composed of exceptional students and non-handicapped students.	

Instructional Management

INTRODUCTION

SPECIAL EDUCATORS have for a long time organized instruction through stated behavioral objectives; at times, regular educators have not. When these educators begin to work together to write the IEP, regular educators feel at a loss because of a lack of familiarity with the language related to setting up and meeting behavioral objectives. Module 9.1 is meant to alleviate the possible difficulties of such a situation by familiarizing regular educators with the language and mode of instruction associated with establishing overt short range and terminal behavioral objectives. The module develops three criteria for appropriately stating objectives, reviews common objectives in relationship to ascending hierarchies of cognition and affectivity, and offers practice in the writing of objectives. Module 9.2 introduces or reviews the concept of task analysis as one way to determine the students' entry skills in relation to the objective chosen, and the kind of instruction needed to assist the students to achieve the objective in terms of their entry skills. This instruction is to be stated in small steps which include both teacher and student behaviors which lead to the successful completion of the terminal goal of the unit or lesson.

Module 9.3 describes mastery learning. Mastery learning is a logical forward step in instruction through behavioral objectives for it takes into consideration the amount of time to accomplish sub and terminal goals. Since students in any class — but more so in a mainstreamed class — need different amounts of time to accomplish any given task in terms of their ability, perseverance, the quality of instruction, and the materials presented, mastery learning is a model for instruction which permits individual rates of learning in the same classroom.

Note: Deena Newman of Syracuse University collaborated in the development of the direct instruction pattern and the observation instrument in this module.

Module 9.4 offers the form and function of the direct instruction pattern, a teaching style that has been suggested for use with less able learners. An observation instrument that measures teacher behaviors in direct instruction is provided so that educators may test the direct instruction pattern with their students.

Module 9.5 emphasizes the value of the computer, specifically CAI, as an instructional tool. An outline of an inservice training model in CAI for interdisciplinary teams is provided.

Module 9.6 focuses on the important concepts of data gathering on instruction and evaluation. It suggests that assessment and evaluation are ongoing processes and that the sequence of assessment (diagnosis), instruction, and evaluation is cyclical in nature leading always to the next cycle, with the evident hope on the part of the educator and student that the cycle will move in upward spirals.

For further information on instructional strategies in the mainstreamed classroom, see the Topic Referenced Bibliography on pages 232 to 262, under the number *8.2*. For evaluation modes, see the number *8.3*. A special bibliography will offer you assistance in combining art with teaching reading, writing and the content areas in the mainstreamed classroom. It is to be found on page 270 to 279.

9.1   WRITING INSTRUCTIONAL OBJECTIVES

Minimum Competency Objectives

1. You will develop a skill in identifying goals for learners that will lead students to behave, act, or perform in certain ways under certain conditions.

2. You will write and use objectives that include three criteria. The objectives are:

1) describe the behavior sought;
2) identify the conditions under which the behavior is expected to occur;
3) state standards for determining whether the level of achievement has been reached.

Rationale

It has been suggested that teachers operate in a state of self-made confusion unless they know exactly what they want students to be able to do at the end of a lesson. While some components of teaching lend themselves to this precision more than others (the cognitive or thinking domain is easier to deal with in objective terms than the affective or feeling domain), teachers can improve instruction by learning to develop and use instructional objectives which are based on overt performances of students. Consequently, educators support the notion that clearly defined performance objectives make it possible to provide a basis for lesson/unit evaluation and the selection and evaluation of appropriate materials, content, and instructional methods for student learning. In fact, the use of objectives makes it easier for school-based interdisciplinary teams consisting of regular and special educators, school psychologists/educational evaluators, guidance counselors, and principals to identify and ensure the specific kinds and levels of academic and social activities they wish exceptional children and youth to experience. Additionally, interdisciplinary team members may use objectives to facilitate the identification of their own role functions in student learning.

Enabling Activities

1. Read the following content section on developing instructional objectives.

2. After reading the section, discuss and share with a colleague your example of one cognitive objective and one affective objective for one child in your class. Ask for a critique in terms of the criteria offered in this module.

DEVELOPING INSTRUCTIONAL OBJECTIVES

I.   Criterion I

    A.   To describe the behavior sought:

        1.   state exactly what the learner will be expected to do as you understand it. (*the terminal behavior*);

        2.   use performance words to exclude the greatest number of interpretations of your intended behavior;

        3.   if you must use words open to varying interpretations, describe what the learner will be doing when he knows the alphabet, enjoys a painting, or appreciates music.

    B.   The best statement of objective(s) is the one that excludes the greatest number of possible interpretations of your goal.

Words Open to Many Interpretations	*Words Open to Fewer Interpretations*
to know	to write
to understand	to differentiate
to fully appreciate	to solve
to grasp the significance of	to construct
to enjoy	to list
to believe	to compare
to explore	to contrast

Example:

What do we mean when we say we want a learner to "know" something? Do we mean that we want him to be able to recite, or to solve, or to construct? Just telling him we want him to "know" tells him little. The word can mean many things.

C. Such words as "understand" and "appreciate" may be included in a statement of an objective, but the statement is not explicit enough to be useful until it indicates how you intend to sample the "understanding" and "appreciating." Until you describe what the learner will be doing when demonstrating that he "understands" or "appreciates," you have described very little at all.

II. Criterion II

A. To identify conditions under which the behavior is expected to occur, specify the factors you will impose on the learners.

B. You sometimes will have to define a terminal behavior further by stating the conditions you will impose upon the learner when he is demonstrating his mastery of the objective. These are examples of conditions you may impose on the learner:

1. Given a problem of the following kind ....

2. Given a list of ....

3. Given any reference of the learner's choice ....

4. Without aid of reference ....

5. With the aid of a slide rule ....

6. Given the story "_____" ....

III. Criterion III

    A.   To state standards for determining whether the level of achievement has been reached, describe how well the learner must perform.

    B.   Specify the criteria (excellence of performance, qualitative or quantitative) by describing how well the learner must perform the activity to be considered acceptable.

    Example:

    1.   Run the 100 yard dash *within a period of 14 seconds.*

    2.   The student must solve correctly *at least 7 out of 10* linear equations.

IV.   Although all three criteria have value for making instructional objectives more specific, it is not always necessary to include all three criteria in each instructional objective.

    The foregoing materials focus on the skill of writing instructional objectives in performance terms. Teachers also need to consider the appropriateness of their objectives for students in relation to learner characteristics, the subject content, and the kinds of learning outcomes expected of students. It is particularly important that instructional objectives include affective as well as cognitive components.

    Benjamin Bloom and David Krathwohl have led recent efforts in developing taxonomies of educational objectives. Their classifications of the cognitive and affective domains are especially useful in helping teachers include a variety of thinking and feeling processes in the educational experiences developed for students.

    A.   Cognitive domain

    The taxonomy of cognitive behavior identifies six levels of thinking. A hierarchical structure emerges, proceeding from the lowest level to the highest level of cognition. The learning at higher levels presupposes ability to perform at the levels below.

    B.   Affective domain

    The taxonomy of affective behavior identifies five levels of attitudes, interests, and/or personal involvement. Progressing from the lowest level to the highest level is predicated on the degree of internalization or the extent of feeling.

V.   There is a direct relationship between the terminal behavior and the levels of learning in the cognitive and affective domains. The illustrations which follow show this relationship as spelled out by Bloom and Krathwohl.

TABLE 9.1A

Relationship Between Terminal Behavior and Cognitive Domain

Cognitive Domain	Terminal Behavior
Knowledge (Level 1)	to recall to recite to list to enumerate
Comprehension (Level 2)	to translate to interpret in own words to edit to extrapolate
Application (Level 3)	to use rules, laws, generalizations in new situations to apply known solutions to new events to apply new skills in effecting solutions to construct models for solving problems
Analysis (Level 4)	to take apart the elements of an object or event to interchange equivalent parts to separate events for more careful study to reorder the parts for clearer conceptualization
Synthesis (Level 5)	to derive a unique approach to a given situation to formulate a hypothesis to produce a new plan of operation to contribute the parts for clearer conceptualization
Evaluation (Level 6)	to render an opinion based on relevant data to give a point of view supported by valid evidence to judge an object or event by means of specified criteria to support a position after careful analysis of the situation

Relationship Between Terminal Behavior and Affective Domain

Affective Domain	Terminal Behavior
Receiving (Level 1)	to listen by following directions to observe by pointing to the event to give attention by sitting up straight to be aware of the assignment by doing it
Responding (Level 2)	to answer a question to perform a task to turn in work to volunteer for a job
Valuing (Level 3)	to follow the school rules to conform to the school dress norms to initiate a task to complete a job on time

TABLE 9.1A (Continued)

Affective Domain	Terminal Behavior
Organization (Level 4)	to resolve conflicting values to change an opinion to alter a belief to adhere to a position
Characterization by a value or value complex (Level 5)	to behave in a predictable manner to demonstrate a life style to behave according to a philosophical principle to demonstrate personality characteristics in harmony with a belief

Assessment

1. With a colleague, write one instructional objective for each of the six levels of the cognitive domain cited by Bloom, and one instructional objective for each of the five levels of the affective domain cited by Krathwohl.

2. Develop and use instructional objectives (cognitive and affective) in a two-day mini-unit related to the teaching of any content area.

During the teaching of the unit, include comments in your lesson plans on the following in terms of your defined objectives:

a. their clarity;
b. their appropriateness in terms of students' defined needs including strengths and weaknesses;
c. their appropriateness in terms of materials selection and use;
d. their appropriateness in terms of teaching methods;
e. their usefulness in student evaluation;
f. their usefulness in unit evaluation.

Provide evidence of student work for the instructor's review, when possible.

3. Reflect on your role in facilitating a student's academic and social learning. With another member of the building interdisciplinary team in your school, write one objective for each of the six levels of Bloom's cognitive domain, and one objective for each of the five levels of Krathwohl's affective domain in terms of facilitative activities for student academic and social learning. Review your objectives with a third member of your building level interdisciplinary team. Talk through your objectives in terms of your perceived role in facilitating student learning. Are your objectives congruent, complementary, or

discrepant with the way other team members perceive your facilitative activities for student learning?

Implications/Applications

The use of objectives provides a framework to be used by teachers as individuals or as members of interdisciplinary teams for two purposes:

1. Objectives, particularly if they are data based, provide a basis for an appropriate academic and social educational program for a youngster.

2. Objectives assist in defining facilitative role function behaviors of teachers and interdisciplinary team members.

A review of Bloom's and Krathwohl's taxonomies reveals that both are somewhat hierarchical in nature. This fact suggests that the higher level objectives may subsume the lower level ones. For example, before students are provided a Level 5 objective — synthesis in the cognitive domain — they should have had some success in working with objectives on Levels 1–4 in the same domain. Therefore, when designing instructional activities for a student or facilitative activities for yourself, keep in mind the ascending levels of these objectives and use this information in designing objectives for different learners for different reasons for varied outcomes. For example in teaching basic skills or concrete content to educable mentally retarded (EMR) learners, the lower level objectives would be most frequently used. If you are designing instructional activities for gifted and talented youngsters in critical thinking skills or abstract content, you might still use the lower level objectives including knowledge, comprehension and application, but would then move up on the taxonomy and concentrate on the higher level objectives (analysis, synthesis, and evaluation). The levels of objectives in the affective domain would be used in the same way as those in the cognitive domain.

Application of Objectives for Students

Most importantly, the application of objectives to student learning must focus on the student's present level of functioning. The following chart provides you with hints as to how the cognitive domain (the most commonly used domain) may be applied to instructional objectives with a mildly handicapped student.

CHART 9.1

Cognitive Domain Applied to Objectives for
the Mildly Handicapped Student

Level	Objective Application
Knowledge	Provide objectives for content, preferably concrete, that students can succeed with.
Comprehension	Provide objectives that include repetition in comprehending the concrete content.
Application	Provide objectives that focus on hands-on activities and functional uses (application) of the information.
Analysis	Provide objectives whereby students may experience the breaking of the whole into parts.
Synthesis	Provide objectives whereby students may experience the putting together of the parts into a whole.
Evaluation	Provide objectives that focus on evaluation in social situations.

Application of Objectives for Interdisciplinary Teams

The objectives by the interdisciplinary team in facilitating student learning may be varied in order to match them with the team member. Since principals are responsible for scheduling, a typical role function of their facilitation objectives may include providing release time for all team members to become better acquainted with school programs and curricula that have been shown to be effective for students. Table 9.1 is affixed to provide some suggestions as to how the cognitive domain may be applied to selected facilitative objectives for interdisciplinary team members in their roles in student learning.

TABLE 9.1B

Examples of the Cognitive Domain Applied to Facilitation Objectives
for Interdisciplinary Team Members in Student Learning

Level	Team Member	Objective/Application
Knowledge	• principal	Provides scheduled release time for the team to visit schools and to review exemplary programs and curricula.

TABLE 9.1B (Continued)

Level	Team Member	Objective/Application
	• teachers (special and regular), guidance counselors, school psychologists, educational evaluators, and principal	After team members visit schools or review school programs and curricula, they will share their learnings concerning observed team member roles in facilitating student learning.
Comprehension	• school psychologists/educational evaluators and guidance counselors	Provide information needed to interpret standardized test data and observational data that would indicate that the schools the team visited and/or the programs and curricula reviewed were effective.
	• principal	Provides information whereby the team will be able to interpret data on student absences and student discipline in schools they visited and programs they reviewed.
	• teachers (regular and special)	Will describe the teaching strategies students received and materials that students used in the schools visited and programs reviewed.
Application	• principal	Provides the needed scheduling and inservice education to assist the team in implementing new teaching strategies and materials.
	• teachers (regular and special)	Will work together to test the use of new strategies and materials.
	• school psychologists/educational evaluators and all teachers	Will gather data on teacher use of new teaching strategies and materials.
Analysis	• school psychologists/educational evaluators and all teachers	Will analyze data on teacher use of new teaching strategies and materials.
	• principal	Will provide basis for the analysis of data, the time needed, and arrangements for appropriate inservice staff development.
Synthesis	• all team members	Will put together a new data-based plan for facilitation for student

TABLE 9.1B (Continued)

Level	Team Member	Objective/Application
		learning to include the use of different teaching strategies, the choice of materials, and the staff development of all teachers.
Evaluation	• all team members	Will set up a plan for individual and team evaluation based on agreed criteria arising from team study observations and program progress.

9.2   TASK ANALYSIS: AN ORGANIZATIONAL TOOL

Minimum Competency Objectives

1. You will be able to systematically identify the components of a task.

2. You will be able to identify learner characteristics/strengths necessary and related to those task components.

3. You will be able to design tasks with specific components to match student readiness for such tasks.

4. You will be able to collaborate with interdisciplinary team members to assist you in using task analysis to make appropriate decisions for organizing instruction for a student.

Rationale

Cognitive psychologists suggest that analyzing the process dimensions of a task (operations through which a learner receives, organizes, and transmits information in concert with task analysis—defined as a means of identifying skills/sequence demands) should provide educators with a skill that is applicable to instructional settings for a variety of learners. Task analysis may be developed through an interdisciplinary team approach that utilizes the varying levels of team members' expertise necessary to assess learner characteristics and to analyze the appropriate skills and processes related to the learner's successful completion of a task. Therefore, the purpose of task analysis is to provide teachers with a decision-making tool for organizing and presenting instruction. As a result of task analysis, teachers may identify trends or patterns in a student's task performance and modify task components during instruction. Additionally, the skill allows teachers to design tasks with specific components to match student readiness for such tasks.

Enabling Activities

Read and study the following content section on Task Analysis.

PROCESS DIMENSIONS

Tasks are composed of 3 dimensions of procession: input, association, and output.

1. *Input* — Students receive and organize directions and materials presented to them. Students use verbal and nonverbal stimuli sets in concert with sensory modalities to receive and organize directions.

Process Dimension Input Modes

	Visual	Auditory	Tactile
VERBAL	Visual-Verbal	Auditory-Verbal	Tactile-Verbal
NONVERBAL	Visual-Nonverbal	Auditory-Nonverbal	Tactile-Nonverbal

Example:

A child is given a picture of a square and a circle. The teacher says, "Look at the circle and the square on the page and circle the square." The substance of the activity describes the input modalities used as visual/nonverbal.

2. *Association* — An internal process that is inferred by looking at input (things we give youngsters to look at and listen to) and output (responses youngsters make) over a range of tasks students have undertaken. If tasks are failed, the educator changes the input stimuli from auditory to visual, and so on.

3. *Output* — Students make the responses they have chosen in a number of ways.

Process Dimension Output Modes

	Vocal	Motor
VERBAL	Vocal-Verbal	Motor-Verbal
NONVERBAL	Vocal-Nonverbal	Motor-Nonverbal

Example:

Students orally read two sentences from a story — vocal-verbal output.

TASK ANALYSIS AND ENTRY BEHAVIORS

Task analysis breaks down and/or sequences the subcomponents or subtasks necessary for learner mastery of an objective. Consider the following example that might be used with a mildly retarded youngster.

The Task — Joe will add two one-digit numbers whose sum is no greater than 10 and report his answer orally and in written form.

Necessary Entry Behaviors
1. Joe can speak.
2. Joe responds to verbal directions.
3. Joe can hold and use a writing implement.
4. Joe can draw a straight, vertical line.
5. Joe can make a plus sign.

Objective 1 — Begin Instruction
Joe will count orally from one to ten in various ways: a. counting from 1–10; b. counting from a number other than 1; c. counting to a number other than 10.

Objective 2 — Subskill
Joe will read a plus sign (+) correctly and will say "plus" when he sees the symbol " + ."

Objective 3 — Subskill
Joe will read a number sentence with lines and signs.

Sample: /// + /// translates to "three plus three."

Objective 4 — Subskill
Joe will read and provide the correct answer to a number sentence with lines, plus sign, and equal sign (=).

Sample: // + // = 4 is read "Two plus two equal four."

Objective 5 — Subskill
Joe will add numbers using vertical lines (////) and plus sign (+).

Terminal Objective — Joe will add two out of three of the following addition problems correctly using vertical lines (////) and plus signs (+).

> "To nine add one."
> "To four add six."
> "To two add five."

NOTIONS RELATED TO TASK ANALYSIS

1. Task analysis enables educators to identify strengths and weaknesses of children in their ability to meet demands.

Example:

Joe is capable of completing the task since it is a task that a typical mildly retarded student can achieve. This assumption is based on the fact that mildly retarded youngsters can achieve successfully when the instructional sequence is formulated to include the use of skills that move from the simple concrete to the complex concrete and then to simple abstract, and instruction that is initiated by small steps and then goes on to larger steps.

2. Teachers will identify the essential subcomponent and/or prerequisites to each task.

Example:

The subcomponents of Joe's task have been broken down into a sufficient number of small steps in order to:

a. attempt to match them with his present level of academic functioning;
b. coordinate them with his ability to process the subtasks verbally and nonverbally; and
c. ensure success with each subcomponent, thereby supporting Joe's academic engagement.

3. Teachers specify instructional objectives for tasks to be taught.

Example:

The instructional objective for the task to be taught Joe is specific and reflects a sequence of difficulty ranging from simple to complex in terms of a hierarchy of skills.

4. Teachers will match learner characteristics with appropriate tasks to support student achievement.

Example:

The task that Joe is to complete should be determined by coordinating his assessment data with an analysis of the curriculum skill to be learned.

5. Task analysis may be helpful in the grouping of children for instruction.

Example:

It may be that other mildly retarded students who are similar to Joe in their assessment data may be grouped for instructional purposes.

MODIFICATIONS IN TASK

If Joe is not successful in meeting the established criterion for completion of this task within a reasonable time frame, it is then necessary to modify the task. The following are some ways to modify a task:

1. Reduce the number of problems that Joe is to compute.
2. Reduce the criterion for acceptable performance to one that may be achieved by Joe.
3. Clarify and limit the number of instructions that are being given to Joe at one time.
4. Change input modes from verbal to visual or vice versa.
5. Combine input modes.
6. Change the output modes.
7. Further break down the task into smaller subtasks.
8. Systematically collect data as the team (or teacher) makes modifications to assist in making further changes in the task if necessary.

Implications/Applications

An examination of the appropriate facets of task analysis should reveal that the classroom teacher will find it next to impossible to accomplish the process successfully without the assistance of an interdisciplinary team made up, for example, of a special education teacher, a school psychologist, a learning disabilities specialist, and/or a curriculum coordinator. The importance of making educational decisions for exceptional children and youth in the regular classroom demands that appropriate administrators/supervisors call together such an interdisciplinary team to work with the classroom teacher.

Table 9.2 is provided to describe the process and skill dimensions of task analysis as they relate to the expertise and typical functions of the identified interdisciplinary team members in a school.

TABLE 9.2

Task Analysis Dimensions Related to Expertise and Typical Functions of Interdisciplinary Team Members in a School

Task Analysis Dimensions	Interdisciplinary Team Member(s)
1. Assessing and interpreting student's academic and social strengths and weaknesses.	1. Regular and special education teachers, school psychologist, educational evaluator, and learning disabilities specialist.
2. Identifying the entry level skills necessary for the task.	2. Primarily regular and special education teachers.
3. Analyzing the process dimension (input and output modes) used by the student.	3. Primarily the school psychologist and learning disabilities specialist.
4. Identifying an appropriate task for a student based on level of difficulty as related to student characteristics.	4. Primarily regular and special education teachers.
5. Analyzing the skill sequencing of the curriculum components of the task.	5. Regular and special education teachers and curriculum coordinator.
6. Establishing an appropriate criterion level of acceptance performance, preferably with a time frame.	6. All team members.
7. Evaluating/monitoring student progress by collecting data and making decisions to bring about positive change in student achievement.	7. All team members.

9.3   MASTERY LEARNING: A MODEL FOR SCHOOL LEARNING

Minimum Competency Objectives

You will be able to recall the appropriate conditions of learning, focusing on allowing for necessary time for school learning, as these conditions are related to an organized, systematic teaching approach known as mastery learning.

2. You will evaluate the relevancy of "necessary learning time" as related to "learning rate" as a source of meeting individual differences when teaching youngsters.

3. You will collaborate with a member(s) of an interdisciplinary team to

better apply mastery learning components for the successful instruction of an exceptional student.

Rationale

Mastery learning assumes that given the "appropriate time" almost all students can and will learn. It suggests classroom procedures whereby almost all (75 percent to 95 percent) can achieve at higher levels within the context of ordinary group-based classroom instruction. In brief, mastery learning is Skinnerian in its orientation in that it breaks down a complex behavior into a chain of component behaviors and ensures student mastery of each link in the chain.

Essentially, John B. Carroll's model of school learning outlines the major factors influencing student success in school learning and indicates how these factors interact.[1]

Full Model:

Degree of learning = f

1. Time Allowed
2. Perseverance
3. Aptitude
4. Quality of Instruction
5. Ability to Understand Instruction

Simple Model:

Degree of learning = f

$$\frac{\text{time actually spent}}{\text{time needed}}$$

The model proposes that under typical school learning conditions, the time spent and the time needed are functions of the characteristics of the individual and his instruction.

Explanation of Terms

Time spent:	Determined by the amount of time the student is willing to spend actively involved in the learning (i.e., his perseverance) and the total learning time he is allowed.
Time needed:	Determined by the student's aptitude for the task, ability to understand instruction, and quality of instruction.
Quality of instruction:	Degree to which the presentation, explana-

1. James H. Block, ed., *Mastery Learning: Theory and Practice* (New York: Holt, Rinehart and Winston, 1971), 29–46.

tion, and ordering of the learning tasks approach the optimum for each learner.

Ability to understand instruction: Student's ability to profit from instruction, closely identified with general intelligence.

Aptitude: Entry behavior.

The model proposes that the quality of instruction multiplied by the ability to understand extends the time needed for task mastery beyond that normally required by the student's aptitude for the task.

> *Example:* Quality of instruction is low × ability to understand is low = additional time.

More simply, if each student is allowed the time needed to learn some level (criterion) and spends the required time, then he/she can be expected to attain the level.

Enabling Activities

1. Read and study the rationale and content sections on mastery learning.

2. With an interdisciplinary team member(s), discuss and give examples of how you may use the broad elements of the mastery learning model with your class.

3. If your interest in the use of the model is sparked, see your instructor for more specific information in regard to the use of the mastery learning approach.

I. *Operating Model*

Bloom transformed Carroll's conceptual model into a working model for mastery learning. Bloom indicated that if aptitudes are predictive of the rate at which a student can learn a given task, it is possible to fix the degree of learning expected of students at some mastery level and to manipulate the relevant instructional variables in Carroll's model so that almost all students attain the mastery level.[2]

---

2. Bloom, Benjamin S. (1971). Mastery learning. In James H. Block. (Eds.) *Mastery Learning: Theory and Practice.* New York: Holt, Rinehart and Winston, 47–63.

BLOOM'S EXAMPLE

Uniform Distribution Per Learner

If a "normal distribution" of students by aptitude are provided uniform instruction (quality instruction + learning time), achievements will be normally distributed.

However, if each learner in the distribution receives optimal quality of instruction and the learning time he/she requires, then a majority of students can be expected to attain mastery.

II. Bloom's Mastery Learning Approach
The mastery learning strategy Bloom proposed to activate these ideas was designed for use in the classroom where the time allowed for learning is relatively fixed.

The Model

A. Develop major objectives (content and cognitive behaviors) that students are expected to exhibit.

B. Develop smaller learning units. The mastery of these unit objectives must be essential for mastery of the major objectives.

C. The units are taught by group-based methods and are supplemented with simple feedback correction procedures (diagnostic-formative tests that cover unit objectives).

D. Supplementary instructional correctives are applied to help students overcome unit learning problems before the group instruction continues.

III. Important Aspects of This Approach

A. Learning units are organized in terms of new content and cognitive processes to be used.

B. Formative tests are used which specifically test mastery of the smaller learning units.

C. Formative evaluation is part of the teaching-learning process. It provides continuous feedback to the teacher and student and enables modification of the process so that the student can attain mastery.

D. Quality of instruction is defined in terms of:
1. clarity and appropriateness of the instructional cues for each pupil;

       2. amount of active participation and practice in the learning time allowed each student;

       3. amount and variety of reinforcements available to each learner.

  E. Correctives include:

       1. small group work;

       2. study sessions;

       3. individualized tutoring;

       4. alternative learning materials (additional texts, workbooks, programmed instruction, A.V. materials, games);

       5. reteaching.

IV. Review of Model: Areas of Strengths

  A. A high level of interest on the part of students is generated.

  B. If performance is adequate, students assume confident behavior, positive attitudes toward learning, and an improved self-concept.

  C. Student learning is more efficient than that caused by conventional approaches. (Student learns more material in less time.)

  D. Model focuses on organizing learning tasks in such a way that all learners will experience some success.

  E. Use of criterion measures is preferred in evaluation of individual performance.

  F. Amount of time needed to reach criterion is observable.

V. Notions Related to Mastery Learning that are Applicable to the Teaching Learning Process in General

  A. Learning rates vary.

  B. Individual differences should be recognized.

  C. Teacher planned and structured learning sequences promote achievement.

  D. Time is a critical variable in learning.

Assessment

To be conducted with a member(s) of an interdisciplinary team in your school.

I. Test your understanding of the mastery learning model with one or more lessons.

A.   Identify major objectives for a particular content/topic. (Include student expected outcomes in terms of content and cognitive skills.)

B.   Divide content/topic into basic components with specific objectives that include criterion measures.

Content Components   *Objectives*
1.
2.
3.

C.   Write specific objectives for one lesson to be taught this week.

1. *Content/Topic*   *Specific Objectives*
                               Content outcomes and
                               cognitive outcomes

D.   Test (diagnostic-formative) students on material taught in C.

1.   Include copy of test.

2.   Record student test results.

E.   List the enrichment materials and activities that you used with students who reached criterion (80% or above).

F.   List the instructional corrections you provided for students who did not reach criterion. (How did you manipulate or manage time for these students?)

G.   Was this an effective teaching strategy for use in your class? Why or why not?

H.   If you use this strategy again, what changes or modifications will you make in terms of its implementation?

Implications/Applications

An important feature of mastery learning allows students the time necessary to learn academic material. In motivational terms, this increased time to learn to the point of mastery or criterion helps students to experience success. Additionally, recent research suggests that academically engaged time-on-task and successful performance are strongly related. Therefore, a series of frequent successes coupled with an increased knowledge base will enable students to exert more effort and to further experience more success. If there is some truth to the adage that the best predictor of future performance is past performance, then mastery learning is an effective instructional management tool that is essentially focused on providing for learning success. Student mastery of academic material is one way of effecting students' positive feelings about themselves.

However, Bloom estimates that half of the variability in achievement on a learning task can be attributed to the cognitive-entry characteristics of the individual. The importance of assessing these entry characteristics before instruction is pressing, particularly since educators today are faced with teaching exceptional children and youth in the regular classroom. The expertise of interdisciplinary team members may be utilized for unbiased assessment of student skills and entry levels. Indeed, the team can contribute to sequencing objectives and curriculum content, and designing evaluation procedures — all necessary elements of mastery learning.

Table 9.3 is provided to describe the broad elements of mastery learning and suggested relationships of these elements in the expertise of interdisciplinary team members.

TABLE 9.3

Mastery Learning Related to the Interdisciplinary Team

Broad Elements of Mastery Learning	Suggested Relationship to Interdisciplinary Team Members
I. Student assessment	1. Regular and special education teachers, school psychologist, educational evaluators, and reading specialist will assess entry characteristics that are cognitive and affective with appropriate instrumentation and methodologies.
II. Division and sequence of curriculum content into units and objectives for teaching	1. Regular and special education teachers and curriculum coordinator will select an instructional unit and then sequence the content for exceptional students. These decisions will be based on the team members' assessment of student's past performance and interests. 2. Regular and special education teachers will select teaching objectives.
III. Managing instruction	1. Regular and special education teachers and school psychologist will determine the prerequisite skills needed for teaching objectives. 2. Regular and special education teachers and school psychologist/educational evaluator will use task analysis to break down objectives (See Module 9.2). 3. Regular and special education teachers and school

TABLE 9.3 (Continued)

Broad Elements of Mastery Learning	Suggested Relationship to Interdisciplinary Team Members
	psychologist will identify and consider different teaching strategies for the stated objectives.
	4. School psychologist with regular classroom teacher will identify the student's learning style.
	5. Regular classroom teacher will assign a peer tutor to assist the exceptional student in learning objectives.
	6. Regular and special education teachers will test alternative grouping procedures (See Modules 8.1 and 8.2).
IV. Evaluation — Phase A	1. Regular and special education teachers and curriculum coordinator will evaluate tests of student's performance. They will check the content validity of the tests to determine whether the test measures what it is intended to measure.
	2. Regular and special education teachers may provide alternative modes for administering the test to the exceptional student. The modes may include an oral test, a written test, or a project.
	3. Regular and special education teachers may modify where and when the test is taken in order to assist the exceptional student to succeed.
V. Evaluation — Phase B *"Clues to Success"	1. If a test demanding reading is used, regular and special education teachers and the reading specialist will assess appropriateness of materials used in terms of readability level, size of print, pictures, etc.
	2. Regular and special education teachers will monitor whether the exceptional student can read the test and understand directions.
	3. Regular and special education teacher will modify test questions according to responses to 1 above.
	4. Regular and special education teachers must be sure that the exceptional student knows what to do and how to do it.
	5. Regular classroom teacher will assign a "buddy" in order to mainstream the exceptional student in how to take tests, answer questions, locate and use materials, etc.
	6. Regular and special education teachers will assist the exceptional student in finding supplementary resources to correct inaccurate responses to test questions.

TABLE 9.3 (Continued)

Broad Elements of Mastery Learning	Suggested Relationship to Interdisciplinary Team Members
	7. Regular and special education teachers will carefully monitor student accuracy. If the exceptional student answers questions incorrectly, clues are provided to assist the student in obtaining the correct answer. The clues provide information on alternative sources for additional exploration and instruction for finding the correct answer to each test question.

*"Clues to success" are systematic corrections of inaccurate answers to questions. They allow students to master more of the material.

Keep in mind that mastery learning is an instructional management tool focused on providing learning success. Its use has been particularly effective with the mildly handicapped student since it permits teachers to provide a kind of individualized instruction within the context of a whole group regular classroom setting.

9.4   DIRECT INSTRUCTION PATTERN: A TEACHING STYLE FOR LESS ABLE LEARNERS

Minimum Competency Objectives

1. You will be able to describe the rationale for a pattern of instruction.
2. You will be able to describe the direct instruction pattern as a workable teaching style.
3. You will be encouraged to apply, with the cooperation of another teacher or school psychologist, the direct instruction pattern with less able learners in regular classrooms, resource rooms or special classes.

Rationale

The theme of meeting students' instructional needs has recently pervaded the language of education. One population of students whose needs have been studied are called "less able learners" in the current research in special education conducted by the National Academy of Science in 1983 and in the research on teacher effectiveness. It is important for teachers to note that the findings from both research perspectives are similar. This is, findings suggest the academic effectiveness of direct instruction for less able learners. Consequently, a description of the direct instruction pattern is offered here as a pragmatic teaching style to be used to support academic gains for less able learners who may be placed in regular classrooms, resource rooms, or special education classes.

Enabling Activities

Read and study the following sections on the direct instruction pattern with other teachers, administrators, and/or school psychologists who may be interested in testing the direct instruction pattern with less able learners.

RATIONALE FOR A PATTERN OF INSTRUCTION

It seems that one of the major domains of teaching performance that appears to be critical to student achievement is how instruction is organized. Researchers in teacher effectiveness, including Nathaniel Gage and Frederick McDonald, have suggested grouping teaching behaviors into patterns of performance or clusters of interrelated teaching behaviors that will affect student achievement.

DESCRIPTION OF DIRECT INSTRUCTION PATTERN

Significant variables reported to be related to academic achievement of less able learners can be characterized by clusters of teacher behaviors which include instructional organization and management in which the teacher is the center of attention in response to pupils and in organizing and presenting materials. The following set of directions to the teacher offers a description of the Direct Instruction Pattern:

Center of Attention

You are the dominant leader and central authority. You are responsible for establishing and enforcing rules for group behavior. It is your responsibility to structure the time in that you give specific directions and instructions as to what to do, how to do it, and when to do it. You are concerned with the educational task and, in order to monitor on-task involvement, you walk around the room and verbally keep students on-task while limiting their socialization with each other. Even though you are in charge, the atmosphere in the room is warm, convivial, democratic, and cooperative.

Response to Pupil

Your responses to pupils' written and oral work include the following observable acts: reinforcement of answers as right or wrong; asking another pupil to give an answer if one pupil fails to answer quickly; prompting by hints; and providing correct responses and reasons.

Organizing and Presenting

When you plan, organize and present materials, the following may be observed: statement of objectives at the beginning of a lesson; presentation of content-related information (data); asking questions that are mostly narrow, direct, and involving recall, with some higher order questions; review of materials; frequent summary throughout the entire lesson; and signals to indicate transition, important points, and movement to new topics.

Examples of Direct Instruction Descriptors

To further clarify and facilitate the use of the direct instruction pattern, the teacher may wish to examine examples of behaviors one may exhibit when implementing this teaching style with two EMR students, Mary, age 11, and Joe, age 12. These examples have been organized under the categories:

      I. Center of Attention
     II. Response to Pupils
   III. Organizing and Presenting Content

I.   Center of Attention
     A.   Rules and Discipline
         1. Teacher establishes. (Examples of teacher statements: "Raise your hand to answer," "No talking when I am talking," "Don't leave your seat unnecessarily.")

2. Teacher enforces. (Examples of teacher statements: "Mary, please sit down," "Remember the rule about raising hands," "Joe, please don't talk when I'm talking.")

B. Structuring Directions, Tasks and Use of Time
Teacher tells students what task to do, how to do it, and when to do it. (Examples of teacher statements: "On page one, silently read the directions because we will begin to work on activities 1–3 in about two minutes," "Activity 3 involves tossing dice. Toss your dice and record your findings on the provided paper. Watch me as I demonstrate.")

C. Monitoring On-Task Behavior (Seatwork)
Teacher actively maintains and reinforces student on-task involvement. (Examples of teacher statements: While teacher is scanning students' work, the teacher says, "Remember, we should be working on Activity 3 now.")

II. Response to Pupil: Monitoring During Discussion

A. Teacher immediately reinforces answer as right or wrong. (Examples of teachers statement: "Mary, that is correct," "No, Joe, that is not the right answer.")

B. Teacher uses hints to elicit correct responses. (Examples of teacher statements: "The answer starts with a 't,'" "The answer rhymes with 'moo.'")

C. Teacher provides correct answers if necessary. (Examples of teacher statement: "The correct answer is 'impossible,'" "Well, to save time, the answer is '6.'")

III. Organizing and Presenting Content

A. Content Input

1. Teacher states objectives at the beginning of the lesson. (Examples of teacher statements: "Today we shall discuss rhyming words," "First of all, we shall say and write the words that rhyme with 'at.'" "You will understand that at least three letters of the alphabet may be used with 'at' to make a new word.")

2. Teacher presents content-related information (data). (Examples of teacher statements: "The chance of getting a 7 on a roll of a single die is always 0 since there is no way to roll a 7. This is an impossible event." "The chance of getting either a 1, 2, 3, 4, 5, or 6 is a certain event.")

3. Teacher reviews/summarizes throughout lesson. (Examples of teacher statements: "The important objective to remember in regard to activities one through four is that when you toss one

die, you are certain to get either a 1, 2, 3, 4, 5, or 6," "Yesterday we did experiments that demonstrated certain events.")

B.   Questions

   1.   Teacher asks narrow, direct, recall, content-focused questions. (Examples of teacher statements: "What are the numbers on a die?" "What is the chance of getting a 7 on a roll of a single die?")

   2.   Teacher asks narrow, direct, recall, noncontent-focused questions. (Examples of teacher statements: "Is it raining?" "What time is lunch today?")

C.   Transition

   Teacher signals transition and introduces new topic. (Examples of teacher statements: "Please clear your desks and get ready to study the number line," "Finish checking your answers, and close your booklets since we will be discussing numbers 1 through 10 next.")

Summary

One can correctly argue that there is no best teaching style that supports achievement in all students; however, the direct instruction pattern points to one tentative answer with regard to an effective teaching style for less able learners.

Assessment

1. From your professional experiences as a teacher, school psychologist, or school administrator, do you feel that such a systematically organized instructional pattern as the direct learning style is too rigid for use with less able learners?

2. Are there other teaching styles you would prefer to use with less able learners? What are they? Why do you prefer them?

3. With what categories of exceptional students might you test the direct instruction pattern? Why?

Implications/Applications

Teachers' experiences with the direct instruction pattern have found the relationship between teacher behavior and student achievement to be an interesting one. Teachers discover that when they are using the direct instruction pattern, including frequent reinforcement, stating objectives, reviewing, and indicating topic transition, students seem to spend more time on task than usual. These experiences suggest that an instructional pattern that supports student time on task appears very promising for improving the academic performance of less able learners.

The following observation instrument shown in Table 9.4 may be used by teachers, school psychologists and administrators to code teacher behavior in testing the direct instruction pattern with less able learners in regular classrooms, resource rooms, or special classes.

Observation Instrument for Direct Instruction

Teachers may wish to use this observation instrument designed to code teacher behaviors in order to test the direct instruction pattern with less able learners. It may be noted that the form contains three general categories: teacher as center of attention; teacher responses to pupils; and teacher as organizing and presenting. Under the general categories are subcategories: rules and discipline; structuring directions, tasks, and use of time; monitoring during discussion, content input, questions, and transition. In addition, the subcategories subsume thirteen specific behaviors that are designed to satisfy specifications suggested in the use of the critical incident methodology.

Briefly, the critical incident methodology uses a large behavior unit while simultaneously dealing with a number of behavior stream attributes. An incident is critical if it makes a significant contribution to the general aim of the activity. This instrument may be used to code episodes in a specified time interval (3 minutes) for a given lesson period of time (30 minutes). Essentially, the critical incident methodology records the presence of specific behaviors relevant to the general aim of the activity in a specified time interval for a specified lesson period. Remember, codings are keyed to teacher behaviors. Each time a critical incident occurs (example: teacher establishes rules and discipline), a tally is recorded in that specified time interval. Naturally, the frequency of tallies within a specified time interval as well as the total tally relative to the critical incident can provide teachers with valuable data. For example, it may be of interest to find out how much time and at what point in the sequence or development of a lesson a particular teacher behavior is demonstrated. Further, it could be valuable for teachers to determine how much time is spent in one kind of behavior relative to another. One question that might be answered concerns how much time a teacher spends enforcing rules and discipline as compared to asking narrow, direct, recall, content-focused questions, and so on?

TABLE 9.4

Observation Instrument for Direct Instruction

Developed by: T. Cicchelli and D. Newman

	3 MINUTE TIME INTERVALS FOR A 30 MINUTE LESSON									
	0–3	4–6	7–9	10–12	13–15	16–18	19–21	22–24	25–27	28–30
I. CENTER OF ATTENTION:										
A. *Rules and Discipline*										
1. Teacher establishes										
2. Teacher enforces										
B. *Structuring Directions, Tasks, and Use of Time*										
Teacher tells student what task to do, how to do it, and when to do it.										
C. *Monitoring On-Task Behavior (Seatwork)*										
Teacher actively maintains and refocuses student on-task involvement.										
II. RESPONSE TO PUPIL MONITORING DURING DISCUSSION:										
A. Teacher immediately reinforces answers as right or wrong.										
B. Teacher uses hints to elicit correct responses										
C. Teacher provides correct answers if necessary										

TABLE 9.4 (Continued)

	3 MINUTE TIME INTERVALS FOR A 30 MINUTE LESSON									
	0–3	4–6	7–9	10–12	13–15	16–18	19–21	22–24	25–27	28–30
III. ORGANIZING AND PRESENTING:										
A. *Content Input*										
1. Teacher states objectives at beginning of lesson										
2. Teacher presents content-related information										
3. Teacher reviews/summarizes throughout lesson										
B. *Questions*										
1. Teacher asks narrow, direct, recall, content-focused questions										
2. Teacher asks narrow, direct, recall, non-content-focused questions										
C. *Transition*										
Teacher signals transition and introduces new topic										

The question of reliability of observation may be of concern; however, it is possible to train people to be reliable in coding behaviors.

9.5 COMPUTER ASSISTED INSTRUCTION (CAI)

Minimum Competency Objectives

1. You will demonstrate basic knowledge about the computer and its administration for instruction.
2. You will define CAI and describe how it operates.
3. You will describe the major modes of CAI and identify why they may be used in instructing exceptional students.
4. You will cooperate with interdisciplinary team members in identifying how CAI may be used as an instructional supplement to ordinary classroom instructional modes.

Rationale

The computer as an instructional tool can no longer be ignored. The instructional value of the computer depends on how educators understand it and learn to use it. It is practical for educators to acquire basic knowledge about the computer and its application to instruction prior to learning how to implement CAI modes as a complement to their teaching. Modes of CAI that can be used to teach exceptional students provide an individualized instructional experience that can meet their unique needs. Interdisciplinary teams may identify why and how CAI modes may be used as an instructional supplement for the teacher to add to ordinary instructional methods.

Enabling Activities

1. Read and study the following section on Basic Knowledge About Computers and Computer Assisted Instruction by yourself, or
2. with members of the interdisciplinary team.

I.   Basic Knowledge About Computers

Computers come in varying sizes and shapes. However, all computers process information and lists of instructions called programs which can be carried out on command. Every computer system ranging from the large mainframe to a tiny microcomputer contains five components.

A. *Central Processing Unit* (CPU) or the "brain" of the computer, consists of an arithmetic and logic unit (ALU) which performs those operations contained within arithmetic and logic, and a control unit which directs the operation of the computer in keeping track of which step the computer is executing.

B. *Memory* locations store data and programs. They may be perceived as a row of empty boxes, or bytes, capable of accepting one symbol, e.g., a letter, a number, or a dollar sign. Memory in microcomputers is measured in thousands of bytes, or kilobytes (Ks). a "64K" computer has 64,000 memory locations. The larger the "K" value, the more data and programs the computer can accept and execute.

C. *Mass storage* is "memory" outside the computer which is typically contained within an ordinary cassette tape used with a cassette player or on a disk (floppy or hard) used with a disk drive. Computer programs stored on cassettes and diskettes are called software.

D. *Input unit* of the computer gets its information from "outside" the computer.

E. *Output unit* takes the information from the computer and presents it in a form that can be understood. A terminal is an input/output device that may print input and output on paper or a screen.

The keyboard is the most frequently used input device, allowing the computer user to type information into the computer which is then displayed on a video screen. Video output units, often called monitors, look like television sets and can project pictures, text, and graphs.

The use of a programming language called BASIC (Beginner's All-purpose Symbolic Instruction Code), the most frequently offered language, allows the computer to respond immediately to program input. The computer has the ability to respond to commands, usually offered in the BASIC language, as well as the capabilities to sort, compare, calculate, retrieve, select, and present data.

Computer use in instruction or computer-assisted instruction may be administered by large mainframe computers connected through telephone lines to in-house terminals as well as by stand-alone microcomputers not requiring a connection to a large computer. Types of computer and peripheral devices such as printers (allowing for hard copy production of work), speech synthesizers, joysticks, and game paddles may assist in the use of commercially programmed materials for instruction.

An important aspect of CAI is the selection and use of appropriate software packages. Educator input is critical and necessary in the selection and use of software. Educators must be encouraged to examine, evaluate, and choose software in the same way they would a textbook, workbook, or other instructional supplements. Features of software that should be reviewed are:

1. soundness of material
2. accuracy of material
3. logical sequencing of material
4. provisions of appropriate reinforcement patterns and responses
5. motivational appeal of the material
6. provisions for appropriate degree of pupil interaction
7. usefulness of the material in terms of meeting a student's individual needs.

II.   What is CAI?

CAI is the use of computers in highly individualized and interactive instruction in which there is direct contact between the learner and the computer. CAI uses the computer for main line academic instruction in that the computer becomes a supplemental instructor which enables students to approach materials in an individual and personal way. CAI supports the assumption that all students learn a range of materials in different ways at varying rates. In fact, CAI may effect or develop the following:

- individualized instruction
- paced learning
- more efficient use of instructional time
- instruction facilitation
- monitoring and recording of student progress
- adjustments/modifications of instruction to suit learner needs
- prescriptions for new materials.

III.   How Does CAI Operate?

The CAI program tailors students' lessons to their achievement levels and increases student motivation to perform better. A student participating in a specified program receives instruction that has been prepared for him/her on the basis of a prescribed data-based need. Questions are not stored in the computer's memory, but are generated by the computer as the student works at a terminal. Since the computer has been programmed to instantaneously check the student's response to an item, it can adjust the instructional level of difficulty while the lesson is in progress. The computer's adjustment of rate is based on the learner's response, and immediate feedback and reinforcement.

Learning theories indicate that drill and practice time in short sessions, regularly distributed over a period of time, is an appropriate and productive way to operate CAI.

IV.   Major Modes of CAI and Their Advantages

A.   *Drill and practice* is the most commonly used form of CAI, particularly as a supplement to the teacher's instruction. Students usually need drill and practice with subject matter that demands mastery in order to facilitate satisfactory performance of higher level skills. Additionally, drill and practice may be needed after concepts related to the skill have been taught, and just prior to the application of skills to higher level skills in the curriculum hierarchy.

Drill and practice programs have typically been used in teaching skills in mathematics, language arts, reading, and foreign language. More importantly, the effective use of drill and practice programs encourage teachers to determine the "who," "why," and "when" that should be addressed when providing for individualized instruction.

In their use of drill and practice programs with exceptional students, teachers must preview the program to determine the appropriateness of the objectives and content organization in terms of meeting the individual learner's needs. The advantages of drill and practice CAI programs for exceptional students include:

1.   The feedback and reinforcement built into this CAI mode provide a positive learning technique which students often find motivating.

2.   Students can control the rate of information presented to them. For example, less able students do not have to accelerate from their comfortable pace of recitation, and more able students do not have to slow down to a rate determined by a teacher or a small group.

3.   The drill and practice mode is a neutral tutor. Responses to a computer limit the frustration and pressure exceptional students may feel when tutored by a person.

4.   Some drill and practice programs are presented in game form. These have a high interest value used to motivate student learning.

5.   Drill and practice provides for overlearning of basic skills, a necessary ingredient in the learning process of less able exceptional students.

B.   The Tutorial CAI program differs from drill and practice in that it can introduce concepts as well as provide practice in using concepts. Tutorial programs are designed to facilitate learner-computer interactions by using a conversational style in either or both written and oral text. The program can:

1. introduce and describe the concept or rule;
2. provide an example; and
3. provide practice using similar examples.

Through this sequence of instruction, the tutorial program imitates the deductive style of teacher presentation of information in the regular classroom.

Tutorial programs are flexible in their design so that less able students may avoid failure and more able students may escape boredom. Less able students benefit from remediation provided by the review and practice of previously learned concepts, and more able learners benefit from learning concepts in areas of special interest not necessarily included in the classroom curriculum. Additionally, tutorial programs are appropriate for learners with strong visual and kinesthetic modalities since concepts can be introduced without the teacher telling or lecturing. Obviously, auditory learners would need the assistance of a teacher or teacher aide when using tutorial programs. Some advantages of tutorial programs are:

1. Programs can be systematically organized to cover curriculum content spanning several grade levels, allowing less able learners a degree of comfort in knowing how to operate the same system.
2. Tutorial programs may be used to serve individual personal interests.

C. Simulations are programs that present an operational model of an event or an experience. The models may represent economic, political, social, interpersonal, ethical, or behavioral events or experiences. Simulation programs allow students to convert the classroom into a mini laboratory, art gallery, World's Fair or Planet Xenon. The use of simulation programs increases cooperation and collaboration among exceptional students and regular students in the mainstreamed class. These programs demand a high level of integration between computer activities and typical classroom activities, such as discussing, planning, and sharing. Since simulation programs are designed to be used by small groups, which may be composed of exceptional and regular students, they provide for the development of appropriate social behaviors as the group members interact with one another and with the computer. In addition to social skills, simulation programs promote skills in language development, problem solving, and decision making. Essentially, the skills and concepts that simulation programs aim at teaching are clearly visible and well defined. In addition, these programs provide post tests to assess achievement in concept and skill areas. Simulation programs offer the following unique advantages:

1. They may be used with small groups.
2. They support affective behaviors.
3. They promote higher level thinking skills through problem solving and decision making activities.
4. They provide opportunities to integrate/correlate content areas easily.
5. They allow teachers to apply different learning objectives for each member in the small group.
6. Students learn how to interact with an environment — even if it has been created.

V. CAI and the Exceptional Student
CAI is a valuable instructional tool that may be used with exceptional students for the following reasons:

A. CAI modes provide exceptional students with chances to make mistakes and correct them without being penalized.

B. In using CAI modes, particularly the drill and practice and tutorial programs, distractions are minimal. Since this is so, students quickly see the correct answer as well as the process by which the answer was derived.

C. CAI modes provide structured programs that are easily adapted to meet a specific student's need.

D. CAI is a communication device that provides exceptional students with auditory and visual stimulations, often including graphics, animations, and voice stimuli.

E. CAI modes come with hardware equipped with special features such as paddles, leaf switches and flat pressure plates, made to assist the physically handicapped learn through the computer.

Table 9.5A is offered as an example of a typical CAI reading program that may be used with Doris D, age 9, who is an EMR student. The program provides drill and practice in the recognition of phonetic spelling patterns.

TABLE 9.5A

Typical CAI Reading Program

a.　　RECOGNITION OF PHONETIC SPELLING PATTERNS

Visual Monitor Display	Audio Message
The program outputs: -AN-AP-AT	(Doris, type /AN/ as in the picture on the screen.)
Doris responds by typing AN	
The program outputs: + ☺	(Doris, that was very GOOD!)
The program outputs: -AP-AN-AT	(Doris, type /AP/ as in tap.)
Doris responds by typing AP	
The program outputs: -AT-AN-AP	(Doris, please type /AN/ as in ran.)
Doris responds by typing AN	
The program outputs: + ☺	(GREAT AGAIN!)

b.　　　　　　　　BUILDING A WORD

The program outputs: -AN-AP-AT　　F-	(Doris, type fan.)
Doris responds by typing FAN	
The program outputs: + ☺	(SUPER!!)
The program outputs: -AT-AN-AP　　S-	(Type sap.)
Doris responds by typing SAT	
The program outputs: //// SAT	(Sorry, Doris, we wanted SAP.)
The program outputs: -AP-AT-AN　　SL-	(Doris, please type slap.)
Doris responds by typing SLAP	
The program outputs: + ☺ ☺ ☺	(EXTRA SUPER!)

The interactive nature of CAI allows exceptional students to relate personally to what this instructional management tool can do in terms of its programmed capabilities for sound, written responses, and dialogue. More importantly, computers enable the exceptional student to interact with and manipulate his/her environment. This sense of internal control over one's environment is certainly a positive factor in the learning process.

Assessment

1. With your interdisciplinary team, discuss the value of CAI as a supplement to the instruction provided by regular and special education teachers.

2. Can every exceptional student benefit from some mode of CAI in some way? With the interdisciplinary team, identify students in your school and describe the benefits of CAI to them.

3. How should team members coordinate their efforts to integrate CAI into the classroom instructional program?

Implications/Applications

The effective use of CAI will depend on how well and to what degree it is integrated as a supplement to the exceptional student's instructional program. Interdisciplinary team members who may use CAI must have a clear understanding of their own objectives for working with CAI, as well as some computer competence in order to identify the appropriate CAI mode and related software necessary to meet the needs of exceptional students. The quality of available software has raised some questions with educators. However, the present research in this area is contributing to the daily development and production of improved software packages. In addition, inservice training programs in computer competence may include sessions on evaluating and modifying software so that it may be adapted to meet educational objectives. The extent and degree to which CAI will be integrated into a student's instructional program may depend on how well trained interdisciplinary team members are with regard to computer competence. Table 9.5B is a training model showing a typical schedule for the inservice training of CAI content and the relationship of this content to interdisciplinary team members' functions.

TABLE 9.5B

**Training Model for the Inservice Education of Interdisciplinary Teams
Concerning CAI in Relation to Their Job Functions**

Sessions	CAI Content	Relationship to Typical Team Member Functions
Session I	General orientation to CAI with hands-on time at the terminals.	All team members are involved in some way in the instructional program for exceptional students.
Sessions II, III, IV	Review of software materials in CAI for specific content areas. Discuss and provide examples of the selection, uses and evaluation of software.	Special and regular teachers, curriculum coordinators, school psychologist, and educational evaluators are involved in matching appropriate materials to student needs.
Session V	Describe the management of CAI.	School administrators and curriculum coordinators who may be responsible for scheduling students in CAI programs are usually responsible for the administration of these programs.
Sessions VI, VII	Describe the operating procedures of a CAI program that include the enrolling of students, the selecting of courses, the obtaining of student reports, the ongoing management of data, and the use of data in the classroom.	Guidance counselors may enroll students and select courses for student in concert with teachers (regular and special) and the school psychologist. Reports may be managed by the guidance counselor, but interpreted by the school psychologist. The interpretation is then presented to regular and special education teachers so that the information may be integrated in planning the instructional program for exceptional students.
Session VIII	Describe the use of CAI modes in the classroom for curriculum content reinforcement or enrichment. Specify the use of CAI as an alternative instruction mode for the teacher.	Curriculum coordinators, school psychologist, educational evaluator, and regular and special education teachers in concert must identify what should be used for whom and why.
Session IX	Design a mini-research project for the classroom using CAI and traditional instruction methods.	The interdisciplinary team should be involved in a classroom research project, no matter how limited, in order to provide professional expertise and support for creative undertakings of this type of instruction.
Session X	Identify educational objectives for each member's unique role and function for	All team members must cooperate and collaborate in their efforts to bring about change in a school.

TABLE 9.5B (Continued)

Sessions	CAI Content	Relationship to Typical Team Member Functions
	the effective integration of CAI into a student's instructional program.	
Session XI	Specify the adoption of CAI into the regular curriculum.	All team members maintain (see above).

Some Implications for Administering and Coordinating the CAI Program

1. The interdisciplinary team must be involved prior to a full-blown commitment to the use of CAI programs in a school.

2. Selection and availability of an appropriate location for the CAI installation is necessary in order to ensure usage.

3. A minimum of 12 terminals should be available in one classroom in order to ease student scheduling problems as well as to encourage the involvement of teachers in activities for the entire class.

4. Selection of appropriate coordinator(s) of the installation and use of the system is necessary.

5. Selecting exceptional students to participate in the program must be coordinated with teachers, guidance counselors, department heads, or others involved with student services.

6. Selecting materials/strands to meet student needs must be a team effort.

7. Scheduling of students to receive CAI instruction must primarily be coordinated by administrators and guidance counselors with teacher input.

8. Team training workshops should be ongoing.

9. Formative evaluation at all times is necessary to monitor the effectiveness of CAI use.

9.6 EVALUATION: AN ONGOING PROCESS FOR MAKING INSTRUCTIONAL DECISIONS

Minimum Competency Objectives

1. You will demonstrate skill in the use of an evaluation model that will allow you to systematically plan for as well as collect data on instruction.

2. You will gather data on student behaviors by using the evaluation model in order to make judgments in regard to instructional decisions.

3. You will contribute to the data base provided by the interdisciplinary team to make decisions for planned change.

Rationale

Instructional decision making may be systematized when based on authenticated data. Appropriate data, gathered by use of an evaluation model, may improve the quality of decision making necessary for improved instruction. The use of a broad data base provided by the interdisciplinary team will contribute to the team process of planning for effective change. Consequently, evaluation is used as a vehicle for examining events in terms of the evaluator's values for the purpose of making better instructional decisions.

Enabling Activities

1. Read and study the following section on evaluation by yourself.

2. Discuss and provide examples with members of the interdisciplinary team on the use of an evaluation model for making instructional decisions.

I.   What is Evaluation?

Evaluation is an examination of events or happenings in terms of one's values and standards. Example of a teacher's use of evaluation: assigning grades to students by testing.

Test — reflects your values as to what is important.

Grade — the student's performance on the test based on your values.

II.

CHART 9.6

Evaluation Model

Objective	Process Plan	Observed Outcome
Entry Conditions		
Methods-Materials Activities		
*Teacher Strategies (your behavior)		
Outcome		

*The role of "teacher" may be played by any member of an interdisciplinary team.

III. Decisions Related to Use of Evaluation Model

A. Process Plan (How to) Section

1. *Objectives as Related to Outcome* — You will determine a series of if-then statements.

If students have certain characteristics (entry behaviors) and are subjected to an instructional procedure (methods, materials, activities, teacher behavior), *then* they will be able to perform in a certain way (outcome). You will identify values (i.e., what is important to know).

2. *Entry conditions* — You will determine the developmental stage of the learner and, by use of diagnosis, select appropriate instruments (tests, inventories, observation, etc.) that will determine the kinds of data you are looking for.

3. *Methods, materials, activities* — You will identify the appropriate materials (additional texts, workbooks, programmed instruction, audio-visual materials, games, etc.), methods and activities (learning centers, small groups, study sessions, peer teaching, individualized instruction, student contracting, simulations, and role playing), and schedule of activities, and match them with entry conditions in order to support student achievement.

4. *Teacher strategies* — You will determine your behavior (questioning techniques, teaching style) and appropriately match it with entry conditions, materials, methods, and activities.

5. *Outcome* — You will determine your prescribed outcome that supports your objectives.

B. Use of Observed Outcome

1. These data should provide a relationship between what was planned and what actually occurred.

2. Analysis of these data enables us to identify problems and their nature.

3. *Sample change decisions* can be made on the basis of data gathered, revise a particular component of the plan, develop additional instruction, and terminate specific aspects of the plan.

IV. Summary

After reading the text above, you will realize that evaluation is an ongoing process in which you are making decisions in regard to presenting a general framework (model plan) for organizing your thoughts about this process.

V. Evaluation

1. Use the described evaluation model for at least one lesson. Provide a description of your instructional plan.

2.   As a result of the observed data collected by use of this model, what decisions did you make that affected or modified your instructional plan?

3.   List the changes, if any, that you made in your instructional plan.

4.   Which component(s) of the model were most helpful to you when making changes in your instructional plan?

5.   How valuable is this model as an instructional tool? Will you use it again? Why? Why not? Would you prefer to use this model on an individual basis or as part of an interdisciplinary team function? Why?

Implications/Applications

Instructional management and evaluation are dynamically related activities. The evaluation model proposed in this module may serve as a framework for gathering data regarding this dynamic relationship which should result in carefully planned change. In testing the model, interdisciplinary team members may examine each of the classes of data, that is, entry conditions, methods/materials/activities, team member strategies, and outcomes to determine the degree of congruence or match between what was planned and what actually occurred. If there is a difference between what was planned and what actually happened, there should be an accompanying change in the observed outcome. It is exactly this kind of information that allows the team to identify problems and their nature. Consequently, the team may use these findings to engage in team planning to make decisions for change.

It should be mentioned that this model may be used to evaluate the instructional management program for the exceptional student as well as to evaluate the functions of interdisciplinary team members who are involved in the student's program. For example, when an exceptional student receives a specialized program designated to promote mastery of the minimum objectives established for all students within a school, evaluation of this special program is necessary. If a student's academic and social learnings are not promoted by this program or these services, then the student has not been appropriately served and the program/services have not been effective. Once again, this kind of information promotes the team process for planning change.

Module 7.0, relating to the IEP, shows the relationship of the typical components of the IEP to the suggested functions of interdisciplinary team members. The evaluation model offered in this lesson also may be used to evaluate the function of team members in the IEP process, as well as to evaluate the IEP in terms of its academic and social benefits to the exceptional student. Whether the evaluation model prepared here is or is not used, it is important for team members to be concerned with assisting one another in defining problems, generating reasonable alternatives (based on available research), evaluating the alternatives in terms of their advantages and disadvantages, identifying a solution, and determining how well the solution works. Naturally, the cycle will repeat itself.

Table 9.6A is an example of how the planning phase of the evaluation model may be used to evaluate the functioning of the interdisciplinary team during the IEP process. Team members may wish to complete the observed phase and conduct an analysis of their findings in order to make decisions for planned change in their respective behaviors during the IEP process.

Since the IEP is a custom-tailored educational program designed to accommodate specific student needs, it requires continuous and systematic monitoring of the progress a student makes in this program. Table 9.6B is an example of how the evaluation model may be used to monitor a piece of the educational program for Jim, age 9½, who is a gifted, talented, physically handicapped student. With a member of the interdisciplinary team, test the model and fill in the blank blocks with some educated guesses. Did your analysis of the findings permit you to make changes in Jim's instructional program?

TABLE 9.6A

Evaluating the Interdisciplinary Team During the IEP Process

Objective: At least 80 percent of the interdisciplinary team, when given the chance to volunteer to collaborate with another team member, will actually collaborate at least one hour per week with regard to the instructional management program of exceptional students.

	Process Plan	Observed Outcome
Entry Conditions	1. The interdisciplinary team has been constituted. 2. Team members are given an opportunity to volunteer to collaborate with one another.	
Methods/ Materials/ Activities	1. Contact other team members. 2. Plan what to monitor. 3. Plan how to monitor. 4. Identify team member responsibilities.	

TABLE 9.6A (Continued)

	Process Plan	Observed Outcome
Team Member Strategies (Example for a parent)	1. Question the school psychologist and education evaluation concerning appropriateness of the assessment phase of the IEP for your child. Include the following questions: a. Were the assessments culture free? b. Was the student's native language or major mode of communication used? c. Were the testers or diagnosticians qualified? d. Was more than one kind of assessment instrument and procedure used?	
Outcome	1. Of the total interdisciplinary team, 80 percent will volunteer. 2. Of those who did volunteer, 80 percent collaborated one hour per week with another team member. 3. Data with regard to instructional management program for a student is obtained.	

TABLE 9.6B

Evaluating a Piece of the Educational Program for an Exceptional Student

Student: Jim, age 9½, is gifted, talented, and physically handicapped. *Grade:* 4		*Objective:* Jim will be able to compute an area for a triangle and apply the formula for computing the area of a triangle to three different kinds of triangles with 90 percent accuracy.	

	Process Plan	Observed Outcome
Entry Conditions	Jim's performance will be assessed to determine if he has:	1. Use of teacher-made tests showed that Jim success-

TABLE 9.6B (Continued)

	Process Plan	Observed Outcome
	1. mastered the minimum competencies required in the 7th grade mathematics program; 2. demonstrated 7th grade level reading ability; 3. demonstrated 90 percent accuracy in computing the area of a rectangle	fully mastered the minimum competencies required in the 7th grade mathematics program. 2. Use of the district-wide reading tests demonstrated Jim is at the 8th grade reading level. 3. Use of a teacher-made test showed that Jim had 95 percent accuracy computing the area of a rectangle.
Methods/ Materials/ Activities	Jim will: 1. complete CAI package on computing the area of a triangle; 2. read elementary geometry textbook by Gray & Co. (1984); 3. engage in tutoring sessions with a high school honors student in mathematics.	1. Jim achieved 75 percent accuracy with the CAI package. 2. Jim has some difficulty comprehending the text. Review of text by a special mathematics teacher revealed that explanations offered were not clear. 3. Jim never engaged in peer tutoring sessions because the high school student never showed up.
Team Member Strategies (Example for a regular classroom teacher)	Teacher will use non-direct teaching style and will behave in a facilitative manner.	
Outcome	Jim will be able to: 1. compute area of triangle with 90 percent accuracy; 2. apply the formula for computing the area of a triangle to three types of triangles with 90 percent accuracy.	

Behavior Management

INTRODUCTION

Classroom management skills related to the social behaviors of students often include behavior management and structured learning. Module 10.1 provides the interdisciplinary team with a brief review of the concepts of Pavlov and Skinner in relation to operant conditioning, and the application of theory to a behavior contract in terms of Premack's principles. Module 10.2 offers an explanation of structured learning and provides practice in working with students who may lack social skills behaviors.

Further information on classroom management skills needed to work with students who may be in lack of social skills behaviors can be found in the Topic Referenced Bibliography on pages 232 to 262 under the number 9 (Classroom Management).

10.1 OPERANT CONDITIONING: A BEHAVIOR MANAGEMENT TOOL

Minimum Competency Objectives

1. You will be able to define the terms used by Pavlov in classical conditioning.

2. You will be able to recall the terms used by Skinner in the stimulus-response (S-R) sequence.

3. You will be able to apply the (S-R) sequence to your teaching.

4. You will be able to design a contingency management contract accord-

ing to Premack's principles with the input of an exceptional student, regular/ special teachers, and the school psychologist.

5. You, as a member of an interdisciplinary team, will assess operant conditioning practices as applied to the teaching-learning process in a main-streamed classroom.

Rationale

Research has indicated that behavior may be learned through operant conditioning. It should be mentioned that there are some educators who are concerned about the ethics of teaching by this process. Others, however, believe concepts and applications of principles of operant conditioning provide teachers with a tool to arrange and manipulate variables so as to support positive learning experiences. The ethical relevance of operant conditioning principles in the instruction and management of exceptional students may be monitored by the broad base provided by an interdisciplinary team in a school.

Enabling Activities

1. Read and discuss the section related to Pavlov, Skinner, and Premack.

2. With a peer, complete the activities relative to Pavlov, Skinner, and Premack.

Background

I.   PAVLOV

Pavlov in his famous 1927 salivation experiments with dogs reached conclusions regarding what is called *classical conditioning.* Briefly, Pavlov rang a bell (new stimulus) immediately prior to introducing food which made the dog salivate (learned stimulus-response sequence). Upon repeated presentation of the ringing bell (conditioned stimulus) without introducing food (unconditioned stimulus) salivation (response) was produced by the dog.

Eventually, the dog came to associate the ringing bell with food, and would salivate when the bell rang and no food was introduced. In fact, once the response was established, salivation (response) would occur (for a period of time) when the bell was rung without the presentation of food.

A. Related Activity to Pavlov (S-R) Classical Conditioning

Fill in the blanks

1. Pavlov experimented with dogs in his _____ experiments.

2. Pavlov's _____ experiments are called classical _____.

3. In his experiments, the *bell* became the new _____ and eventually became the _____ stimulus.

4. The "old" or _____ stimulus was _____.

5. The conditioned stimulus (bell) was always introduced _____ to introducing food (unconditioned stimulus).

6. Upon repeated ringing of the _____ (conditioned stimulus) without the food, the dog would produce _____.

B. Summary of Classical Conditioning

In brief, the following notions summarize Pavlov's work:

1. Systematic environmental manipulation produces new associations.

2. When these associations between conditioned and unconditioned stimuli become established, presentation of the conditioned stimulus (bell) produces an unconditioned response (saliva) and a new association.

3. These new associations between stimulus and response are called classical conditioning.

II. SKINNER

In 1957, Skinner and others further suggested that reinforcing a stimulus-response sequence supported the probability that the sequence would occur again. Conversely, if the sequence (S-R) is repeated and not reinforced, the probability of its occurring is weakened.

Briefly, Skinner's approach involves four primary concepts. They are as follows:

A. *Positive reinforcement* or rewards given to responses are likely to be repeated.

B. *Negative reinforcement* (aversive events) given to responses that are free from painful situations are likely to be repeated.

C. *No reinforcement* (the occurrence of no event) given to responses is *not* likely to be repeated, and in fact may be extinguished.

D. When *punishing,* responses that lead to unpleasant consequences will be repressed, but can appear if reinforcement contingencies are altered.

It should be mentioned that research has indicated that habits or behaviors are maintained and are more lasting with partial reinforcement. For example, if a teacher is interested in strengthening a behavior, a partial schedule of reinforcement should be maintained. Similarly, extinction of a behavior occurs quickly when behavior maintained under a 100% reinforcement schedule is no longer reinforced.

Moreover, Skinner's *operant conditioning,* which involves eliciting those behaviors through manipulating and then reinforcing stimuli, may be used to shape and fade behaviors. Skinner suggested that behaviors may be analyzed by breaking them down into steps and then ordering them into a sequence. Furthermore these steps (or smaller behaviors) in the sequence are reinforced. Consequently, shaping and fading are accomplished by reinforcing those steps that lead to the ultimate behavior.

E.   Related Activity to Skinner (S-R)

1. *Fill In The Blanks*

a. Skinner suggested that _____ a _____ _____ sequence increases the chance that the sequence will occur again.

b. If an S-R sequence is not reinforced, the chance that it will occur again is _____.

2. Skinner's approach involves four primary concepts. Please match the following:

a. Punishment   response likely to occur that provides relief from painful situation _____.

b. No Reinforcement   response likely to be repeated. _____.

c. Negative Reinforcement   response not likely to be repeated _____.

d. Positive Reinforcement   responses are repressed, but can appear if reinforcement contingencies are altered _____.

3. *True or False*

_____ Partial reinforcement maintains more lasting behaviors.

_____ When 100 percent reinforcement schedules are no longer in effect, behaviors are maintained.

_____ Operant conditioning does not involve reinforcement.

_____ Steps or smaller behaviors of a large behavior may be reinforced in order to help shape the larger behavior or desired behavior.

_____ A behavior modification sequence may be used to fade out behaviors.

The Skinnerian model of S-R has direct application to teaching, particularly when viewed as a 3-step process. These 3 steps include the following sequence:

FIGURE 10.1

S-R Patterns

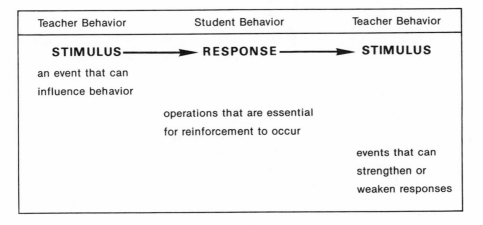

Teacher Behavior	Student Behavior	Teacher Behavior
STIMULUS ⟶	**RESPONSE** ⟶	**STIMULUS**
an event that can influence behavior		
	operations that are essential for reinforcement to occur	
		events that can strengthen or weaken responses

F. *Related Activity to Teaching a 3-Step Process*

Please fill in the following:

FIGURE 10.1A

S-R Activity

Teacher Behavior	Student Behavior	Teacher Behavior
STIMULUS ⟶	**RESPONSE** ⟶	**STIMULUS**
"Who was the first president of the U.S.?"	_____	"Good. Your answer is correct."
"How much does a dime and a nickel equal?"	"$.15 "	_____
_____	No response	No consequence

III.   PREMACK

Premack, in 1959, offered the idea that a preferred activity can enforce a less preferred activity. More simply stated, watching television (a preferred activity) can be used as a reinforcer for doing math drills (a less preferred activity).

Some examples of his principles are:

• "Let's finish problems 1 to 3, and then we will play a game."
• "Sit down quietly for two minutes, then you can talk to a friend for two minutes."

What occurs in these kinds of situations is the existence of conditions for reinforcement to occur (contingent reinforcement).

In the above examples, the conditions are, "finish the problems," and "sit down quietly."

The *reinforcements* are, "play a game," and "talk to a friend."

Contingent reinforcement is reinforcement that depends upon the occurrence of a response. With this in mind, educators can utilize contingency management by providing reinforcement for the appropriate situation and withholding reinforcement if the situation is not appropriate.

The Premack principle profiles an effective tool for identifying and utilizing reinforcers to modify student behavior. Numerous researchers have used this principle in designing contingency contracts with students. However, they offer the following suggestions when designing systematic contracts with students:

• The reward should come early in the learning situation.
• Behaviors may be shaped by rewarding small approximations of the larger goal.
• Easy-to-reach goals should be established in order to shape the desired behavior.
• Rewards may be frequent and in small amounts.
• Reward the desired behavior after it occurs.
• The terms of the contract should be clear, concise, honest, and positive.

It would appear that in order to increase the chance of a successful contract, both student and teacher should determine contract conditions and reinforcers according to Premack's principle.

Conditions may be described as those behaviors that you wish to support (accent the positive).

Examples are:

    • finishing work;
    • raising a hand to signal a desire to speak;
    • getting along with peers.

Reinforcers may reflect the particular interest and needs of the student.

Examples are:

- tangible/material items;
- privileges;
- social responses — deliberate praise;
- tokens — tangible items that include material and social reinforcers.

More specifically, the following suggestions are offered to assist in designing a contingency management contract.

- Select a specific behavior that you want to modify/change that may be described, observed, and measured.
- Design a plan for evaluating the behavior, (i.e., recording behavior and setting criteria for determining the goal).
- Select appropriate reinforcers.
- Determine a systematic schedule for reinforcement.
- Systematically review student's progress based on collected data.

A. *Activity Related to Premack's Principle as Applied to Contracts*

Design a blueprint for a contract that includes the conditions and reinforcers that you would use in a contingency management plan for one of your students.

Assessment

1. *Evaluation*

    a. How and with whom might you utilize the principles of operant conditioning?

    b. Specifically translate the principles of operant conditioning into a teaching activity that you may use with one child or a whole class.

    c. With another teacher (in either regular or special education) and the school psychologist, discuss and apply Premack's principle to the following case study.

    CASE STUDY OF ANN A.

    Ann A., a mildly retarded fifth grade student mainstreamed into a regular classroom, gets out of her seat and walks to the pencil sharpener. Mr. Zee, her teacher, responds, "Ann, go back to your seat. You have been out of your seat five times today. Get back and don't get out." A few minutes pass and Ann casually gets out of her seat, sits on her friend's desk and starts a conversation. Mr. Zee (in a loud tone) says, "Ann, what's the matter with you? Don't you understand English? Can't you do anything right?" Ann starts crying and runs out of the classroom. How would you have reacted to Ann's leaving her seat for the sixth time after teacher correction? What should Mr. Zee do? How can you manage Ann's out-of-seat behavior?

d.   How do you feel about the effectiveness of operant conditioning in the teaching-learning process? Why?

e.   In what ways can the interdisciplinary team use operant conditioning practices in the mainstreamed classroom?

Implications/Applications

Operant conditioning, or the arrangement of variables to support learning, may be orchestrated by the interdisciplinary team for instructing as well as managing exceptional students. Essentially, the operations of stimulus manipulations, reinforcement, shaping, and fading can be implemented in the teaching-learning environment through the use of various modes of classroom organizations and instructional management, as well as the use of materials. Specifically, task analysis (Module 9.1), mastery learning (Module 9.3), the direct instruction pattern (Module 9.4), and computer assisted instruction (Module 9.5) are some examples of operant conditioning instructional practices. The interdisciplinary team may wish to examine and assess the effectiveness of these practices during and after their application. It is important to suggest that the interdisciplinary team also assess the uses of operant conditioning in order to monitor and halt its undesirable consequences, such as excessive control or manipulation that may unjustifiably occur.

Table 10.1 is an instrument that may be used by interdisciplinary teams to examine and assess operant conditioning practices applied to the teaching-learning environment. It represents a sample application to Gwen, a 10-year-old EMR student who has been mainstreamed full-time in a regular classroom. The instrument should be completed by three members of the interdisciplinary team. Academic progress may be assessed by criterion-referenced tests, achievement scales, general assessment of student production, and performance on contracts. Social progress may be assessed by observation instruments, anecdotal records, and performance on contracts.

The use of a contingency contract is a technique that applies the general principles of operant conditioning to develop student achievement and appropriate social behavior.

TABLE 10.1

Assessment of Operant Conditioning Practices in Classroom Organizations, Materials, and Instructional Management

Student: Gwen, 10 years old — EMR

Team Member: Terry C — regular class teacher

Dates	Subject	Class	Class Organization	Materials	Instructional Management Behavior/Instructional Goals	Student Progress + = evidence of progress − = no evidence of progress Academic	Social
Jan. 1–15	Math	Regular Class	Large Group	programmed insntruction	Direct Instruction Pattern used in Mastery Learning	+	+
Jan. 16–30	Math	Regular Class	Small Group	worksheets for drill and practice	Non-Direct Teaching Style. Teacher facilitates instruction	+	+
Feb. 1–15	Math	Regular Class	Large Group	contracts (academic)	Teacher facilitates contracts (academic)	−	−

Contracts provide mildly handicapped students with structure, whereby they know what is expected of them academically and socially. They are a visual on-going progress report for the student. The school psychologist and regular and special education teachers can develop the contract together, providing a bridge between the regular class and the special class for the mainstreamed student. The following are examples of behaviors that team members would include in a contract for Phil, age 9, who is mildly physically handicapped with limitations in his fine motor coordination.

2. *Contract Goal*

Phil will write a sentence with three words.

a. Reinforce his paper and pencil contact.
b. Reinforce his approximation of a letter in the alphabet.
c. Reinforce his rough imitation of the letter.
d. Reinforce for connecting letters.
e. Reinforce for completing one word.
f. Reinforce for completing two words.
g. Reinforce for completing three words.

Naturally, the contract would include the realistic reinforcers and conditions the student and teacher mutually agreed upon.

10.2 STRUCTURED LEARNING: BEHAVIOR MANAGEMENT

Minimum Competency Objectives

1. You will be able to explain structured learning as an alternative perspective on behavior management. Behavior management places emphasis on providing youngsters with the means to succeed in challenging personal situations.

2. The interdisciplinary team will be able to propose a plan to use the structured learning approach with a selected group of students. The social skill training will include negotiation, self-control, relaxation, and response to anger.

Rationale

Presently, discipline problems are given a priority position in national polls and by individual educators when asked to comment on critical issues in teaching and learning. Consequently, the need to identify and test student behavior management approaches is recognized and appropriate.

In recent years, theorists are suggesting a behavior deficiency model to describe deviant behavior. In this model, behavior problems of children are viewed as deficiencies in essential skills; behavioral deficits are thought to be the result of histories of inadequate reinforcement and instruction rather than the consequence of some hypothetical internal psychopathology. Furthermore, when the desired behaviors do not already exist in students' repertoires, the teaching of more adaptive and socially acceptable behaviors is necessary to remediate their deficits. A method to develop the desired behaviors is to shape these behaviors through selective reinforcement of successively closer approximations to the desired behaviors. Educators utilize performance guides in the form of appropriate verbal or behavioral modeling clues.

Enabling Activities

1. Read and discuss with the interdisciplinary team the rationale and background sections of this module. Together, provide examples from your own teaching or other professional experience relative to modeling, role playing, social reinforcement, and transfer training.

2. The team will write out a plan to use the structured learning approach for a selected group of exceptional students. (See the evaluation section and consult with the instructor.)

Structured learning is a psychoeducational approach that is designed to teach pro-social behavior skills to aggressive, acting out youngsters. The model is focused on teaching students to recognize those situations that create anxiety for them and then to apply a variety of alternative, non-aggressive responses.

Essentially, this approach is concerned with pro-skill training in negotiation, self-control, relaxation, and responding to anger.

Operating the Model

Structured learning is an approach to skill training. It consists of four components: modeling, role playing, feed-back, and transfer training. Each of these components is a well established behavior change procedure.

By use of these components, youngsters are taught how to interact more effectively with others, how to deal with fear, anger and other feelings, and are instructed in the use of appropriate skills for handling stressful situations.

Model Components

1. *Modeling* refers to providing youngsters with a demonstration or example of the skill behaviors you wish them to learn. Small groups of students are shown numerous specific and detailed displays (commercial and/or teacher developed) including: audiotapes, videotapes, slides, etc., of the person (the model) performing the skill behavior you wish them to acquire. This activity is repeated with the use of different modeling materials as many times as is determined necessary by the teacher.

2. Once the skill models have been presented, students are given considerable opportunity and encouragement to rehearse or practice the modeled behaviors in a manner relevant to their own real-life situation. The students use *role playing* to do so. The student engages in role playing of the desired skill behaviors which takes place several times. Then the student observes other group members role playing the same behavior.

3. Students are provided with positive feedback, approval, or reward as their role playing behaviors become more and more like the behaviors of the model. This is called *social reinforcement* or *feedback.*

4. What students learn in the training session will be applied to homework assignments involving real-life practice of the skills rehearsed in the group, and then systematically reported upon in subsequent meetings of the group. This process is called the *transfer training.* This phase of structured learning (SL) is practiced several times in a real life context by students as part of their formal homework assignments in response to adult and/or peer leader coaching.

Factors Related to the Operating of the Model

1. Teachers may develop their own modeling materials that reflect the problems and/or issues that are relevant to the daily lives of their students.

2. Respected students may be used as group leaders. Apparently, when youngsters teach others a skill, their own level of skill acquisition is enhanced.

3. A scheduled, specific time period must be established for the use of this approach in an organized, systematic way.

4. The implementation of the four components of this approach takes time. Meanwhile teachers may collect and chart data on student behaviors while the approach is in operation.

Assessment

(If you choose to do this activity, see instructor for assistance.)

1. Undertake a needs assessment of your class to identify those stu-

dents who lack positive behaviors that would enhance their performance as students. Analyze your data in order to group students according to similar needs. Groups should contain a mix of exceptional students with regular students.

2. Identify and describe a basic skill and its components with which your pilot group will be working.

Example: Skill Options for Belligerent Behavior:
- accepting authority roles
- supporting someone
- negotiating
- avoiding trouble
- understanding your rights

3. Write behavioral objectives which include affective objectives.

4. Write out a plan to be used with your pilot group that includes the operating components of the structured learning approach.

5. Develop and produce appropriate modeling and role playing materials that match the social skill to be taught.

6. Establish a specific period of time in which you will meet with one group on a pilot basis to test the structured learning approach described in this lesson.

7. Test your plan for a specified period of time.

8. Collect data on the behavior of group members while the plan is in progress.

9. Analyze your data and modify your plan, if necessary.

10. See instructor for further directions.

The organization and implementation of the structured learning approach requires the active involvement of the interdisciplinary team, particularly regular and special education teachers, guidance counselors, and school psychologists. Their participation can only increase the probability of success in using this approach.

Implications/Applications

Behavior problems in the classroom create a challenge to educators. Unfortunately, this challenge tends to evoke responses from regular and special education teachers that often aggravate the problem. Ineffective responses include feelings of helplessness, feelings of misplaced power which results in more authoritarian approaches in the classroom, and attitudes which place blame on exceptional students for their behavior. Teachers who blame students for deviant behaviors assume that students want to cause trouble, are not interested in learning, do not really want to be in school, or are disruptive for hostile reasons. This attitude reinforces teachers' negative expectations of their students and ultimately reinforces students' disruptive behaviors.

Research results generally indicate that social learning techniques are more effective than traditional punitive actions for helping exceptional students acquire more positive behaviors. The use of structured learning for behavior management may be particularly useful in working with exceptional students who are often referred to as "discipline problems." Interdisciplinary teams are a valuable asset to the regular and special education teachers in operating structured learning in mainstreamed classes. The following script is provided as an example of how structured learning may operate with a trio of discipline problems named Amy, Adam, and Eve.

Assumptions

1. Amy, Adam, and Eve are perceived by a regular classrsoom teacher to be exceptional students who have not yet been classified. They probably exist in every classroom.

2. The interdisciplinary team members will work in pairs in the actual implementation of a structured learning program in the classroom. One member may serve as a "teacher" and the other an observer. The pairs will work together in the action-reaction activities of role playing and feedback in which effective skill behaviors are first rehearsed (role played) and then critiqued (feedback). The teaching pairs in this script are a special education teacher and a guidance counselor.

I. One Piece of a Structured Learning Script to Teach Self-Control

    A. Teacher and counselor present an overview of self-control.

        1. Teacher and counselor will discuss self-control before showing models of self-control.

        2. Teacher and counselor will solicit definitions of self-control from Amy, Adam, and Eve.

            a. "Amy, what is self-control?"

            b. "Eve, what does self-control mean to you?"

            c. "Adam, can you define self-control?"

        3. Teacher and counselor will present a model of self-control. The model may be a prepared vignette that emphasizes self-control. It may consist of:

            a. a film about a student yelling and cursing at a teacher when the teacher may be harsh in his/her critical remarks;

    b. a film strip about a student who is using a way to control himself/herself when when Mom and Dad forbid something that is desired; and

    c. a story about a student who controls himself/herself when a friend is seen rummaging through his/her desk.

Teacher and counselor will follow up vignette with a discussion focused on the example of self-control depicted in the vignette. They will ask Amy, Adam, and Eve when they have had to use self-control.

Teacher and counselor will assist Amy, Adam, and Eve in identifying situations they have already encountered in which they used self-control. They will ask Amy, Adam, and Eve what situations they think they will encounter in the future that will demand that they use self-control.

4. Teacher and counselor will discuss the steps Amy, Adam, and Eve may take in order to learn self-control (a kind of task analysis).

    a. "Amy, what is going on inside of you that signals or alerts you to the fact that your are losing your self-control?" (Hints from teacher and counselor: "Do you feel jumpy, angry, nervous?")

    b. "Adam, what occurred to make you feel that you were losing your self-control?" (Hints from teacher and counselor: "Did anything happen at home or did you think of a situation that bothered you?")

    c. "Eve, take some guesses as to ways in which you can control yourself?" (Hints from teacher and counselor: "How do you slow down?")

5. Teacher and counselor will identify ways in which Amy, Adam, and Eve may control themselves. The ways may be:

    a. slow down—take a deep breath and realize you are "racing";

    b. count to 10;

    c. assert yourself;

    d. leave the scene;

    e. move on to a new activity;

    f. other ways may be generated by Adam, Eve, and Amy.

B. Teacher and counselor will follow up with several vignettes depicting self-control. Several sessions may be spent on exposure to vignettes or other models. They will identify and discuss with students the instances of the uses of self-control in the vignettes.

Teacher and counselor will ask, "Amy, Adam, Eve, what specific ways or steps did Mr. X take in the vignette so that he could control himself when . . . . ?"

C.   Teacher and counselor will solicit the involvement of Amy, Adam, and Eve in the discussion of self-control in terms of how self-control modeled in the vignettes reminds them of situations involving their use of self-control at home, at school, or with friends.

   1.   Teacher and counselor ask:

      a.   "Adam, did anything that you saw in vignette #1 remind you of a time when you had to use self-control?"
      b.   "Eve, what did Mrs. Y do in the vignette to use self-control?" "What do you do in school when you have to use self-control?"
      c.   "Amy, when in particular have you had to use self-control?"

D.   Teacher and counselor will organize for the role playing. The teacher and counselor will continue to teach the skill of self-control with basically the same dialogue for the role playing, feedback, and transfer training components of the model.

Note: For a comprehensive description of how a structured learning program may be operationalized, Goldstein et al. (1980). *Skill-streaming the adolescent.* Champaign, Illinois: Research Press Co. See also Manuele, C. and Cicchelli, T. (1983), "Discipline revisited: Social skills programs and methods for the classroom." *Contemporary Education* 5, 104–109.

Attitudes

INTRODUCTION

Public Law 94-142 invites a new collaboration among educators, parents, and students. Module 11.0 investigates the appropriate interactions in a school among these groups and suggests some practical applications of theory to be investigated by regular and special educators for bringing parents, students and educators together, as they should and must be in a "real" world.

For further information on this topic, see the Topic Referenced Bibliography on pages 232 to 262 under numbers: *3, 4, 5, 6, 7, 8.2* and *9.* Also see the bibliography on Literature for and About Children with Special Needs prepared by Arlene M. Pillar on pages 263 to 267.

11.1 POSITIVE ATTITUDES TOWARD HANDICAPPED AND NON-HANDICAPPED CHILDREN AND YOUTH

Minimum Competency Objectives

1. You will be able to recall how and why the interaction of handicapped youngsters with non-handicapped youngsters contributes to positive attitudes towards peers.

2. You will be able to interpret goal setting and the implementation thereof as a vehicle for promoting cooperative relationships between the handicapped and the non-handicapped.

3. You will demonstrate how collaboration of special education teachers with regular education teachers and other interdisciplinary team members

can contribute to the mainstreaming of handicapped youngsters with non-handicapped youngsters.

Rationale

PL 94-142 may very well be one of the most important pieces of human rights legislation in recent history. In compliance with its provisions, handicapped youngsters will be integrated with non-handicapped youngsters in the everyday functioning of classroom and school life. Consequently, non-handicapped children and youth may be exposed to behaviors that are unfamiliar to them. It is therefore incumbent upon educators to provide and implement well-functioning integration activities that support positive constructive relationships and attitudes between the handicapped and non-handicapped.

Enabling Activities

1. Read and discuss the following section of this module.
2. In class, debate the implications of PL 94-142 in terms of its affecting positive and/or negative attitudes of school administrators, teachers, parents, and students toward mainstreaming.

Peer Relationships

Peer relationships between the handicapped and non-handicapped should contribute to an interaction process that promotes the sharing of values, skills, and attitudes. These relationships provide the handicapped with models and role playing experiences that may shape the necessary social behaviors for their survival in the "real world." Consequently, the interaction process between the handicapped and non-handicapped may provide for the following for both groups:

- reduction of social isolation;
- contributions to psychological development by reduction of egocentrism and the encouragement of the ability to perceive broader horizons;
- positive influence on social and academic aspiration and goals.

Interdependence — Mutual Goals

At this time, there is mixed evidence concerning the effects of placing the handicapped with the non-handicapped. What we have learned is that the simple physical integration of these peers is not enough. What appears to be important are the context and influences that determine and support attitudes that are characterized as accepting, liking, and caring. Primary concern must be directed toward situations or contexts that promote interdependent goals that support collaboration, positive cathexis toward self and others, and expectations for rewards for future interactions. What becomes critical, then, is the manner in which teachers structure goals since they will set the stage for the manner in which students will interact. Emphasis should be placed on small heterogeneous learning groups having joint tasks designed to assure mastery of such tasks. The goal structure should contain criteria for success as well as the same reward for all group members.

Operating Procedures for Goals and Collaborative Learning

The operating procedures for goal setting and collaborative learning are:

- Specify appropriate goals that are realistic and can be attained successfully by all group members. The goal must be attained through the collaboration of the group. Research has shown that when the work is a joint venture, rather than a matter of each student doing his/her *own* thing, true interaction takes place.
- Explain goals and tasks necessary to complete them.
    - •• Identify criteria for success.
    - •• Identify incentives and rewards.
- Maximize the heterogeneity of the group.
- Physically arrange group so that they are close together.
- Provide appropriate resources.
- Monitor and facilitate positive student interaction. Intervene if necessary to assist group in problem solving.
- Gather data on individual as well as group activities so that group members may assist one another if necessary.
- Provide appropriate feedback in order to support and encourage collaborative group interaction.

Activities for Goals and Collaborative Learning

Since goals should be designed to support the interaction of the handicapped with the non-handicapped, the following activities may be used in the goal planning-collaborative learning design:

- simulations and role playing that demonstrate individual differences as well as similarities in students;
- information (first-hand knowledge) provided by handicapped persons;
- achievements of handicapped persons;
- nonstructured social contacts between the handicapped and non-handicapped;
- activities that support objectives in the affective domain (i.e., attitudes);
- use of appropriate software that is designed to affect opinions;
- specification of joint goals through developing a newsletter, solving a math problem, solving a problem concerning economic/survival concerns, setting class rules, etc.

The Teaming and Collaboration of Regular and Special Education Teachers and Interdisciplinary Team Members

Regular and special education teachers and interdisciplinary team members need to engage in new professional relationships in order to facilitate the interactive process between the handicapped and non-handicapped youngster. Together they may work in the following ways:

- completion of IEPs;
- team teaching;
- planning and implementing joint activities
    - •• structuring learning tasks for the handicapped and non-handicapped youngster;
    - •• facilitating non-structured social events for handicapped and non-handicapped youngsters;
    - •• observing and gathering data on student and group performance; and
    - •• co-teaching for tutorial services.

Special and regular education teachers in particular, should become part of handicapped and non-handicapped students' total environment. Additionally, the interaction of special and regular education teachers and other interdisciplinary team members encourages and supports the integration process of handicapped and non-handicapped youngsters.

Summary

The interaction of the handicapped youngster with the non-handicapped youngster provides the non-handicapped with entry opportunities into "real world" experiences. Moreover, these real-life experiences benefit the non-handicapped student as well. When peers work together, realistic dynamic perceptions of one another develop. Collaboration, rather than competition, is supported. Equality does not mean sameness, and the recognition of individual uniqueness contributes to a richness in a real-life society.

Assessment

I.   In pairs, regular and special educators may conduct a structured interview with some handicapped and non-handicapped youngsters. Ask questions related to the following:

   - kinds of collaborative activities that include handicapped with non-handicapped;
   - description of resources (hardware and software) available for instructional purposes;
   - role and function of teacher when working in small heterogeneous groups; and
   - discussion of students' feelings regarding mainstreaming.

II. As a member of an interdisciplinary team, plan a mini-unit for a small heterogeneous group of handicapped and non-handicapped youngsters. Collaboratively design group goals, activities, materials, teaching techniques, and assessment procedures.

III. Design an inventory intended for regular and special education that may be used for gathering data concerning attitudes toward exceptional children and youth. (See your instructor for assistance.)

Implications/Applications

People tend to model their behavior on what others do and not on what they say. Teacher behavior that reflects attitudes toward exceptional students will play a large part in determining student attitudes. A few current findings regarding attitudes toward mainstreaming suggest the following:

- Teacher and student attitudes are more positive when handicapped students are introduced to non-handicapped students as individuals, rather than as a group.
- Physically handicapped and learning disabled students are more easily accepted for mainstreaming by regular and special education teachers than are mentally retarded and emotionally disturbed students.
- Teachers are more willing to deal with severe attention and management problems when students have not been labeled mentally retarded and emotionally disturbed.
- The selection of a "most likely to succeed" student for mainstreaming by regular and special education teachers increases teachers' positive attitudes towards handicapped students.

Other information on attitudes indicates that there are general processes that regular and special education teachers may use with their students to influence attitude learning. They are as follows:

- Students must see the desired behavior modeled.
- Students must see the model display/experience satisfaction with the attitude.
- Students should be provided an opportunity to interact with the object of an attitude.

Obviously, the model described in the attitude learning sequence is the teacher and the object is the handicapped student.

The findings of research on attitudes in concert with the attitude learning model provide a framework by which regular and special education teachers may prepare themselves and their students for successful mainstreaming to occur. The following case study dilemma is presented to regular and special educators and interested interdisciplinary team members as an extreme example to be used to test the application of this framework. But, prior to solving the dilemma, the following assumptions are offered:

1. Interdisciplinary team members, particularly regular and special education teachers, have experienced techniques (e.g. values clarification) to increase their self-awareness with regard to stereotyping.
2. Regular and special education teachers have had experiences in team teaching, cross-grouping, and simulated role playing.
3. Students, both handicapped and non-handicapped, have had experiences in

cross grouping, peer tutoring, simulated role playing, and interacting together in schoolwide activities.

Case Study — Dilemma

Two special education classes in School X are to be abolished as a result of a sharp decrease in the school's enrollment. As a result, each regular education class will receive some special education students. The regular class that you will be working with is designated to receive nine new students. The addition of these new students will bring the class enrollment up to twenty-five. The following students were selected by the COH as likely candidates for mainstreaming to the regular class that you are involved with. They are:

1. June, age 8 — EMR (labeled)
2. Don, age 8½ — EMR? (unlabeled)
3. Bette, age 9½ — Emotionally disturbed? (unlabeled)
4. Alan, age 10 — Learning disabled (labeled)
5. Carol, age 9½ — Physically handicapped (labeled — moderately hearing impaired)
6. Steve, age 8½ — Emotionally disturbed (labeled — mildly)
7. Lisa, age 9½ — Multihandicapped (labeled)
8. Jack, age 8 — EMR (labeled)
9. Ed, age 9 — Physically handicapped? (unlabeled — mildly hearing impaired)

Two weeks prior to their placement in the regular class, the enrollment figures in School X increased because of an influx of non-handicapped students from another school district. As a result of this enrollment shift, only six students will be selected for placement in the regular class with which you are working.

As a member of an interdisciplinary team, which six students would you select? Why did you select the students that you did? Were your selections in agreement with other team members? How would you work with other interdisciplinary team members in preparing for and actually implementing these placements for effective mainstreaming to take place? How would you work with the handicapped and non-handicapped students in the placement process in order to promote positive attitudes toward mainstreaming? If a student's handicap is not obvious, would you point this out in your preparation of students (both non-handicapped and handicapped) for the mainstreaming process? Would you prepare students (handicapped and non-handicapped) for the placement of the more obviously handicapped student in the regular class? How would you, with interdisciplinary team members, evaluate your use of the suggested framework in solving this dilemma?

Servicing the Bilingual Exceptional Child:
Issues and Directions

INTRODUCTION

THIS MODULE will focus your attention on the bilingual exceptional child. Who is this child? How does this child acquire meaning in various settings? What aptitudes (characteristics that promise success in educational tasks), have become critical across the continuum of exceptionalities described in Module 3.3? As a result of doing this module, you will become more familiar with other terms that attempt to capture the important characteristics of this individual (e.g., "limited English proficient" (LEP), "bilingual handicapped," "partial bilingual"). Due to the special characteristics of the population of bilingual exceptional children — language proficiency in more than one language, cultural differences from the majority culture, and language minority status — a plethora of terms has come into use. Sometimes these terms may add more confusion than clarity to one's understanding of the bilingual exceptional child. Nevertheless, they do reflect the current level of our knowledge of bilingualism, second language acquisition, and dynamic, complex, and tentative handicapping conditions.

Module 12.1 stimulates you to think about the issues and controversies that have become evident about the most appropriate ways to service the bilingual exceptional child. You will learn about the projections of LEP children by language group and the difficulties in estimating exact figures within each language group. Despite the lack of precise data on the population of bilingual exceptional children, three essential principles are formulated as guides in making decisions about servicing bilingual exceptional students.

Note: At the request of the authors, Richard Baecher of Fordham University contributed this timely module specifically focused on educating the bilingual exceptional student. Dr. Baecher is a respected educator who consistently promotes and attempts to provide equality of educational opportunity for bilingual children and youth.

Module 12.2 introduces you to a model that is presently in operation in New York City. This scheme will broaden your view of the range and diversity of educational services for LEP students with handicapping conditions. You'll also become familiar with such terms as intensive ESL, bilingual instruction, and many others.

Module 12.3 summarizes some recent thinking on the issue of assessment of the bilingual exceptional child. You'll quickly discover that language proficiency is a critical factor in placing, servicing, and instructing LEP students. Although researchers and practitioners working in the areas of second language learning, applied linguistics, and bilingualism have different conceptions about the meaning and measurement of language proficiency, much progress has been made that is useful to relevant assessment. An illustration of one approach used to assess the relative language proficiency of bilingual children will show you some of the issues in this area and the new directions in which language assessment in headed.

Once you have completed this module in its entirety, it is hoped that you'll be encouraged to pursue its topics in greater depth by consulting the references. Indeed, we are at the threshold of an exciting development in special education, bilingual education and regular instruction. The confluence of these three areas can only result in more appropriate and better servicing for the bilingual exceptional child.

12.1 SOME ISSUES AND PRINCIPLES IN TEACHING THE BILINGUAL EXCEPTIONAL CHILD

Minimum Competency Objectives

1. Given some recent figures on the projection of limited English proficient children in our schools, you will interpret these data in terms of implications for school policies, impact on school organization, curriculum, and need for qualified personnel.

2. Having reviewed Module 1.1 about recent litigation, specific court cases (*Lau v. Nichols*), and PL 94-142, you will articulate and relate some basic principles that can operate in the delivery of services to the bilingual exceptional child.

Rationale

Recent census data have identified more accurately than ever the numbers of language minority persons in the total population of the United States.

A current definition of language minority persons refers to them as individuals of any age whose usual or second language is not English, or, if over 14 years of age, whose mother tongue is other than English (National Center for Education Statistics Bulletin, 1978). The most current projections, collected as part of the Congressional mandate under Part C of the Title VII Elementary and Secondary Education Act (Bilingual Education), are included in Table 12.1. These data have enormous implications for teaching language minority students.

TABLE 12.1

Projections of LEP Children by Language Group, Ages 5–14, in Thousands

(National Center for Education Statistics, 1981)

Language	1976	Projection Years 1980	1990	2000
Chinese	34.4	31.3	33.0	36.2
Filipino	36.4	33.2	35.0	38.3
French	97.6	89.0	93.9	102.9
German	97.4	88.8	93.7	102.6
Greek	29.0	26.5	27.9	30.6
Italian	104.1	94.9	100.1	109.6
Japanese	14.5	13.3	14.0	15.3
Korean	13.4	12.2	12.8	14.1
Navajo	26.6	24.3	25.6	28.1
Polish	26.3	24.0	25.3	27.7
Portuguese	26.1	23.8	25.1	27.5
Spanish	1,789.5	1,727.6	2,092.7	2,630.0
Vietnamese	27.3	24.9	26.2	28.7
Yiddish	24.6	22.5	23.7	26.0
Other LEP	154.4	140.8	148.6	162.7
Total	2,520.4	2,394.2	2,795.9	3,400.0

Note: Due to the technique used to disaggregate LEP estimates into language groups, reported totals do not equal the sum of individual LEP estimates across languages. The reported totals are more accurate than individual language estimates because they are based on a larger sample population.

A number of significant implications and inferences can be made from the data in Table 12.1 These have immediate impact on one's attitude toward the instruction of language minority persons, in particular the bilingual exceptional child, and the need to recognize essential principles in mainstreaming such a child.

Enabling Activities

1. Review the projections of LEP children in Table 12.1 and interpret them with these areas in mind: school policy, school organization, curriculum, and qualified personnel.

2. Read those sections in PL 94-142 about non-discriminatory assessment and least restrictive environment. What guidelines can you derive from *Lau v. Nichols* (1974) about the local educational agency's responsibility in the teaching of language minority students? Review the *Jose P. v. Ambach* (1979) case and discuss your findings about this case with a colleague on the interdisciplinary team.

3. Read and reflect on the section below, noting the importance of having essential principles in establishing educational services for bilingual exceptional children.

The projections of Table 12.1 indicate that the size of the non-English language background population in the United States is expected to increase from 30 million in 1980 to approximately 39.5 million in the year 2000. Children between the ages of 5 and 14 of non-English language background are expected to increase from 3.8 million in 1976 to 5.1 million in the year 2000. Within this time period, the total number of LEP children is expected to increase from 2.5 million to 3.4 million. Table 12.1 points out the projected numbers of limited English proficient children by language group for the years 1976 through 2000.

The largest group of LEP individuals in the United States are Spanish speaking. Current Bureau of the Census reports give a count of 13.2 million. Of that total, 60 percent are of Mexican origin, 14 percent Puerto Rican, 6 percent Cuban, 8 percent Central or South American and 12 percent other Spanish-language origin. Although more precise estimates are forthcoming, it is estimated that more than one-third of the language minority population and 60 percent of language minority school-age children are of Spanish-speaking background. The remaining 40 percent are composed of a variety of linguistic and cultural groups, both native-born and immigrant populations.

While these figures project the need and demand for educational services, various court decisions have pointed out the obligations of state and local educational agencies to handicapped students of limited English proficiency. Peter Ross (1983) has summarized the more important obligations.

1. The LEA is obligated to service handicapped LEP children as stipulated in PL 94-142. Its regulations provide the primary authority for issues of identification, evaluation, child find, and parental rights.

2. An LEA must take special steps to locate handicapped LEP pupils as part of its "child find" obligation. Activities such as door-to-door canvassing, radio and newspaper advertising, etc., must be undertaken in the predominant languages of the district. See *Jose P. v. Ambach* (1979) for more information.

3. Tests and evaluations of students for purpose of placement must be conducted in the students' primary language, unless clearly not feasible. Testing and evaluation should be done by someone trained in the assessment of linguistically and culturally different students and fluent in the child's language.

This summary of obligations on the part of LEAs and projected figures of Table 12.1 have led to the formulation of essential principles in the delivery of appropriate educational interventions. Although others can be applied, these three are crucial:

1. educational services are provided in the least restrictive environment which is appropriate to meet a student's special education needs;

2. educational services should emphasize the educational needs of students rather than only focusing on the handicapping conditions for appropriate grouping; and

3. educational services are built on an appropriate evaluation which reflect the level of support, related, and/or instructional services required to meet the individual educational needs of students.

(New York City Board of Education, 1984)

These principles reflect one approach that an LEA can take in organizing its educational services for bilingual exceptional children with handicapping conditions.

Assessment

(to be conducted with a member of the interdisciplinary team)

1. Review Table 12.1 and state your interpretations of the available data. Why was there a decrease in LEP children in 1980 and an increase in subsequent years? Locate more recent data on the bilingual exceptional child and, using the continuum of exceptionalities in Module 3.2, estimate the current percentages. Compare some of your findings with actual figures in your school district.

2. Use the following chart to formulate your thinking about the implications of Table 12.1. Compare them with a team member. Rank order your list if you have written more than three in each box.

CHART 12.1

Activity on Impact of Projected LEP Figures

Area		Impact/Implications
School Policy	1.	
	2.	
	3.	
	4.	
School Organization	1.	
	2.	
	3.	
	4.	
Curriculum	1.	
	2.	
	3.	
	4.	
Qualified Personnel	1.	
	2.	
	3.	
	4.	

3. In what ways are the three basic principles translated into sound educational practice in your school or school district?

Interview some decision makers in the superintendent's office, COH, or bilingual office about their reactions to these principles. Are there others that you think are more important? Collect your findings and discuss them with a colleague.

Implications/Applications

The projections of LEP children demonstrate the magnitude of the need for appropriate services and the diversity of children and adults in the years ahead. This means vast transformations are necessary, both conceptually and operationally. Only an approach which does not lose sight of each individual's uniqueness and individual differences will be feasible and relevant in servicing the bilingual exceptional child.

This summary of Oxford, Pol, Lopez, Stupp, Gendell, and Peng (1981) highlights the educational implications of LEP children projections:

> The total number of LEP children, ages 5–14, will increase overall in the period 1976–2000 (2.5 to 3.4 million), although there was a temporary drop to 2.4 million in 1980 and 1985. Spanish, Asian and combined non-Spanish and non-Asian LEPs all experienced slight declines during the decade of the 1980s but are projected to rise strongly until the year 2000. Spanish LEPs moved from having 71 percent of all LEPs in 1976 to 77 percent in 2000. Highest LEP rates (LEP/NELB—non-English language background persons ratio) among non-English language groups were found among Spanish (.75), Vietnamese (.75), Navajo (.66), and Yiddish (.60), as compared with the usual rate ranging from .41 to .53. California and Texas will show overall LEP increases until the year 2000 (California, .6 million in 1976 to .9 in 2000; Texas, .5 million in 1976 to .9 million in 2000); New York, however, began and ended with .5 million, with a slight decline to .4 million lasting at least for the decade of the 1980s. Not only did the proportion of all LEPs residing in California, New York, and Texas increase, but the percentage of Spanish language LEPs living in these three states also increased.

These projections have definite implications for bilingual education planning. First, Spanish LEPs will become an increasingly important constituency in educational planning over the next two decades. Spanish language background persons are already the largest group of non-English language background persons, and their share of LEPs will increase. This is due in part to the fact that they have higher LEP rates than do most other NELBs, indicating that a greater percentage of the Spanish language background children ages 5–14 are limited in English than children of the same ages from most other NELB groups. These facts, then, indicate that educational planners in many agencies will need to find ways to meet the bilingual education needs of a growing Spanish clientele.

Nevertheless, sheer numbers of Spanish NELBs and LEPs should not conceal the needs of other groups. The very high LEP rates among smaller groups, such as Vietnamese, Navajo, and Yiddish, are important for educational planning. Planning for these groups in areas where their concentration is low most certainly will present difficulties.

The geographic concentration of NELBs and LEPs within three states, California, Texas, and New York, should exercise much influence on the allocation of educational funds and programs for the next few decades. An important caveat, however, is that the projections cannot foresee and take into account such phenomena as the increasing Cambodian refugee influx or the massive Cuban sea-lift operation, both of which have affected geographic concentrations of LEPs in untold ways. In addition, changes in United States immigration policy would certainly affect our projections.

One interesting result that affects educational planning is that LEP children and younger NELB groups temporarily decreased in numbers during the decade of the 1980s, although they are projected to increase again by the end of the century. This reflects the projected temporary decline of younger age groups in the total United States population and is a factor in educational planning.

12.2   A MODEL OF EDUCATIONAL SERVICES
FOR HANDICAPPED LIMITED ENGLISH PROFICIENT STUDENTS

Minimum Competency Objectives

1. Presented with one model of educational services for handicapped pupils, you will become familiar with the range of educational services being planned for LEP pupils with handicapping conditions and their particular meanings.

2. Discovering how these services will be implemented for handicapped LEP pupils is another objective. You will learn what such terms as "bilingual resource room" and "full bilingual education" mean in the context of servicing the bilingual exceptional child.

Rationale

Once the interdisciplinary team develops its IEP (see Module 7.1), it must determine how and where the program can be provided. A number of service delivery models are possible. The one from New York City (1984) indicates the spectrum of services being offered for the handicapped LEP pupil.

Enabling Activities

1. Carefully analyze Figure 12.2A and learn the definitions of the components of educational services.

2. Read the following section of this module and carefully examine Table 12.2 on bilingual services.

Although the bilingual, English as a second language (ESL), and special education staff are responsible for bilingual exceptional children, the major accountability lies with special education services. Bilingual exceptional children must have access to all special education services. At the same time, having access to them should not preclude them from bilingual or ESL assistance. Victoria Bergin (1980) delineates the division of responsibility for bilingual youngsters in the following manner. She points out that minority language children are not necessarily exceptional or handicapped children. While they may be entitled to a bilingual or English-as-a-second-language program so that they can learn to their full potential, such programs are not considered special education programs. These same children, however, may also be handicapped or exceptional, thereby entitling them to both bilingual assistance and special education services. In both cases, their linguistic abilities must be taken into account.

This distinction focuses on the need to merge services and the creation of a unified entity rather than the sum of two mutually exclusive efforts. In other words, bilingual services that do not account for the exceptionality are misdirected, just as special education programs that do not consider cultural, linguistic, and personal experiences are misinformed.

Figure 12.2A (New York City Board of Education, Division of Special Education, 1984) displays the range of educational services presently recommended for handicapped students.

For a better understanding of this model, these terms need to be defined:

General education with supplementary services: the first option in the continuum of educational services. It must be noted "that the placement of a student with handicapping condition into a special class, school or more restrictive environment occurs only when the severity of the educational needs makes placement into general education classes with the use of supplementary aids and services not an appropriate educational program." (New York City Board of Education, Division of Special Education 1984, p. 27).

Transitional support services: those temporary services designed for either a regular or special education teacher to assist the teacher in providing appropriate education services to a student with a handicapping condition who is transferring to a regular program or to a program or services in a less restrictive environment. These services are meant primarily for regular education teachers who are receiving a handicapped student who has been in a special class or school and is being considered for decertification.

Related Services: provided only when considered essential for that student with a handicapping condition so as to benefit from the primary educational program. Related services are speech pathology, audiology, psychological services, physical therapy, occupational therapy, counseling services and other support services. Assessment for these services must be made by an appropriately certified evaluator.

These components of the model are essential to the diverse educational services for handicapped students. Figure 12.2A also indicates, by a broken ar-

FIGURE 12.2A

Model of the Original Special Education Cascade
THE ORIGINAL SPECIAL EDUCATION CASCADE*

LIMITED EDUCATIONAL ENVIRONMENTS OUTSIDE OF THE SCHOOL[†]
- SPECIAL TREATMENT AND DETECTION CENTERS
- HOSPITALS
- "HOMEBOUND" INSTRUCTORS

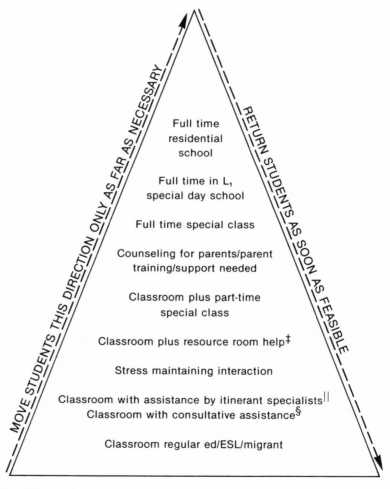

* Reynolds and Birch 1982.

[†] This special set of environments is included here in set-aside fashion because students are usually placed in these settings for reasons other than educational. For example, they go to detention centers on court orders due to conviction of some criminal offense, or they go to hospitals or are held at home because of health problems. Special educators often work in these *limited* environments and some degree of specialization in education is required. But in the

row, the types of services offered for handicapped students of limited English proficiency.

Table 12.2A presents an overview of educational services for LEP pupils.

TABLE 12.2A

Overview of Services for Students Limited in English Proficiency

Bilingual Services

Educational Recommendation	Service	Setting	Provider	Instructional Components
Related Services	LEP students who are receiving full bilingual services within general education or special education will receive speech/language therapy and counseling in their native language. Providers of the other related service categories may require a translator's assistance in providing services for these students.	• Not applicable	(When applicable) • Bilingual speech/ language specialist • Bilingual counselor • Translator	• Not applicable
Resource Room	Bilingual resource room	• General education bilingual class • Bilingual resource room	• General education bilingual teacher • Bilingual special education teacher	• Academic/ subject area skills and strategies

main, there is strong preference, from an educational point of view, for return of the students to regular school environments as soon as feasible.

‡A resource classroom is a special station in a school building that is manned by a resource teacher who usually offers *some direct* instruction to selected students, but also usually offers consulting services to regular teachers. Sometimes resource teachers are categorical (such as resource teacher for the blind) but increasingly resource teachers are employed for a more generic, noncategorical role.

‖Itinerant specialists commonly include, for example, speech and hearing therapists and mobility instructors for the blind. They offer *some direct* instruction to the students involved.

§Consultative assistance might be offered, for example, by school psychologists, consulting teachers, resource room teachers, supervisors, or others. The term "consultant" denotes only *indirect* services and *no direct* service or instruction to the child by the consultant.

Source: Perlman, Zabel, and Zabel, 1982, p. 83.

TABLE 12.2A (Continued)

Educational Recommendation	Service	Setting	Provider	Instructional Components
Special Class or Special Class/ Special School	Full bilingual education	• Self-contained bilingual special education class	• Bilingual special education teacher	• Intensive ESL • Substantive subject areas — Native Language • Native language arts
	Partial bilingual education (dual language approach — transitional)	• Self-contained bilingual special education class	• Bilingual special education teacher	• Intensive ESL • Substantive subject areas — English • Native language arts
ESL Only		• Self-contained monolingual English) special education class	• Monolingual special education teacher • Teacher ESL • Bilingual paraprofessional (when appropriate)	• All subject areas instruction — English • ESL • Subject area summary native language • Mainstreaming general education bilingual

Source: New York City Board of Education, Division of Special Education, 1984, p. 21.

These services will consist of combinations of these three elements:

1. intensive instruction in English as a second language;
2. instruction in substantive subject areas in the student's native language; and
3. reinforcement and development of native language arts skills.

Bilingual education is the common term used for an educational program which provides all three of these elements. Its primary goal is to increase the student's level of independent functioning within the total school environment (New York City Board of Education, Division of Special Education, 1984, 18–20). The particular service category of Table 12.2A includes a variation of the three elements of ESL, native language arts development, and instruction in substantive areas in the student's native language.

Assessment

(to be conducted with a member of the team)

1. Analyze Figure 12.2A (taken from Perlman, Zabel, and Zabel, 1982, p. 83). What assumptions can you identify in the model? Exchange and discuss your responses with another team member or your instructor.

2. Since no model is to be viewed as *the* final solution, carefully study the three models illustrated below (Perlman, Zabel, and Zabel, 1982, p. 85). Each model allows the integration of specialized curriculum materials in the first and second language and mainstreaming to either a bilingual or monolingual regular education program. Identify the salient features of each model (Bilingual Support, Coordinated Services and Integrated Bilingual Special Education models). What model(s) does your local school/district follow? Which model, in your opinion, is the best solution in your circumstances?

How does each model satisfy the linguistic and cultural needs of the bilingual exceptional child?

Implications/Applications

The continuum of educational services and models presented in this module highlight the various approaches and directions in which special services are headed. They all have in common the assumption that placements are not permanent and that regular education classrooms can be adapted to serve most handicapped children with support services provided either indirectly through their teachers, or directly, on a part-time basis, from specialized staff. This also holds for bilingual exceptional children.

12.3 RELATIVE LANGUAGE PROFICIENCY ASSESSMENT

Minimum Competency Objectives

1. You will learn about some unresolved issues in identifying and instruct-

FIGURE 12.2 B

Three Models of Alternative Services for LEP Students

BILINGUAL SUPPORT MODEL

SPECIAL EDUCATION TEACHER (Monolingual)

- Sequenced L_2 Instruction (ESL)
  - Oral language (receptive, expressive)
  - Reading (word attack, comprehension)
  - Spelling/writing (based on oral language)
- Math Instruction in L_2
  - Based on concrete experiences
  - Building language & cognitive development together
- Other IEP Objectives (self-help, vocation, gross/fine motor, visual/auditory perception)

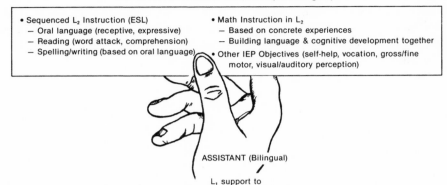

ASSISTANT (Bilingual)

L_1 support to
any of the above

COORDINATED SERVICES MODEL

SPECIAL EDUCATION TEACHER (Monolingual)

- Sequenced L_2 Instruction (ESL)
- Design Intervention Program (content & sequence)
  - Ameliorate specific learning problems
- Implementing IEP Objectives to be Accomplished in L_2

BILINGUAL CLASSROOM TEACHER

- Sequenced L_1 Instruction
  - Oral language, reading, spelling and writing in primary language
- Math Instruction in L_1
- Other IEP Objectives Specified for L_1

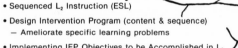

INTEGRATED BILINGUAL SPECIAL EDUCATION MODEL

BILINGUAL SPECIAL EDUCATION TEACHER

- Comprehensive Language Development Program

L_1	Oral Language Reading Spelling/Writing
L_2	Oral Language Reading Spelling/Writing

- Math Instruction (L_1, L_2)
- Other IEP Objectives (L_1, L_2)

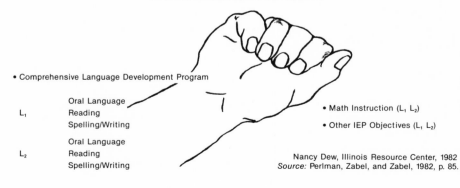

Nancy Dew, Illinois Resource Center, 1982
Source: Perlman, Zabel, and Zabel, 1982, p. 85.

ing the bilingual exceptional child, and how researchers and practitioners approach the assessment of language proficiency.

2. By means of a specific illustration of the assessment of language proficiency in bilingual children, you will become familiar with the concept of assessment, relative language proficiency, and principles of language assessment as they bear on the bilingual exceptional child.

Rationale

Due to the lack of agreement on the appropriate treatment of bilingual exceptional children, educators have raised a number of serious questions. Does a limited proficiency in English, in itself, constitute a handicap? How are handicapped bilingual children identified? How does one decide when a bilingual child's difficulties in meeting the demands of the instructional program result from limitations in proficiency rather than from actual learning impairments? Which is the most suitable language of instruction? All these questions revolve around one's definition of language proficiency.

Enabling Activities

1. Review and critically analyze some of the definitions of language proficiency summarized in the following section. Note how these definitions are similar and different.

2. Carefully study Jim Cummins' (1981) notion of language proficiency and his representation of the content of the communication act.

Confusion and conflicting theoretical beliefs characterize the language assessment landscape as currently understood and practiced. With particular attention to bilingual contexts, such terms as, "language dominance," "language ability," "comparably limited," and "semilingual versus alingual" have been used to clarify language proficiency, usually resulting in more confusion than clarity. here are some definitions that are germane to bilingual students (Richard Baecher, 1981) and their functioning:

> ". . . the degree to which an individual exhibits control over the use of the rules of a language for one, some, or all of its numerous and diverse aspects." (Marina Burt and Heidi Dulay, 1978 cited in Baecher, 1981)
> ". . . the student's language skills in English which are learned in both school and natural settings . . . It is not necessarily dependent upon specific instruction

> or content . . . language achievement is more likely to be dependent upon proficiency than vice-versa." (Ed DeAvila and Sharon Duncan, 1980, cited in Baecher, 1981)

> ". . . a single factor of global language proficiency seems to account for the lion's share of variance in a wide variety of educational tests including nonverbal and verbal I.Q. measures, achievement batteries and even personality inventories and affective measures . . . The results to date are preponderantly in favor of the assumption that language skill pervades every area of the school curriculum even more strongly than was ever thought by curriculum writers or testers." (John Oller and Kyle Perkins, 1980, cited in Baecher, 1981).

> ". . . the ability to make effective use of the cognitive functions of the language, i.e., to use language effectively as an instrument of thought and represent cognitive operation by means of language." (Jim Cummins, 1979, cited in Baecher, 1981).

The list of definitions demonstrates the variation in meanings assigned to language proficiency or communicative competence. For example, the definition of Burt and Dulay implies a model of language proficiency consisting of 64 separate components. In contrast, the Oller and Perkins description views language proficiency as a single, unitary factor. Current language tests and approaches reflect this diversity and lack of consensus.

One theoretical framework that promises to be useful and relevant to bilingual exceptional children is that advocated by Cummins (1983). Since it meets the criterion of a developmental perspective, distinguishes between school-related tasks and interpersonal ones outside the school, and allows the developmental relationships between Language 1 and Language 2 proficiency to be described, Cummins' framework merits consideration. Figure 12.3 portrays his view of relative language proficiency.

According to Cummins, language proficiency can be viewed along two continuums. One continuum relates to a range of contextual support available for expressing or receiving meaning. The terms "context-embedded" versus "context-reduced" communication describe the extremes of this continuum. In context-embedded communication, the participants can actively negotiate meaning, for example, providing feedback that the message has not been understood; the language is supported by a wide range of meaningful nonverbal and situational cues. In context-reduced communication, on the other hand, the participants rely heavily on linguistic cues to meaning and may in some cases involve suspending knowledge of the "real world" in order to interpret (or manipulate) the logic of the communication appropriately. Examples of communicative behaviors going from left to right along the continuum might be: engaging in a conversation, writing a letter to a close friend, reading an academic article. "Clearly, context-embedded communication is more typical of the everyday world outside the classroom, whereas many of the linguistic demands of the classroom

FIGURE 12.3

Range of Contextual Support and Degree of Cognitive Involvement in Communicative Activities

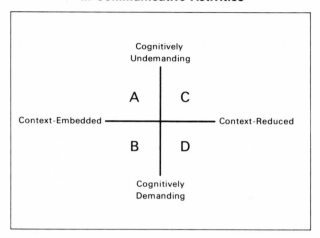

Source: Seidner, Stan, 1983, p. 11.

reflect communication which is closer to the context-reduced end of the continuum." (Jim Cummins, 1983, p. 11).

The vertical continuum addresses the developmental aspects of language proficiency in terms of the degree of active cognitive involvement in the task or activity. Cognitive involvement can be conceptualized in terms of amount of information that must be processed simultaneously or in close succession by the individual in order to carry out the activity. With reference to figure 12.3, the upper parts of the vertical continuum entail communicative tasks and activities in which the linguistic tools have become largely automatized (mastered) and therefore require little active cognitive involvement for appropriate performance. At the lower end of the continuum are tasks and activities in which the communicative tools have not become automatized, and thus require active cognitive involvement. Illustrations of such activities might include persuading another person that one's own point of view, rather than hers/his, is correct, or writing an essay on a complex theme.

Specific linguistic tasks and skills travel from the bottom to the top of the vertical continuum. There tends to be a high level of cognitive involvement in task or activity performance until mastery has been achieved. For example, learning the sound system and syntax of Language 1 requires considerable cognitive involvement for two and three-year-old children and so, such tasks would be placed in quadrant B (context-embedded, cognitively demanding). As mastery of these skills develops, however, tasks involving them would move from quadrant B to quadrant A since performance becomes increasingly automatized and cognitively undemanding. The same type of developmental progression occurs in a second language context.

Cummins proposes this framework as a way to visualize the complexity of L1-L2 relationships and the interdependence of academic skills in L1 and L2. Moreover, it provides a basis for a task-analysis of language proficiency measures and activities. Nevertheless, these task characteristics must be considered in combination with the characteristics of particular language users and their cognitive styles (Richard Baecher, 1981).

Assessment

(to be conducted with a member of the interdisciplinary team)

1. Carefully read the following quote about assessment biases. Do you agree or disagree with its major points? What precautions need to be taken to avoid some of these baises? Share your reactions and responses with a colleague.

> Because assessment is such an important and complex factor in designing educational programs, the performance of traditional assessments of language minority students can become problematic and discouraging. All too often, traditional evaluation procedures result in little useful information due to the inherent bias of the methods themselves. Biases can arise from:
>
> 1. inadequate representation of language minority children in the test-item selection population, which results in questions that are biased culturally, experientially, and linguistically toward the majority groups;
> 2. insufficient representation of minority students when norming the instrument;
> 3. problems during administration of the test (e.g., a lack of test sophistication on the part of the examinees, examiner ethnicity, etc.); and
> 4. misinterpretation of the student's performance.
>
> (Perlman, Zabel, and Zabel, 1982, p. 41)

2. Using Cummins' theoretical framework of communicative activities (Figure 12.3), locate the quadrant for these tasks:

a. an explanation of how to set a table;
b. describing an adventure one had on a field trip;

c. identifying the correct subject pronouns (he, she, it, they) in a written story;

d. the discussion that takes place during a science experiment; and

e. reading assignments of content usually found in textbooks.

3. Select one test currently used to diagnose bilingual exceptional children and analyze it in terms of contextual support and degree of cognitive involvement in communicative activities. Share your findings with another team member.

Implications/Applications

The concept of relative language proficiency has taken on extreme significance for identifying bilingual exceptional children. The framework briefly described in this module has many implications for bilingual servicing. One is its predictive value, whereby the more context-reduced and cognitively demanding a language task is, the more it will be related to academic achievement. Relative language proficiency will continue to exercise much influence in deciding on the best educational services for the bilingual exceptional child.

SELECTED BIBLIOGRAPHIES

TOPIC REFERENCED BIBLIOGRAPHY

Key to Numbers

Number	Topics Included
1.	Historical Perspectives American Education Educating the Exceptional Child
2.	Legal Aspects Laws Due Process Hearings
3.	New Roles for Educational Personnel and Parents Administrators Supervisors Special Educators Regular Educators School Psychologists Social Workers Guidance Counselors Therapists Medical Personnel Parents Students
4.	Attitudes/Labeling
5.	Strengths and Needs of Exceptional Children and Youth
6.	Current Models for Planning Education for Exceptional Children and Youth

Key to Numbers (Continued)

Number	Topics Included
7.	Current Programs of Collaboration in Management of Programs for Exceptional Children and Youth
8.	Writing the IEP
8.1	Assessment Processes
8.2	Instructional Strategies
8.3	Evaluation Strategies
9.	Classroom Management

Bibliography

Abeson, A., et al. (1975). A primer on due process: Education decisions for handicapped children. *Exceptional Children,* 42, 68–74.   1.

Abidin, Richard R. (ed). (1980). *Parent education and international handbook.* New York: Charles C. Thomas.   2, 3.

Aiello, Barbara. (1976). *Mainstreaming: Teacher training workshops on individualized instruction.* Reston, Virginia. The Council for Exceptional Children.   8.2.

Allan J. (1982). Preparation for mainstreaming: A new role for counselors. *Elementary school guidance and counseling.* 16, 193–201.   3.

Allport, Gordon W. (1954). *The nature of prejudice.* Cambridge, Massachusetts: Addison-Wesley.   4.

Amary, Issam. (1980). *The rights of the mentally retarded/developmentally disabled to treatment and education.* New York: Charles C. Thomas.   1, 2.

Ameruso, Frank A. (1978). *Concordance for the implementation of P.L. 94-142.* Pittsburgh, Pennsylvania: Allegheny Intermediate Unit, Exceptional Children's Programs.   1, 2, 3.

Anderson, Carl M. (1974). *Classroom activities for helping children with special needs: Classroom activities for modifying misbehavior in children.* West Nyack, New York: Center for Applied Research in Education, Inc.   9.

Anderson, N., and R. D. Laird. (1972). Teaching the deaf child to read. *Audiovisual Instruction,* 17, 19–20.   5, 8.1, 8.2.

Apter, S.J. (1977). Application of ecological theory: Toward a community special education model. *Exceptional Children,* 43, 367–73.   1, 6.

Bateman, Barbara. (1980). *So you're going to a hearing*. Northbrook,
Illinois: Hubbard.   2, 3.

Baum, R. Bruce, and Richard F. Frazita. (1979). Educating the exceptional child in the regular classroom. *Journal of Teacher
Education*, 30, 20–21.   8.2.

Beery, K. E. (1972). *Models for mainstreaming*. Sioux Falls, South
Dakota: Dimensions Publishing Company.   6, 7.

Behr, Marcia Ward, Alice Boston Snyder and Anna S. Clopton. (1979).
*Drama integrates basic skills: Lesson plans for the learning
disabled*. Springfield, Illinois: Charles C. Thomas.   5, 8.2.

Benton, A. L., and D. Pearl (Eds.). (1978). *Dyslexia: An appraisal
of current knowledge*. Rockville, Maryland: National Institute of Mental Health.   5.

Bergin, V. (1980). *Special education needs in bilingual programs*.
Roslyn, Virginia: National Clearinghouse for Bilingual
Education.   1, 5.

Berk, Ronald A. (1980). *Criterion-referenced measurement: The state
of the art*. Baltimore, Maryland: The Johns Hopkins University Press.   8.1.

Berry, Sharon R. (1981). *Legal considerations in the education of the
handicapped. An annotated bibliography for school administrators*. Washington, D.C.: National Association of State
Directors of Special Education.   1, 2, 3.

Bersky, S., Shaw, A., Gouse, H. Baker, B. Dixon, and Beane, W.T.
(1980). Public law 94-142 and stress: A problem for educa-
tors, *Exceptional Children*, 47, 27–29.   1, 2, 3, 4, 8.

Bertness, H. J. (1976). Progressive inclusion: The mainstream move-
ment in Tacoma. In M.C. Reynolds (Ed.), *Mainstreaming:
Origins and implications*. Reston, Virginia: The Council for
Exceptional Children.   3, 6, 7, 8.

Best, Gary A. (1978). *Individuals with physical disabilities: An introduction for educators*. St. Louis, Missouri: Mosby/Times
Mirror.   5.

Biklin, Douglas. (1977). *The elementary school administrator's practical guide to mainstreaming*. Syracuse, New York: Syracuse
University Human Policy Project.   1, 2, 3, 6, 7, 8.

Biklin, Douglas. (1974). *Let our children go*. Syracuse, New York:
Human Policy Press.   1.

Binet, A. and Simon, L. (1910). L'intelligence des imbeciles. *L'Annie
Psychologique*, 15, 1–147.   1, 8.1.

Birch, Jack W. (1974). *Mainstreaming: Educable mentally retarded
children in regular classrooms*. Reston, Virginia: The Coun-
cil for Exceptional Children.   1, 2, 6, 8.

Birch, Jack W. (1975). *Hearing impaired children in the mainstream.* Reston, Virginia: The Council for Exceptional Children.   1, 2, 5, 8.

Birch, Jack W. (1978). Mainstreaming that works in elementary and secondary schools. *Journal of Teacher Education,* 29, 18–22.   6, 7, 8, 9.

Bishop, L. J. (1979). *Staff development and instructional improvement: Plans and procedures.* Boston, Massachusetts: Allyn and Bacon.   6, 7.

Bishop, Virginia E. (1978). *Teaching the visually handicapped child.* Springfield, Illinois: Charles C. Thomas.   5, 8.1, 8.2, 8.3.

Blackwell, P.M., et al. (1978). *Sentences and other systems: A language and learning curriculum for hearing impaired children.* Washington, D.C.: Alexander Graham Bell Association for the Deaf.   5, 8.1, 8.2, 8.3.

Blaney, N., et al. (1977). Interdependence in the classroom: A field study. *Journal of Educational Psychology,* 69, 121–27.   9.

Blankenship, C. and Lilly, S. (1981). *Mainstreaming students with learning and behavior problems.* New York: Holt, Rinehart and Winston.   6, 8.2.

Blanton, R. L., Odon, P. and McIntyre, C. (1970). *Symbolic and linguistic processes in the deaf: Final report.* Nashville, Tennessee: Vanderbilt University. ERIC Document Reproduction Service.   5, 8.1, 8.3.

Blatt, B. (1970). *Exodus from pandemonium: Human abuse and a reformation of public policy.* Boston, Massachusetts: Allyn & Bacon, Inc.   1.

Blatt, B., Biklen, D. and Bogdan, R. (Eds.) (1977). *An alternative textbook in special education.* Denver, Colorado: Love Publishing Company.   5, 6.

Blatt, B. (1979). A drastically different analysis in mainstreaming all sides to an issue. *Mental Retardation.* 17, 303–6.   1, 6.

Blatt, B. (1981). *In and out of mental retardation.* Baltimore, Maryland: University Park Press.   1.

Bloom, B. (1956). *Taxonomy of educational objectives. Handbook I: Cognitive domain.* New York: McKay.   5, 8, 8.2, 8.3.

Bloom, B. (1971). Mastery learning. In J. Block (Ed.), *Mastery learning: Theory and practice.* New York: Holt, Rinehart and Winston.   5, 8, 8.2, 8.3.

Bloom, B., Hastings, J. and Madaus, G. (1971). *Handbook on formative and summative evaluation of student learning.* New York: McGraw-Hill.   5, 8.1, 8.2, 8.3.

Boardman, Sharon G. (Ed.) (1980). *Inservice programs for helping regular classroom teachers implement public law 94-142.* Washington, D.C.: Clearinghouse on Teacher Education.   3, 6, 7.

Bogdan, R. and Biklin, D. (1988). Handicapism. *Social Policy,* 45, 14–19.

5.

Bohart, A. C. (1977). Role playing and interpersonal conflict reduction. *Journal of Counseling Psychology,* 24, 15–24.

4, 8.2.

Brewer, G. and Kakalek, J. (1979). *Handicapped children — strategies for improving services.* New York: McGraw Hill.

1, 6.

Bronson, S., Cassidy, S., Schiffman, G. and Tablin, G. (1982). Personal computers for the learning disabled. *Journal of Learning Disabilities,* 15, 42–46.

8.2.

Brophy, J. E., and Good, T. L. (1970). Teachers communication of differential expectation for children's classroom performance. *Journal of Educational Psychology,* 61, 365–74.

4.

Burg, Leslie and Kaufman, Maurice. (1980). Laws about special education: Their impact on the use of reading specialists. *The Reading Teacher,* 34, 187–91.

1, 2, 3, 6.

Burrello, L. and Sage, D. (1979). *Leadership and change in special education.* New Jersey: Prentice Hall.

1.

Burt, M., and Dulag, H. (1978). Some guidelines for the assessment of oral language proficiency and dominance. *TESOL Quarterly* 12, #2, 177–92.

8.1.

Burwell, Melvin A. (1980). An administrative perspective on implementing a learning disabilities program under P.L. 94-142. *The Forum,* New York State Federation of Chapters of the Council for Exceptional Children. 6, 122–26.

3.

Byford, Evelyn M. (1979). Mainstreaming: The effect on regular teacher training programs. *Journal of Teacher Education,* 30, 23–34.

3.

Carlson, B. and Ginglend, D. (1961). *Play activities for the retarded child.* Nashville, Tennessee, Abingdon Press.

8.2.

Carroll, J. (1971). Problems of measurement related to the concept of learning for mastery. In J. Block (Ed.) *Mastery learning: Theory and practice.* New York: Holt, Rinehart and Winston.

8, 8.1, 8.2.

Chaffin, J. (1974). Will the real mainstreaming program, please stand up! *Focus on Exceptional Children.* 6. 1–18.

6.

Chaiken, A., Sigler, E., and Derleger, V. (1974). Non-verbal mediators of teacher expectance effects. *Journal of Personality and Social Psychology,* 30, 144–49.

4.

Chaiken, W., and Jarper, M. (1979). *Mainstreaming the learning disabled adolescent: A staff development guide.* Springfield, Illinois: Charles C. Thomas.

6, 7, 8.1, 8.2, 8.3.

Champagne, D. and Goldman, R. (1975). *Handbook for managing individualized learning in the classroom.* Englewood Cliffs, New Jersey: Educational Technology Publishers.

7, 8.1, 8.2, 8.3.

Charrow, V. R. (1974). *Deaf English: An investigation of the written competence of deaf adolescents.* Technical Report No. 236. Stanford, California: Stanford University. ERIC Document Reproduction Service.   5.

Charrow, V. R. and Fletcher, J. D. (1974). English as the second language of deaf children. *Developmental Psychology,* 10, 463–70.   5, 8.1.

Childs, R. E., (1975). Review of the research concerning mainstreaming. *Journal for Special Educators of the Mentally Retarded.* 11, 106–12.   1, 2, 3, 4, 6, 7.

Chinn, P. C., Winn, J. and Walters, R. (1978). *Two-way talking with parents of special children.* St. Louis, Missouri: Mosby/Times Mirror.   3, 4.

Cicchelli, T. and Newman, D. (1981). *The effects of instructional patterns, aptitude and academic engagement on student academic performance.* Paper presented at the meeting of the American Education Research Association, Los Angeles, California.   8.1, 8.2.

Cicchelli, T. (1982). Effects of direct and indirect instruction patterns and prior achievement on post-course achievement. *Journal of Instructional Psychology,* 9, 176–89.   8.1, 8.2.

Cicchelli, T. (1983). Forms and functions of instruction patterns: Direct and nondirect. *Instructional Science,* 12, 343–83.   8.1, 8.2.

Cicchelli, T. (1983). Implementing the direct instruction pattern: A study with primary grade low SES children. *Urban Education,* 17, 419–30.   3, 8.1, 8.2.

Cicchelli, T. and Baecher, R. (1983). Concerns, uses systems: Data-based inservicing for change. Paper presented at the meeting of the American Education Research Association, Montreal, Canada.   1, 7, 8.2.

Cicchelli, T. and Baecher, R. (1984). Microcomputers in the classroom. A study of teacher concerns. *Journal of Computing Research.* 1, 55–65.   7, 8.2.

Clarizio, H. and McCoy, G. (1970). *Behavior disorders in school-aged children.* Scranton, Pennsylvania: Chandler Publishing Co.   5, 8.1, 8.2, 8.3.

Clay, M. (1980). *The early detection of reading difficulties: A diagnostic survey with recovery procedures.* Exeter, New Hampshire: Heinemann Educational Books, Inc.   8.1, 8.2, 8.3.

Clymer, T. (1969). *Reading 360.* Boston, Massachusetts: Ginn and Company.   8.1.

Cochrane, P. and Westling, D. (1977). The principal and mainstreaming: Ten suggestions for success. *Educational Leadership,* 34, 506–10.   3, 6, 7.

Cohen, S. B. (1983). Assigning report card grades to the mainstreamed child. *Teaching Exceptional Children,* 15, 86–99.   8.3.

Cohn, M. (1979). *Helping your teen-age student: What parents can do to improve reading and study skills.* New York: E.P. Dutton.   5, 6, 7, 8.2.

Connell, D. (1980). *ITL (Integrated Total Language).* Novato, California: Academic Therapy Publication.   8.1, 8.2, 8.3.

Connelly, A., Natchman, W. and Pritchett, E. (1971). *Key math: Diagnostic arithmetic test.* Circle Pines, Minnesota: American Guidance Services.   8.1.

Connor, James P. (1974). *Classroom activities for helping children with special needs: Classroom activities for helping hyperactive children.* West Nyack, New York: Center for Applied Research in Education.   8.2.

Conrad, R. (1970). How do the deaf remember words? *Teacher of the Deaf,* 68, 3–12.   8.2, 8.3.

Cook, J. E. and Earley, F. (1979). *Remediating reading disabilities: Simple things that work.* Germantown, Maryland: Aspen Systems Corporation.   5, 8.1, 8.2, 8.3.

Cooper, H. M. (1979). Pygmalion grows up: A model for teacher expectations, communication and performance influence. *Review of Educational Research,* 49, 389–410.   4.

Corrigan, Dean. (1978). Political and moral contexts that produced P.L. 94-142. *Journal of Teacher Education,* 29, 10–14.   1, 2, 4.

Corrigan, P. and Howey, K. (1980). *Special education in transition: Concepts to guide the education of experienced teachers.* Reston, Virginia: Council for Exceptional Children, V–VI.   1, 7.

Cruickshank, W. M. (1977). Myths and realities in learning disabilities. *Journal of Learning Disabilities,* 10, 57–64.   5.

Cruickshank, W. M., Morse, W. and Johns, J. (1980). *Learning disabilities: The struggle from adolescence toward adulthood.* Syracuse, New York: Syracuse University Press.   5, 8.2.

Cruickshank, W. (1981). *Concepts in special education: Selected writings, volume I.* Syracuse, New York: Syracuse University Press.   1.

Cruickshank, W. (1981). *Concepts in learning disabilities: Selected writings, volume II.* Syracuse, New York: Syracuse University Press.   5.

Cruickshank, W. and Kliebham, J. M. (Eds.) (1984). *Early adolescence to early adulthood.* Syracuse, New York: Syracuse University Press.   1.

Cummins, J. (1983). Conceptual and linguistic foundations of language assessment. In S. Seidner (Ed.) *Issues of language assessment. Vol. II: Language assessment and curriculum planning.* Illinois State Board of Education.   5, 8.1.

Cummins, J. (1979). Linguistic interdependence and the educational development of bilingual children. *Review of Educational Research,* 49, 222–51.

Das, J. P. and Baine, D. (1978). *Mental retardation for special educators.* Springfield, Illinois: Charles C. Thomas. 5.

Davis, J. (1977). *Our forgotten children: Hard-of-hearing pupils in the schools.* Minneapolis, Minnesota: Audio Visual Library Service, University of Minnesota. 5, 8.1, 8.2, 8.3.

Davis, M. (1980). *Typing keys for remediation of reading and spelling.* Novato, California: Academic Therapy Publications. 8.2.

Davis, O. L., et al. (1977). Curriculum materials used by eleven-year-old pupils: An analysis using the Annehurst Classification System. A paper presented at the annual meeting of the American Educational Research Assn., New York. 8.1.

Davis, W. E. (1980). *Educator's resource guide to special education.* Rockleigh, New Jersey: Longwood, Allyn and Bacon. 7, 8.1.

Deal, T. E. and Celotti, L. (1980). How much influence do (and can) educational administrators have on a classroom? *Phi Delta Kappan,* 61, 471–73. 3, 6, 7.

DeAvila, E. and Duncan, S. (1980). The language minority child: A psychological, linguistic, and social analysis. In J. Alatis (Ed.). *Current issues in bilingual education,* Georgetown University Round Table on Language and Linguistics. Washington, D.C.: Georgetown University Press. 5, 8.1.

DeAvila, E. and Duncan, S. (1977). *Language assessment scales.* Monterey, California: Publishers Test Service. 8.1.

Degler, L. and Risko, J. (1979). Teaching reading to mainstreamed sensory impaired children. *The Reading Teacher,* 32. 8.1, 8.2.

De Haan, R. F. and Kough, J. (1956). *Helping children with special needs, Volume II.* Chicago, Illinois: Science Research Associates, Inc. 5, 8.2.

Deno, E. N. (Ed.). (1974). *Instructional alternatives for exceptional children.* Reston, Virginia: Council for Exceptional Children. 6, 7, 8.2.

Deno, E. (1978). Educating children with emotional, learning and behavior problems. Minneapolis: University of Minnesota, National Support Systems Project. 6, 7, 8.2.

DesJardins, C. (1971). *How to organize an effective parent group and move bureaucracies.* Chicago, Illinois: Coordinating Council for Handicapped Children and Governor's Committee on the Handicapped. 1, 2, 4, 6, 7.

DesJardins, C. and Hull, R. (1977). *Rights handbook for handicapped children and adults.* Chicago, Illinois: Coordinating Council for handicapped children and Governor's Committee on the Handicapped. 2.

DeVries, D. and Edward, K. (1974). Student teams and learning games: Their effects on cross-race and cross-sex interaction, *Journal of Educational Psychology,* 66, 741–49. 4, 8.2, 9.

Dewar, R. K. (1982). Peer acceptance of handicapped students, *Exceptional Children,* 14, 188–93.   4, 8.2, 9.

Dexter, B. L. (1977). *Special education and the classroom teacher: Concepts, perspectives, and strategies.* Springfield, Illinois: Charles C. Thomas.   3, 6, 7, 8.

Di Rise, W. J. and Butz, G. (1979). *Writing behavioral contracts.* Bellevue, Washington: Edmark Associates.   9.

Dixon, B., Shaw, S. and Bersk, J. (1980). Administrator's role in fostering the mental health of special services personnel, *Exceptional Children,* 47, 30–34.   3.

Dolson, D.P. (Project team leader) (1981). *Schooling and language minority students: A theoretical framework.* Los Angeles Evaluation, Dissemination, and Assessment Center, California State University, Los Angeles.   1, 5, 6.

Donaldson, J. (1980). Changing attitudes toward handicapped persons: A review and analysis of research. *Exceptional Children,* 46, 504.   4.

Doyle, W. (1977). Learning the classroom environment: An ecological analysis, *Journal of Teacher Education,* 28, 51–55.   6, 9.

Drew, M. E. (1979). On using methods and materials for the physically disabled with the learning disabled. *Kappa Delta Pi Record,* 16, 45–47.   8.2.

Dulay, H., Burt, M. and Krashen, S. (1982). *Language two.* New York: Oxford University Press.   5.

Dunn, L. and Markwardt, F. (1979). *Peabody individual achievement test (PIAT).* Circle Pines, Minnesota: American Guidance Service.   8.1.

Dunn, R. S. and Cole, R. W. (1979). Inviting malpractice through mainstreaming. *Educational Leadership,* 36, 302–5.   2.

Durast, W., et al. (1971). *Metropolitan achievement test (MAT).* New York: Harcourt Brace Jovanovich.   8.1.

Ehly, S. and Larsen, S. (1982). *Peer tutoring for individualized instruction.* Rockleigh, New Jersey: Longwood Division, Allyn and Bacon.   8.2, 9.

Ensher, G., Blatt, B. and Winschel, J. (1977). Headstart for the handicapped: An audit of the congressional mandate. *Exceptional Children,* 43, 202–13.   1, 8.1.

Erickson, J. G. and Omark, D. R. (Eds.). (1981). *Communication assessment of the bilingual bicultural child: Issues and guidelines.* Baltimore, Maryland: University Park Press.   1, 8.1.

Evans, D. and Hall, J. (1978). *The delivery of educational services*

. . . *and the special child.* Palo Alto, California: VORT Corporation.   2, 6, 7.

Evans, J. and Hall, J. (1980). *Exceptional children: A reference book.* New York: Jeffrey Norton Publishers, Inc.   2, 5, 8.1, 8.2, 8.3.

Falik. L., et al. (1971). Evaluating the impact of the counseling-learning team on the elementary school. *School Counselor,* 19, 25–37.   3, 6, 7.

Fant, L. J. (1972). *Ameslan: An introduction to American sign language.* Northridge, California: Joyce Motion Picture Company.   8.2.

Farrald, R. R., et al. (1979). *A diagnostic and prescriptive technique-handbook II; Disabilities in arithmetic and mathematics/ approaches to diagnosis and treatment.* Sioux Falls, South Dakota: Adapt Press.   8.1, 8.2, 8.3.

Fenton, K. S., et al. (1977). *Role expectations: Implications for multi-disciplinary pupil programming.* Washington, D.C.: Office of Education, Bureau of Education for the Handicapped, Division of Innovation and Development, State Programs Studies Branch.   3, 6, 7.

Fenton, K. S., et al. (1978). *Recognition of team goals: An essential step toward rational decision making.* Washington, D.C.: U.S. Office of Education, Bureau of Education for the Handicapped, Division of Innovation and Development, State Programs, Studies Branch.   6, 7.

Feuerstein, R., Rand, Y. and Hoffman, M. (1979). *The dynamic assessment of retarded performers: The learning potential assessment device, theory instruments and techniques.* Baltimore, Maryland: University Park Press.   5, 8.1.

Feuerstein, R. (1980). *Instructional enrichments: An intervention program for cognitive modifiability.* Baltimore, Maryland: University Park Press.   5, 8.2.

Finn, J. and Resnick, K. (1984). Issues in the instruction of mildly mentally retarded children. *Education Research,* 13, 9–11.   1.

Fox, J. (1978). Personal perspectives on educating handicapped children. *Journal of Teacher Education,* 29, 10–15.   3.

Frith, U. and Vogel, J. (1980). *Some perceptual prerequisites for reading.* Newark, Delaware: The International Reading Assn.   5, 8.1, 8.2, 8.3.

Frostig, M., Lefeuer, W. and Whittlesey, J. (1964). *Marianne Frostig developmental test of visual perception.* Palo Alto, California: Consulting Psychologists Press.   8.1.

Frostig, M. and Horne, D. (1964). *The Frostig program for the development of visual perception.* Chicago, Illinois: Follett.   5, 8.1, 8.2.

Frymier, J. R. (1977). *The Annehurst curriculum classification system: A practical way to individualize instruction.* West Lafayette, Indiana: Kappa Delta Pi.   8, 8.1, 9.

Gallagher, P. A. (1971). *Positive classroom performance: Techniques for changing behaviors.* Denver, Colorado: Love Publishing Co.   9.

Gardner, M. (1979). *Expressive one-word picture vocabulary test.* Novato, California: Academic Therapy Publications.   8.1.

Gardner, W. (1977). *Learning and behavior characteristics of exceptional children and youth: A humanistic behavioral approach.* Boston, Massachusetts: Allyn and Bacon.   5, 9.

Garton, M. D. (1974). *Teaching the educable mentally retarded.* Springfield, Illinois: Charles C. Thomas.   5, 8.2.

Gay, G. (1980). Conceptual models of the curriculum planning process in Arthur W. Foshay (Ed.), *Considered action for curriculum improvement.* Alexandria, Virginia: Association for Supervision and Curriculum Development, 120–42.   6, 7.

Geoffrton, L. D. and Schuster, K. (1980). *Auditory handicaps and reading: An annotated bibliography.* Newark, Delaware: The International Reading Assn.   8.1, 8.2, 8.3.

George, W. C. (1980). *Educating the Gifted: Acceleration and enrollment.* Baltimore, Maryland: The Johns Hopkins University Press.   5, 8, 8.2.

Gerber, A. and Bryer, D. (Eds.). (1981). *Language and learning disabilities.* Baltimore, Maryland: University Park Press.   5, 8.1, 8.2., 8.3.

Gilliam, J. E. (1979). Contributions and status rankings of educational planning committee participants. *Exceptional Children,* 45, 466–68.   4, 6, 7.

Gingold, W. and Gingold, P. (1973). *Individualization of instruction.* Minneapolis, Minnesota: Paul S. Amidon and Associates, Inc.   8.2, 9.

Gladstone, G. S. (No date given). *A dialogue on education and control of human behavior,* Six Audio Cassettes which contain the remarks of Carl R. Rogers and B. F. Skinner. New York: Jeffrey Norton Publishers, Inc.   4, 9.

Gliedman, J. and Roth, W. (1980). *The unexpected minority: Handicapped children in America.* Report by the Carnegie Council on Children, New York: Harcourt Brace Jovanovich.   1, 2, 4.

Glover, J. A. and Gary, A. L. (1976). *Mainstreaming exceptional children: How to make it work.* Pacific Grove, California: The Boxwood Press.   1, 2, 6, 7, 8.

Goldbaum, J. and Rucker, C. (1977). *Assessment data and the child study team training program;* Book of readings. Austin, Texas: Special Education Associates.   6, 7, 8.1.

Golden, J. and Anderson, S. (1979). *Learning disabilities and brain dysfunction: An introduction for educators and parents.* Springfield, Illinois: Charles C. Thomas.   5, 8.2.

Goldenberg, E. P. (1979). *Special technology for special children: Computers as prostheses to serve communication and autonomy in the education of handicapped children.* Baltimore, Maryland: University Park Press.   8.2, 9.

Goldstein, et al. (1980). *Skill-streaming the adolescent.* Champaign, Illinois: Research Press Co.   5, 8.2, 9.

Golick, M. (1978). *Deal me in! The use of playing cards in teaching and learning.* New York: Jeffrey Norton Publishing, Inc.   8.2.

Gollay, E. and Bennett, A. (1976). *The college guide for students with disabilities.* Cambridge, Maryland: Abt Publications.   2.

Golumb, C. and Cornelius, C. (1974). Symbolic play and its cognitive significance. *Developmental Psychology,* 11, 313–20.   8.2, 9.

Goodman, L. and Hammill, D. (1973). The effectiveness of the Kephart-Getman activities in developing perceptual-motion cognitive skills. *Focus on Exceptional Children,* 9, 1–9.   9, 1–9, 8.2.

Gormley, K. A. and Franzen, A. M. (1978). Why can't the deaf read? Comments on asking the wrong questions. *American Annals of the Deaf,* 123, 542–47.   5, 8.1.

Gorton, R. A. (1980). *School administration and supervision: Important issues, concepts and case studies.* Dubuque, Iowa: Wm. C. Brown Company.   3, 6, 7.

Gould, E. (1978). *Arts and crafts for physically handicapped and mentally disabled.* New York: Charles C. Thomas.   8.2.

Graham, M. D. (1978). *Cleft palate: Middle ear disease and hearing loss.* Springfield, Illinois: Charles C. Thomas.   5, 8.1.

Grant, W. D. (1978). *The Brill educational achievement test.* A review, *American Annals of the Deaf,* 123, 522–23.   8.1.

Gray, L. (1978). *Peer teaching handbook.* Pittsburgh, Pennsylvania: Peer Teaching project.   9.

Gregory, M. K. (1978). *Perceptions of school psychologists on interdisciplinary teams.* A paper presented at the national association of school psychologists conference, New York, New York.   4, 6, 7.

Grzynkowicz, W. (1979). *Basic education for children with learning disabilities.* Springfield, Illinois: Charles C. Thomas.   6, 7.

Grzynkowicz, W. (1980). *Guidelines for the preparation of teachers in compliance with U.S. public law 94-142.* Harrisburg, Pennsylvania: Pennsylvania Dept. of Education.   6, 7, 8, 9.

Guinagh, B. (1980). The social integration of handicapped children. *Phi Delta Kappan,* 62, 27–29.   4, 9.

Gumaer, J., et al. (1975). Affective education through role playing. *The Personnel and Guidance Journal,* 53, 604–8.   8.2, 9.

Guthrie, J. (Ed.). (1980). *Aspects of reading acquisition.* Baltimore, Maryland: The Johns Hopkins University Press.   8.1, 8.2, 8.3.

Hagen, E. (1980). *Identification of the gifted.* New York: Teachers College Press, Columbia University.   5, 8.1, 8.3.

Hagerty, R. and Howard, T. (1978). *How to make federal mandatory special education work for you: A handbook for educators and consumers.* Springfield, Illinois: Charles C. Thomas.   1, 2, 6, 7.

Haisley, F. B. and Gilberts, R. D. (1978). Individual competencies needed to implement P.L. 94-142. *Journal of Teacher Education,* 29, 30–33.   3.

Halliday, C. and Kurzhals, I. (1976). *Stimulating environments for children who are visually impaired.* New York: Charles C. Thomas.   8.2, 9.

Hamby, J. D. (1977). *Instructional exceptional prescriptions.* Birmingham, Alabama: Ebsco Curriculum Materials.   8.

Hammill, D. and Wiederhalt, J. (1973). Reveiw of the Frostig visual perception test and the related training program in L. Mann and D. A. Sabatino (Eds.). *The first review of special education.* Philadelphia, Pennsylvania: J. S. E. Press.   8.1.

Hammill, D. and Larsen, S. (1974). The effectiveness of psycholinguistic training. *Exceptional Children,* 41, 5–14.   8.2.

Haring, N. (1974). *Behavior of exceptional children: An introduction to exceptional children.* Columbus, Ohio: Charles E. Merrill.   5, 9.

Harley, R., Henderson, F. and Truan, M. (1979). *The teaching of braille reading.* Springfield, Illinois: Charles C. Thomas.   8.2.

Harper, R. and Kilarr, G. (1978). *Reading and the law.* Newark, Delaware: International Reading Assn. ERIC/RCS.   2.

Harris, N. M. (1980). *Improving staff performance through inservice education.* Rockleigh, New Jersey: Longwood Division of Allyn and Bacon.   6, 7.

Hasazi, S. E., Rice, P. D. and York, R. (1979). *Mainstreaming: Merging regular and special education.* Bloomington, Indiana: Phi Delta Kappa Fastbacks.   3.

Hedley, E. (1971). *Boating for the handicapped.* Albertson, New York: National Center for Employment of the Handicapped at the Human Resources Center.   4, 5.

Herlihy, J. G. and Herlihy, M. T. (Eds.). (1980). *Mainstreaming in the social studies.* Washington, D.C.: National Council for the Social Studies.   8.2.

Hertel, P. M. and Hertel, N. W. (1977). *Learning disabilities: Getting into the mainstream.* Johnstown, Pennsylvania: Mafex Publications.   5, 8.2.

Hewett, Frank M. (1974). *Education of exceptional learners.* Westport, Connecticut: Technomic Publishing Co.   1, 6, 7, 9.

Hilliard, A. G. (1974). Mainstreaming: Assessment issues in Patrick O'Donnell and Robert H. Bradfield (Eds.). *Mainstreaming: Controversy and Consensus,* San Rafael, California: Academic Therapy Publications.   8.1.

Hively, Wells and Reynolds, M. C. (1975). *Domain-referenced testing in special education.* Reston, Virginia: The Council for Exceptional Children.   8.1.

Hoback, J. and Perry, P. (1980). Common sense about educating the gifted and talented. *Educational Leadership,* 37, 346–50.   5, 6, 7, 8, 9.

Hobbs, N. (1979). *The futures of children.* San Francisco, California: Jossey-Bass, Inc.   4, 8.1.

Hoffman, P. L. (1979). Mainstreaming in education: A new challenge. *The Forum,* The New York State Federation of Councils for Exceptional Children, 5, 14.   1, 2, 6, 7, 9.

Hofmeister, Alan. (1984). *Microcomputer applications in the classroom.* New York: Holt, Rinehart and Winston.   5, 8.2.

Hogenson, D. (1973). A multidisciplinary approach to the in-school management of acutely anxious and depressed students in a large urban senior high school setting. *Pupil Personnel Services Journal,* 3, 29–31.   6, 7, 9.

Holmann, H. W., et al. (1979). The spelling proficiency of deaf children. *American Annals of the Deaf,* 121, 489–93.   5, 8.1., 8.2.

Homme, L., et al. (1978). *How to use contingency contracting in the classroom.* Champaign, Illinois: Research Press.   9.

Howath, L. J. (1978). *The effects of parental requests on the selection of educational placements by child study team members.* Unpublished doctoral dissertation, University of Connecticut.   3, 6, 7.

Hull, D. and Reuter, J. (1977). Development of charitable behavior in elementary school children. *Journal of Genetic Psychology,* 131, 147–53.   4, 8.2, 9.

Hull, D., and Reuter, J. (1962). *Human ecology and susceptibility to the chemical environment.* Springfield, Illinois: Charles C. Thomas.   5, 8.1.

Hyman, I., et al. (1973). Patterns of inter-professional conflict resolution in school child study teams. *Journal of School Psychology,* 11, 187–95. 3, 6, 7.

Hynd, G. W. (Ed.). (1983). *The school psychologist.* Syracuse, New York: Syracuse University Press. 2, 3, 7, 8.1, 8.3.

Iano, R., et al. (1974). Socio-metric status of retarded children in an integrative program. *Exceptional Children,* 40, 267–72. 4.

Iano, R., et al. (1980). IEP development: The cost in time and money. Information Bulletin, NYSUT, #798016, 1–3. 2, 3.

Iano, R., et al. (1980). Inservice resources to improve learning opportunities for handicapped children. Inservice, Newsletter of the National Council of States on Inservice Education. Syracuse, New York, 6. 1–6. 2.

Jamison, D., Suppes, P. and Wells, S. (1974). The effectiveness of alternative instructional media: A survey. *Review of Educational Research,* 44, 1–67. 5, 8.2.

Jastak, J. and Jastak, S. (1965). *Wide range achievement test* (WRAT), Wilmington, Delaware: Guidance Associates. 8.1.

Jeffers, J., and Bailey, M. (1979). *Look, now hear this: Combined auditory training and speedreading instruction.* Springfield, Illinois: Charles C. Thomas. 5, 8.2.

Johnson, D. W. and Johnson, R. T. (1975). *Learning together and alone: Cooperation, competition and individualization.* Englewood Cliffs, New Jersey: Prentice-Hall. 8.2, 9.

Johnson, S. and Johnson, R. B. (1970). *Developing individualized instruction material.* Palo Alto, California: Westinghouse Press. 8.2, 9.

Jones, Philip. (1981). *A practical guide to federal special education law.* New York: Holt, Rinehart and Winston. 3.1.

Jones, R. L. (Ed.). (1976). *Mainstreaming and the minority child.* Reston, Virginia: The Council for Exceptional Children. 4, 8.1.

Jordan, June B. (Ed.). (1978). *Exceptional students in secondary schools.* Reston, Virginia: The Council for Exceptional Children. 4, 6, 7, 8, 8.1, 8.2.

Joyce, B. and Harootunian, B. (1967). *The structure of teaching.* Chicago, Illinois: Science Research Associates. 8.2.

Joyce, B. and Weil, M. (1980). *The models of teaching.* Englewood, New Jersey: Prentice-Hall. 8.2.

Joyce, B. R. (Ed.). (1978). *Involvement: A study of shared governance of inservice teacher education.* Syracuse, N.Y.: National Dissemination Center at Syracuse University. 6, 7.

Kaufman, A. S. (1981). The WISC-R and learning disabilities assessment: State of the art. *Journal of Learning Disabilities,* 14, 520–25.   8.1.

Keiffer, L. I. (1979). Mainstreaming: The challenge of professional preparation. *The Forum,* New York State Federation of Councils for Exceptional Children, 5, 9.   6, 7.

Keller, G. (1974). *Flexibility language dominance test, Spanish/English.* Monterey, California: Publishers Test Service.   8.1.

Kelly, E. J. (1976). *Parent-teacher interaction: A special education perspective.* New York: Special Education Publications, A Division of Bernie Straub Publishing Co.   3, 6, 7, 8.1, 8.2, 8.3.

Kephart, M. (1966). *The Purdue perceptual motor survey.* Columbus, Ohio: Charles Merrill.   8.1.

Kester, S. and Letchworth G. (1972). Communication of teacher expectations and their effects on achievement and attitudes of secondary school students. *Journal of Education Research,* 66, 51–55.   4.

Kirk, S., McCarthy, J. and Kirk, W. (1968). *The Illinois test of psycholinguistic abilities.* Urbana, Illinois: University of Illinois Press.   8.1.

Kirk, S. A., Kliebman, J. M. and Lerner, J. (1978). *Teaching reading to slow and disabled learners.* Boston, Massachusetts: Houghton Mifflin Company.   5, 8.2.

Kirp, D. L., Buss, W. and Kuriloff, P. (1974). Legal reform of special education: Empirical studies and procedural proposals. *California Law Review,* 62, 40–155.   2.

Kirschenbaum, L. (1977). *Advanced values clarification.* La Jolla, California: University Associates.   4, 8.2.

Klein, A. F. (1956). *Role playing in leadership training and group problem solving.* New York: Association Press.   4, 6, 7.

Kline, J. A. (1974). *Classroom management.* Duluth, Minnesota: The Instructor Publications, Inc.   4, 8.2, 9.

Klovekorn, M. R. (1980). P.L. 94-142 and its impact on educating our handicapped children and youth. *Kappa Delta Pi Record,* 17, 53–54.   1, 2.

Knoblock, P. (1973). Open education for emotionally disturbed children. *Exceptional Children,* 39, 358–65.   5, 6.

Krathwohl, D., Bloom, B. and Masia, B. (1964). *Taxonomy of educational objectives. Handbook II: Affective domain.* New York: McKay.   8.1, 8.2, 8.3.

Kretschmer, R. R. and Kretschmer, L. W. (1971). *Language development and intervention with the hearing impaired.* Baltimore, Maryland: University Park Press.

Kroth, R. L. and Scholl, G. T. (1978). *Getting schools involved with parents.* Reston, Virginia: The Council for Exceptional Children.   3, 6, 7, 8.1, 8.2, 8.

Kunzelman, J. and Koenig, C. (1980). *REFER; Rapid exam for early referral.* Columbus, Ohio: Charles E. Merrill.   8.1.

Lambert, N. M., Windmiller, M., Cole, L. J. and Figueroa, R. A. (1975). *AAMD adaptive behavior scale manual* (Rev. ed.). Washington, D.C.: American Association on Mental Deficiency.   8.1.

Lambert, W. E. and Tucker, G. R. (1972). *Bilingual education of children: The St. Lambert experiment.* Rowley, Massachusetts: Newburg House.   5, 6.

Lee, L. (1971). *Northwestern syntax screening test.* Evanston, Illinois: Northwestern University Press.   8.1.

Lemleck, Johanna Kasin. (1979). Preparation for individualized educational programming: The communication gap. *Journal of Teacher Education,* 30, 21–23.   4, 6, 7, 8.

Lerner, Janet W. (1975). Remedial reading and learning disabilities: Are they the same or different? *Journal of Special Education,* 9, 119–31.   3, 8.1., 8.2, 8.3.

Lerner, J., Dawson, D. and Horvath, L. (1980). *Cases in learning and behavior problems: A guide to individualized education programs.* Boston, Massachusetts: Houghton Mifflin Company.   5, 8.2.

Lerner, J. (1981). *Learning disabilities* (3rd ed.). Boston, Massachusetts: Houghton Mifflin Company.   5.

Lindsay, Z. (1972). *Art and the handicapped child.* New York: Van Rostrand Reinhold Co.   8.2.

Linton, T. E. and Juul, K. D. (1980). Mainstreaming: Time for reassessment. *Educational Leadership,* 37, 433–37.   1, 2.

Lipham, J. M. and Hoch, J. A. Jr. (1974). *The principalship: Foundations and functions.* New York: Harper and Row.   3, 6, 7.

Lippman, L., and Goldberg, I. I. (1973). *Right to education.* New York: Columbia University, Teachers College.   2.

Lockhard, G. (1978). Mainstreaming: One child's experience. *Phi Delta Kappan,* 59, 527–28.   4, 8.1, 8.2.

Lockridge, C. (1978). *Mainstreaming: Answers to your classroom management questions.* New York: Guidance Associates.   9.

Losen, S. M. and Diament, B. (1978). *Parent conferences in the schools: Procedures for developing effective partnership.* Boston, Massachusetts: Allyn and Bacon.   4, 6, 7.

Love, H. D. (1975). *Educating exceptional children in regular class-rooms*. Springfield, Illinois: Charles C. Thomas.   3, 8, 9.

Love, H. D. (1978). *Teaching physically handicapped children: Methods and materials*. Springfield, Illinois: Charles C. Thomas.   8.2, 9.

Love, Ruth (1981). Involving the community in the schools. *Education Update*, 8, 1-3.   6, 7.

Lowenbraun, S. and Affleck, J. Q. (1976). *Teaching mildly handicapped children in regular classes*. Columbus, Ohio: Charles E. Merrill Publications.   5, 8.1, 8.2, 8.3.

Maehr, Martin L. (1974). *Sociocultural origins of achievement*. Monterey, California: Brooks/Cole Publishing Company.   4.

Mager, R. G. (1973). *Measuring instructional intent*. Belmont, California: Fearon Publishers, Inc.   8.1, 8.3.

Mahon, T. (1981). *Assessing children with special needs*. New York: Holt, Rinehart, and Winston.   8.1.

Mann, P. H. and Suiter, P. (1974). *Handbook in diagnostic teaching: A learning disabilities approach*. Boston, Massachusetts: Allyn and Bacon, Inc.   8.1, 8.2, 8.3.

Mann, P. H. (1980). Inservice for mainstreaming: Educational services as continuous process. *New England Teacher Corps Exchange*, 1-2.   6, 7.

Manuele, C. and Cicchelli, T. (1983). Discipline revisited: Social skills programs and methods for the classroom. *Contemporary Education*, 5, 104-9.   5, 8.2, 9.

Masoodi, Bashir and Ban, J. R. (1980). Teaching the visually handicapped in regular classes. *Educational Leadership*, 37, 351-55.   8.1, 8.2, 8.3, 9.

Mauser, A. J. (1977). *Assessing the learning disabled: Selected instruments*. Guilford, Connecticut: Special Learning Corporation.   8.1.

Mauser, A. J. (1980). Maximizing teacher impact on the evaluation and placement of children with handicapping conditions. NYSUT *Information Bulletin*, June.   4, 6, 7.

McCabe, R. (1978). *Mc Cabe's test handbook*. Tigard, Oregon: C.C. Publications.   8.1.

McCarr, D. (1977). Individualized reading for junior and senior high school students. *American Annals for the Deaf*, 118, 488-95.   5, 8, 8.1, 8.2, 8.3.

McCarr, D. (Ed.). (1974). *Teacher recommended materials for use with hearing impaired students*. Las Cruces, New Mexico: Southwest Regional Media Center for the Deaf.   8.2.

McCarthy, F. E. (1978). Remedial reading and learning disabilities in battle. *The Reading Teacher*, 31, 484-86.   3.

McCarthy, M. M. (1971). The right to education: From Rodriguez to Gross. *Educational Leadership,* 33, 519-21.   1, 2.

McClelland, D. (1973). Testing for competence rather than for intelligence. *American Psychologist,* 28, 1-14.   8.1.

McKean, R. and Taylor, R. L. (1977). Supervisors help with mainstreaming. *Educational Leadership,* 34, 320.   3.

McKenzie, Hugh. (1976). Special education in Vermont: The consulting teacher approach in Patrick A. O'Donnell and Robert H. Bradfield (Eds.), *Mainstreaming: Controversy and consensus.* San Rafael, California: Academic Therapy Publications, 115-28.   6, 7, 8.

McLoughlin, J.A., Edge, D. and Strensky, B. (1978). Establishing new roles for parental involvement in the education process. *Journal of Learning Disabilities,* 2, 291-96.   3.

Meisgeier, Charles. (1976). The Houston plan: A program that works in Patrick O'Donnel and Robert H. Bradfield (Eds.), *Mainstreaming: Controversy and consensus.* San Rafael, California: Academic Therapy Publications, 99-114.   6, 7, 8.

Mercer, J. R. (1979). *System of multicultural pluralistic assessment (SOMPA) technical manual.* New York: Psychological Corporation.   8.1.

Messick, S. (1984). Assessment in context: Appraising student performance in relation to instructional quality. *Educational Researcher,* 13, 3-8.   8.1.

Meyen, Edward L. (1980). *Instructional based appraisal system.* Bellevue, Washington: Edmark Associates.   6, 7.

Meyers, C. E. (Ed.). (1978). *Quality of life in severely and profoundly mentally retarded people: Research foundations for improvement.* Washington, D.C.: American Association on Mental Deficiency.   4, 5.

Michaelis, C. T. (1980). *Home and school partnerships in exceptional education.* Gaithersburg, Maryland: Aspen Systems Corporation.   3, 6, 7.8.

Miller, W. H. (1978). *Reading diagnosis kit.* West Nyack, New York: Center for Applied Research in Education, Inc.   8.1.

Milofsky, D. (1977). Schooling for kids no one wants. *New York Times,* magazine section, January 2.   1, 2, 4.

Minskoff, E. (1982). Training L.D. students to cope with the everyday world. *Academic Therapy,* 17, 311-16.   5, 8.2.

Minskoff, E. (1982). Sharpening language skills in secondary L.D. students. *Academic Therapy,* 18 (1), 53-60.   5, 8.2.

Molloy, L. (1975). The handicapped child in the everyday classroom. *Phi Delta Kappan,* 56, 337-40   8.1, 9.

Moran, M. R. (1978). *Assessment of the exceptional learner in the regular classroom.* Denver, Colorado: Love Publishing Co.   8.1.

Morehead, D. M. (1976). *Normal and deficient child language.* Baltimore, Maryland: University Park Press.   8.1.

Mullins, J. B. (1979). *A teacher's guide to management of physically handicapped students.* Springfield, Illinois: Charles C. Thomas.   5, 8.2, 9.

Murray, F. B., and Pikulski, J. J. (1978). *The acquisition of reading: Cognitive, linguistic, and perceptual prerequisites.* Baltimore, Maryland: University Park Press.   8, 8.1, 8.2, 8.3.

Musgrave, R. G. (1975). *Individualized instruction: teaching strategies focusing on the learner.* Rockleigh, New Jersey: Longwood Division of Allyn and Bacon.   8.1, 8.2, 8.3, 9.

Myers, D. G., and Sinco, M. E. (1979). *Individual education programming for all teachers of the special needs learner.* Springfield, Illinois: Charles C. Thomas.   6, 7, 8, 8.1, 8.2, 8.3.

National Association of State Directors of Special Education Publications:

   An analysis of public law 94-142. Washington, D.C. (1977).   2.
   Education of the handicapped litigation brought under PL 94-142 and section 504. Washington, D.C. (1978).   2.
   Due process in special education: A case record. Washington, D.C. (1978).   2.
   Assistive devices for handicapped students. Washington, D.C. (1980).   2.

National Center for Education Statistics Bulletin: Geographic distribution, nativity and age distribution of language minorities in the United States, Spring 1976. *NCES,* 78–134.   1.

Neale, D., Bailey, W. J. and Rose, B. E. (1980). *Strategies for school improvement: Cooperative planning and organization development.* Rockleigh, New Jersey: Longwood Division of Allyn and Bacon.   3, 6, 7.

Neisworth, J. T., et al. (1977). *Student motivation and classroom management.* Bellevue, Washington: Edmark Associates.   9.

Nelson, R. (1978). *Creating community acceptance for handicapped people.* Springfield, Illinois: Charles C. Thomas.   4.

New York City Board of Education, Division of Special Education (April, 1984). *Special education instructional services and related services.* Part 200 Series Regulations of the NYS Commissioner of Education. Working Draft.   5, 8.1.

New York State Education Department Publications:

Committee on the handicapped, handbook for the committee members. Albany, N.Y. (1978). 3, 4.

The individualized education program—A guide for development. Albany, N.Y. (1979). 6, 7, 8.

The role of the school board member in the education of children with handicapping conditions. Albany, N.Y. (1980). 2, 3.

Regulations of the Commissioner of Education—Part 200—handicapped children. Albany, N.Y. (1980). 2.

Helping children with handicapping conditions in New York State (1980–1981).

The State Plan. Albany, N.Y. (1980). 2.

Your child's right to an education. Albany, N.Y. (1980). 2.

Noland, R. L. (1972). *Counseling parents of the mentally retarded.* New York: Charles C. Thomas. 3, 4.

Norduff, P., and Robbins, C. (Eds.). (1971). *Music therapy in special education.* New York: The John Day Co. 8.2, 9.

Northcott, W. H. (1973). *The hearing impaired child in a regular classroom: Pre-school, elementary, and secondary years.* Washington, D.C.: Alexander Graham Bell Associates. 5, 7, 8, 8.1, 8.2.

Oakland, T. M. (1977). *Psychological and educational assessment of minority children.* New York: Brunner Co. 8.1.

Oakland, T. M., Tombari, M. and Acker, E. (1978). *Factors influencing reading and math achievement: An examination of social class and racial-ethnic differences.* Paper presentation at the meeting of the American Psychological Association, Toronto, Canada. 5.

Oakland, T. M., and Feigenbaum, D. (1980). Comparisons of the psychometric characteristics of the adaptive behavior inventory for children for different subgroups of children. *Journal of School Psychology, 18,* 307–16. 8.1.

O'Donnell, Patrick, and Bradfield, R. H. (1976). (Eds.). *Mainstreaming: Controversy and consensus.* San Rafael, California: Academic Therapy Publications. 1, 2, 3, 4, 5, 6, 7, 8, 9.

Ogletree, E. J. and Garcia, D. (Eds.). (1975). *Education of the Spanish speaking urban child.* Springfield, Illinois: Charles C. Thomas. 1, 2, 8.

Oller, J. W., Jr. (1979). *Language tests at school: A pragmatic approach.* London: Longman. 8.1.

Oller, J. W., Jr., and Perkins, K. (1980). *Research in language testing.* Rawley, Massachusetts: Newburgh House. 8.1.

Omark, D. R., and Erickson, J. G. (Eds.), (1983). *The bilingual exceptional child.* San Diego, California: College-Hill Press. 5.

Owen, Louise. (1978). The placement and preparation of the handicapped child in the regular classroom. *Kappa Delta Pi Record,* 15, 58–59. 8, 8.1, 8.2, 8.3, 9.

Oxford, R., Pol, L., Lopez, Stupp, P., Gendell, and Peng, S. (1981). Projections of non-English language background and limited English proficient persons in the United States in the year 2000: Educational planning in the demographic context. *NABE Journal* V, #3, 1–30. 1.

Padilla, R. (Ed.). (1981). *Bilingual education technology.* Ethnoperspectives in bilingual education, research series, Vol. III. Department of Foreign Languages, Eastern Michigan University, Ypsilanti, Mi. 5.

Papert, S. (1980). *Mindstorms.* New York: Basic Books. 8.2.

Parke, B. (1983). Use of self-instructional materials with gifted students. *Gifted Child Quarterly,* 10, 442–525. 8.2.

Parker, C. A. (1975). *Psychological consultation: Helping teachers meet special needs.* Reston, Virginia: The Council for Exceptional Children. 6, 7, 8.

Paul, J. L., Turnbull, A. P. and Cruickshank, W. M. (1979). *Mainstreaming: A practical guide.* New York: Schocken Books. 6, 7, 8.

Pavlov, I. (1927). *Conditioned-reflexes.* (Translated by G. V. Anep). London: Oxford University Press. 5, 8.2.

Payne, R. and Murray, C. (1974). Principals' attitudes toward integration of the handicapped. *Exceptional Children,* 41, 123–25. 3, 4.

Pennwright, S. (1979). Mainstreaming from the view of a physical education teacher. *The Forum,* The New York State Federation of Councils of Exceptional Children, 5, 16. 3, 4, 8, 9.

Perlman, R., Zabel, M. and Zabel, R. (Eds.). (1982). *Special education for exceptional bilingual students: A handbook for educators.* Midwest National Origin Desegregation Assistance Center, University of Wisconsin-Milwaukee. 5.

Pfeiffer, S. I. (1978). *The interdisciplinary team in the schools: Recurring problems and some possible solutions.* Paper presented at the Council for Exceptional Children, Dallas, Texas. 3, 6, 7.

Piaget, J. (1951). *Play, dreams and imitation in childhood.* New York: Norton. 8.1, 8.2.

Piper, T. (1974). *Classroom management and behavioral objectives: Applications for behavior modification.* Belmont, California: Lear Siegler, Inc. and Fearon Publishers. 8.2, 9.

Piper, T. (1974). *Materials for classroom management.* Belmont, California: Lear Siegler, Inc. and Fearon Publishers.   9.

Pipes, L. (Ed.). (1977). *Teacher centers as an approach to staff development in special education.* Arlington, Virginia: ERIC Document Reproduction Service,   6, 7.

Platt, J. M. and Platt, J. S. (1980). Volunteers for special education: A mainstreaming support system. *Teaching Exceptional Children,* Fall, 31.   3.

Popham, W. and Roy, R. (1969). Implications of criterion-referenced measurements. *Journal of Educational Measurement,* 6, 1–9.   8.1, 8.2, 8.3, 9.

Popham, W. (Ed.). (1971). *Criterion-referenced measurement—An introduction.* Englewood Cliffs, New Jersey: Educational Technology Publishers.   8.1, 8.2, 8.3, 9.

Premack, D. (1965). *Reinforcement theory.* D. Levine (Ed.). Nebraska symposium on motivation. Lincoln, Nebraska: University of Nebraska Press.   5, 8, 8.2, 9.

Reid, B. A. and Reid, W. R. (1974). Role expectations of paraprofessional staff in special education. *Focus on Exceptional Children,* 7, 1–14.   3, 4.

Reschly, D. and Gresham, F. (1983, June). *Use of social competence measures to facilitate parent and teacher involvement and nonbiased assessment* (final report). Washington, D.C.: Department of Education, Office of Special Education.   8.1.

Reschly, D. (1984). Beyond I.Q. test bias: The national academy panel's analysis of minority EMR overrepresentation. *Educational Researcher,* 13, 15–19.   8.1.

Rettig, E. B. (1973). *ABC's for parents: An educational workshop in behavior modification.* Van Nuys, California: Research Press.   3, 4.

Reynolds, C. and Jensen, A. R. (1983). WISC-R subscale patterns of abilities of blacks and whites matched on full scale IQ. *Journal of Educational Psychology, 75,* 207–14.   5, 8.1.

Reynolds, C. and Wilson, V. (1984). Relationship between age and raw score increases on the Kaufman-Assessment battery for children. *Psychology In The Schools, 21,* 19–24.   5, 8.1.

Reynolds, M. (1976). Mainstreaming: Historical perspectives in Patrick O'Donnell and Robert H. Bradfield (Eds.). *Mainstreaming: Controversy and consensus.* San Rafael, California: Academic Therapy Publications.   1.

Reynolds, M. and Birch, J. W. (1982). *Teaching exceptional children in all America's schools.* Reston, Virginia: The Council for Exceptional Children.   1, 2, 3, 4, 5, 6, 7, 8, 9.

Reynolds, M. C. (1980). The expanding implications of public law
    94-142, *Inservice,* Newsletter of the National Council of States
    in Inservice Education, October, 15–18.   2.

Risley, T. (1972). Spontaneous language and the preschool in J. C.
    Stanley (Ed.). *Preschool programs for the disadvantaged.*
    Baltimore, Maryland: Johns Hopkins University Press.   5, 7, 8.2.

Roberson, J. B. (1979). Teacher education and mainstreaming: A status
    report from the south. *Phi Delta Kappan,* 61, 70.   3, 6, 7.

Roberts, J. and Hawk, B. (n.d.). *Legal rights primer for the handi-
    capped: In and out of the classroom.* Novato, California:
    Academic Therapy Publications.

Rogers, V. (1979). Chris Rogers: Special teacher. *Phi Delta Kappan,*
    61, 57.   3, 4.

Rogers, V. M. and Atwood, R. K. (1974). Can we put ourselves in
    their place. *National Council of Social Studies Yearbook,*
    44. 80–111.   4, 8.2.

Rosenberg, J. E. (1980). *Behavior modification for the classroom
    teacher.* Bellevue, Washington: Edmark Associates.   8.2, 9.

Rosner, J. (1975). *Helping children overcome learning difficulties—
    A step-by-step guide for parents and teachers.* New York:
    Walker and Co.   8.2.

Ross, S., De Young, H. and Cohen, J. S. (1971). Confrontation: Special
    education and the law. *Exceptional Children,* 4, 5–12.   1, 2.

Ross, P. D. (1983). *The handicapped, limited English proficient stu-
    dent: A school district's obligation.* Mimeo distributed by Na-
    tional Origin Desegregation Assistance Center, School of
    Education, University of Miami, Coral Gables, Florida.   1, 5.

Roubinek, D. L. (1978). Will mainstreaming fit? *Educational Leader-
    ship,* 35, 410–12.   3.

Rubenstein, R. and Goldenberg, E. P. (1978). Using a computer
    message system for promoting reading and writing in a school
    for the deaf. *Proceedings of the Seventh Annual Conference
    on Systems and Devices for the Handicapped.*

Rucker, C. N., Howe, C. E. and Snider, B. (1969). The participation
    of retarded children in junior high school academic and
    nonacademic regular classrooms. *Exceptional Children,* April,
    617–23.   1.

Safer, D. J. and Allen, R. (1976). *Hyperactive children: Diagnosis
    and management.* Baltimore, Maryland: University Park
    Press.   8.1, 9.

Safer, N., Morissey, P., Kaufman, P. and Lewis, L. (1978). Imple-
    mentation of IEP's: New teacher roles and requisite support
    systems. *Focus on Exceptional Children,* 10, 1–20.   2, 3, 6, 7, 8.

Salvia, J. and Ysseldyke, J.(1978). *Assessment in special and reme-dial education.* Dallas, Texas: Houghton Mifflin. 8.1.

Sandoval, J. and Miille, M. (1980). Accuracy of judgements of WISC-R item difficulty for minority groups. *Journal of Consulting and Clinical Psychology,* 48, 249–53. 5, 8.2.

Sandoval, J., Zimmerman, I.L. and Woo-san, J.M. (1983). Cultural differences on WISC-R verbal items. *Journal of School Psy-chology. 21,* 49–55. 5, 8.1.

Sandoval, J. (1982). Hyperactive children: 12 ways to help them in the classroom. *Academic Therapy, 18,* 107–13. 8.2.

Sapir, S. G. and Wilson, B. (1972). *A professional guide to working with the learning disabled child.* New York: Bauhner/ Mazel. 8, 8.1., 8.2, 8.3.

Sapon-Shevin, M. (1978). Another look at mainstreaming: Excep-tionality, normality, and the nature of difference. *Phi Delta Kappan,* 60, 119–21. 8.2.

Sarason, I. G. (1974). *Constructive classroom behavior: A teacher's guide to modeling and role playing techniques.* New York: Behavioral Publications. 3, 4, 8.2, 9.

Sarason, S. (1983). *Schooling in America: Scapegoat and salvation.* New York: The Free Press. 1.

Saunders, G. (1983). *Bilingual children: Guidance for the family.* Multilingual Matters Ltd., Bank House, England.

Sawyer, D. J. (Ed.). (1980). *Disabled readers: Insight, assessment in-struction.* Newark, Delaware: The International Reading Assn. 8.1, 8.2, 8.3.

Sawyer, W. E. and Wilson, B. A. (1979). Role clarification for re-medial reading and learning disabilities teachers. *The Read-ing Teacher,* 33, 162–66. 3, 4.

Schiffer, W. (1979). Overview of the legislation, P.L. 94–142. *School Media Quarterly,* 8, 17–21. 1, 2.

Schulman, J., and Decker, M. (1979). Multilevel captioning: A sys-tem for preparing reading materials for the hearing impaired. *American Annals of the Deaf,* 124, 559–67. 8.2.

Schwartz, J. I. (1980). Teaching reading to the hearing impaired child, in Diane J. Sawyer (Ed.), *Disabled readers: Insight, assess-ment, instruction.* Newark, Delaware: International Reading Association, 117–27. 5, 8.2.

Sedlock, R. and Weiner, P. (1973). Review of research on the Illinois test of psycholinguistic abilities. In L. Mann and D. Saba-tino (Eds.). *The first review of special education.* Philadelphia, Pennsylvania: JSE Press. 8.1.

Semmel, D. S., et al. (1978). *The contribution of professional role to group decision making in a simulated pupil-planning team setting.* Washington, D.C.: U.S. Office of Education, Bureau

of Education for the Handicapped, Division of Innovation
and Development of State Programs Studies Branch.   3, 4, 5, 7.

Semmel, M. I., Gottlieb, J. and Robinson, N. M. (1979). Mainstreaming: Perspectives on educating handicapped children in the public schools, in David C. Berliner (Ed.). *Review of research in education,* Washington, D.C.: American Educational Research Association.   4.

Sergiovanni, T. J. and Carver, F. D. (1980). *The new school executive: A theory of administration,* second edition. New York: Harper and Row.   3, 4, 6, 7.

Shotel, J. R., Iano, R. P. and McGettigan, J. E. (1972). Teacher attitude associated with the integration of handicapped children, *Exceptional Children,* 38, 677–83.   4.

Simoes, A. (Ed.). (1976). *The bilingual child.* New York: Academic Press.   1, 5.

Simon, S. B. and O'Rourke, R. (1975). Getting to know you: Values clarification strategies. *Educational Leadership,* 32, 524– 56.   4, 8.2.

Singer, J., Bossard, M. and Watkins, M. (1977). Effects of parental presence on attendance and input of interdisciplinary teams in an institutional setting. *Psychological Reports,* 41, 1031– 34.   3, 4, 6, 7.

Skinner, B. F. (1953). *Science and human behavior.* New York: Macmillan.   5, 8.2.

Skinner, B. F. (1968). *The technology of teaching.* New York: Appleton.   5, 8.2.

Smith, D. (1980). *The classroom teacher and the special child.* New York: Jeffrey Norton Publishers, Inc.   1, 2, 3, 4, 5, 6, 7, 8, 9.

Smith, F. M. (1976). *Parent growth through group experience: A study guide for families of children with special learning needs.* San Rafael, California: Academic Therapy Publications.   3, 4.

Smith, J., and Smith, D. (1970). *Classroom management.* New York: Learning Research Associates.   9.

Solomon, E. L. (1977). New York City's prototype school for educating the handicapped. *Phi Delta Kappan,* 59, 7–10.   6, 7.

Snow, R. (1984). Placing children in special education: Some comments. *Educational Research,* 13, 12–14.   1, 8.1.

Sosne, M. (1973). *Handbook of adapted physical education equipment and its use.* New York: Charles C. Thomas.   8.2, 9.

Spache, George D., McIlroy, K. and Berg, P. C. (1981). *Case studies in reading disability.* Boston, Massachusetts: Allyn and Bacon.   8.1, 8.2, 8.3.

Stainback, S. N. and Stainback, W. C. (1977). *Classroom discipline: A positive approach.* Springfield, Illinois: Charles C. Thomas.   8.2.

Stauffer, R. G. (1979). The language experience approach to reading instruction for deaf and hearing impaired children. *The Reading Teacher,* 33, 21–24.   8.2.

Steenburger, F. (n.d.). *Steenburger quick math program.* Novato, California: Academic Therapy Publications.   8.1, 8.2, 8.3.

Sterling, H., Mutti, M., Spaulding, N. (n.d.). *Quick neurological screening test five years to adult.* Novato, California: Academic Therapy Publications.   8.1.

Sternberg, L., et al. (1978). *Essential math and language skills.* Northbrook, Illinois: Hubbard.   8, 8.1, 8.2, 8.3.

Stoefen, J. M. (1980). Instructional alternatives for teaching content reading to mainstreamed hearing impaired students. *Journal of Reading,* 24, 141–43.   8.2.

Stuckless, E. R. and Pollard, G. (1977). Processing of fingerspelling and print by deaf students. *American Annals of the Deaf,* 122, 475–79.   8.2.

Sunderlin, S. (Ed.). (1979). *The most enabling environment: Education is for all children.* Washington, D.C.: Association for Childhood Education International.   1, 2.

Swanson, H. L. and Reinert, H. R. (1979). *Teaching strategies for children in conflict.* St. Louis, Missouri: Mosby/Times Mirror.   1, 2.

Sweeney, J. (1980). Principals vs. teachers, *Phi Delta Kappan,* 61, 565–66.   3, 4.

Tarnopol, L. and Tarnopol, M. (Eds.). (1977). *Brain function and reading disabilities.* Baltimore, Maryland: University Park Press.   8.1.

Taylor, R. (1980). *The computer in the school: Tutor, tool, tutee.* New York: Teachers College Press.   8.2.

Terman, L. (1911). The Binet-Simon scale for measuring intelligence: Impressions gained by its application. *Psychological Clinic,* 5, 199–206.   1, 8.1.

Thorndike, E. (1927). *The measurement of intelligence.* New York: Teachers College Press.   1, 8.1.

Thurman, R. L. (1980). Mainstreaming: A concept to be embraced. *The Educational Forum,* 44, 285–94.   1, 2.

Tolkoff, E. (1980). Mainstreaming: A promise gone away. *The New York Teacher,* January, 9–14.   1, 2, 6, 7.

Tractenberg, P. (1979). A response to Dunn and Cole. *Educational Leadership.* 36, 306–7.   1.

Tucker, J. A. (1980). Ethnic proportions in classes for the learning disabled: Issues in nonbiased assessment. *Journal of Special Education.* 14, 93–105.   1, 8.1.

Tunrek, R., Platt, J.S. and Bowan, J. (1980). Rural community attitudes toward the handicapped: Implications for mainstreaming. *Exceptional Children,* 46, 549.   4.

Turnbull, H. (1977). Legal implications in A. J. Papanikan and J. L. Paul (Eds.). *Mainstreaming emotionally disturbed children.* Syracuse, N.Y.: Syracuse University Press.   2, 5.

Turnbull, P. J. and Cruickshank, W. (1977). *Mainstreaming: A practical guide.* Syracuse, New York: Syracuse University Press.   6.

Turnbull, A. and Cruickshank, W. (1979). *Mainstreaming: A practical guide.* New York: Schocken Books.   6.

Turnbull, A. and Schulz, J. (1979). *Mainstreaming handicapped students: A guide for the classroom teacher.* Boston, Massachusetts: Allyn and Bacon.   6.

Valett, R. E. (1973). *Learning disabilities — diagnostic-prescriptive instruments.* Belmont, California: Fearon Publishers.   8.1.

Valett, R. E. (1980). *Dyslexia: A neuropsychological approach to educating children with severe reading disorders.* Belmont, California: Fearon Publishers.   8.1, 8.2, 8.3.

Van der Honert, D. (1977). A neuropsychological technique for training dyslexics. *Journal of Learning Disabilities,* 10, 21–27.   8.2.

Vellutino, F. R. (1979). *Dyslexia: Theory and research.* Cambridge, Massachusetts: The MIT Press.   8.1.

Vygotsky, L. S. (1976). Play and its role in the mental development of the child, in J. Bruner, A. Jolly, and K. Sylvia (Eds.). *Play: Its role in development and evolution.* New York: Basic Books.   8.2.

Wagonseller, B. R. (1980). *The art of parenting.* Bellevue, Washington: Edmark Associates.   3.

Wallace, G. (1976). Interdisciplinary efforts in learning disabilities. *Journal of Learning Disabilities,* 9, 59–65.   3, 6, 7.

Wallace, G. and Larsen, S. C. (1978). *Educational assessment of learning problems: Testing for teaching.* Rockleigh, New Jersey: Longwood Division of Allyn and Bacon.   8.1, 8.2, 8.3.

Ward, M., and McCormick, S. (1981). Reading instruction for blind and low vision children in the regular classroom. *The Reading Teacher,* 34, 434–44.   8.1, 8.2, 8.3.

Warnot, W. I. (1978). In-service education: Key to PL 94-142's service to handicapped children and youth. *Educational Leadership,* 35, 434–79.   6, 7.

Webster, E. (Ed.). (1976). *Professional approaches with parents of handicapped children.* Springfield, Illinois: Charles C. Thomas.

Wechsler, D. (1939). *The Wechsler-Bellevue Intelligence Scale,* New
York: Psychological Corp.   8.1.

Weigel, R., Wise, P. and Cook, S. (1975). The impact of cooperative
learning experiences on cross-ethnic relations and attitudes.
Journal of Social Issues, 31, 219–44.   1, 5.

Weintraub, F. J., Abeson, A., Ballard, J. and Lanor, M. L. (Eds.).
(1976). *Public policy and the education of exceptional children.* Reston, Virginia: The Council for Exceptional Children.   1.

Werner, P. H., Burton, E. C. (1979). *Learning through movement:
Teaching cognitive content through physical activities.* St.
Louis, Missouri: Mosby.   8.2.

Whitmore, J. R. (1980). *Giftedness, conflict and underachievement.*
Rockleigh, New Jersey: Longwood Division of Allyn and
Bacon.   4, 8.1, 8.2.

Wiederholt, J. L., Hammil, D. D. and Brown, V. (1978). *The resource
teacher:* A guide to effective practices. Boston, Massachusetts:
Allyn and Bacon.   3, 8.

Williams, R. (1973). *The BITCH-100: A culture-specific test.* Paper
presented at the meeting of the American Psychological Association, Honolulu, Hawaii.   8.1.

Winschell, J. F. and Laurence, E. A. (1975). Short-term memory: Cur-
ricular implications for the mentally retarded. *The Journal
of Special Education, 9,* 395–408.   8.2.

Winschell, J. F. and Ensher, G. L. (1978). Educability revisited: Cur-
ricular implications for the mentally retarded. *Education and
Training for the Mentally Retarded,* 13, 131–38.   8.2.

Wirtz, M. A. (1977). *An administrator's handbook of special education: A guide to better education of the handicapped.* Springfield, Illinois: Charles C. Thomas.   3, 6, 7.

Wolfgang, Charles H. (1980). *Solving discipline problems: Strategies for classroom teachers.* Rockleigh, New Jersey: Long-
wood Division of Allyn and Bacon.   8.2, 9.

Woodcock, C. C. (1974). A sensory stimulation center for blind children. *Phi Delta Kappan,* 55, 541.   8.2, 9.

Woodward, D. M. (1981). *Mainstreaming the learning disabled adolescent: A manual of strategies and materials.* Gaithersburg,
Maryland: Aspen Systems Corporation.   8, 8.1, 8.2, 8.3, 9.

Yang, D. (1975). Welcome the handicapped to your classroom and
enrich it. *Teacher,* 93, 13.   4.

Yarger, S. (1978). An exploratory model for program development
in inservice education. In Yarger et al. (Eds.). *Creative authority and collaboration: Report IV.* Syracuse, N.Y.: National
Dissemination Center at Syracuse University.   6.

Yates, V. V. (1977). *Mainstreaming of children with a hearing loss: Practical guidelines and implications.* Springfield, Illinois: Charles C. Thomas.   8.1, 8.2, 8.3.

Yoshida, R. K., Fenton, K. S., Maxwell, J. P. and Kaufan, M. J. (1978). Group decision making in the planning team process: Communication of planning team decisions to program implementation. *Journal of School Psychology,* 16, 178–83.   3, 4, 6, 7.

Ziff, L. (1974). Utilization of visually oriented media to motivate language facility in hearing impaired children. *Volta Review,* 76, 178–81.   8.2, 9.

REFERENCES REGARDING COURT DECISIONS AND LAWS

Brown v. *Board of Education of Topeka.* (1954).

PL 85-926: National Defense Education Act. (1958).

PL 87-276: Special Education Act. (1961).

PL 88-164: Retarded Facility and Community Center Construction Act. (1963).

PL 89-10: Elementary and Secondary Education Act. (1965).

PL 89-313: Amendment to Title I of the Elementary and Secondary Education Act. (1966).

Hobson v. *Hanson in Washington, D.C.* (1968).

PL 91-320: The Learning Disabilities Act. (1969).

Diana v. *California State Board of Education.* (1970).

Pennsylvania Association for Retarded Citizens (PARC) v. *the Commonwealth of Pennsylvania.* (1972).

Mill v. *District of Columbia Board of Education.* (1972).

PL 93-112: The Vocational Rehabilitation Act. (1973).

PL 93-380: The Education Amendments Act. (1974).

Lau v. *Nichols*—Supreme Court Decision. (1974).

Serna v. *Portales Municipal Schools.* (1974).

Aspira v. *New York City Board of Education.* (1974).

PL 94-142: Education for All Handicapped Children Act. (1975).

New York State Education Law: Chapter 853. (1976).

Rios v. *Read in New York.* (1977).

Reid v. *New York City Board of Education.* (1977).

PL 95-561: Gifted and Talented Education Act. (1978).

Jose P. v. *Ambach in New York.* (1979).

Lora v. *New York City Board of Education.* (1979).

Cyrcia v. *New York City Board of Education.* (1980).

BOOKS FOR AND ABOUT CHILDREN WITH SPECIAL NEEDS

Prepared by Arlene M. Pillar

Adams, Barbara. (1979). *Like it is: Facts and feelings about handicaps from kids who know.* New York: Walker, Grades 4–6.

Anderson, Clarence W. (1971). *Blind connemara.* Illustrated by C. W. Anderson. New York: Macmillan, Grades 4–6.

Armer, Alberta. (1975). *Screwball.* New York: Grosset & Dunlap, Grades 4–6.

Arthur, Catherine. (1979). *My sister's silent world.* Illustrated by Nathan Talbot. Chicago: Children's Press, Preschool–Grade 3.

Barber, Elsie M. (1949). *Trembling years.* New York: Macmillan, Grades 7 and up.

Bates, Betty. (1980). *Love is like peanuts.* New York: Holiday, Grades 7–12.

Bawden, Nina. (1966). *Witch's daughter.* New York: J. B. Lippincott, Grades, 4–6.

Bialk, Elisa. (1948). *The horse called Pete.* Boston: Houghton Mifflin, Grades 3–5.

Bloom, Freddie. (1979). *The boy who couldn't hear.* Illustrated by Michael Charlton. Lawrence, Massachusetts: Merrimack Book Service, Preschool–Grade 1.

Branscum, Robbie. (1979). *For love of Jody.* New York: Lothrop, Grades 7–12.

Bridges, Christina. (1980). *The hero.* Illustrated by Linda Batten. Northridge, California: Joyce Media, Grades K–6.

Brooks, Jerome. (1979). *The big dipper marathon.* New York: Dutton, Junior and senior high school.

Brown, Fern G. (1977). *You're somebody special on a horse.* Illustrated by Darrell Wiskur. Chicago: Albert Whitman & Co., Grades 4–8.

Brown, Irene B. (1978). *Run from a scarecrow.* St. Louis, Missouri: Concordia, Grades 5–9.

Brown, Marion and Crone, Ruth. (1963). *The silent storm.* Nashville, Tennessee: Abingdon, Grades 6–8.

Burnett, Frances H. (1962). *The secret garden.* New York: J. B. Lippincott, Grades 4–6.

Butler, Beverly. (1972). *Gift of gold.* New York: Dodd, Grades 4–8.

Butler, Beverly. (1970). *Light a single candle.* New York: Archway, Grades 7–9.

Callen, Larry. (1979). *Sorrow's song.* Illustrated by Marvin Friedman. Boston: Little, Brown & Co., Grades 4–6.

Cavanna, Betty. (1974). *Joyride.* New York: William Morrow & Co., Grades 7 and up.

Churchill, David. (1979). *It, us and the others.* New York: Harper and Row, Grades 4–6.

Cole, Sheila. (1974). *Meaning well.* Illustrated by Paul Raynor. New York: Franklin Watts, Inc., Grades 4–7.

Colman, Hila. (1980). *Accident.* New York: William Morrow & Co., Junior and senior high school.

Cookson, Catherine. (1980). *Go tell it to Mrs. Golightly.* New York: Lothrop, Lee & Shepard, Grades 5 and up.

Corbin, William. (1955). *Golden mare.* New York: Coward, McCann & Geoghegan, Grades 5–7.

Corcoran, Barbara. (1974). *A dance to still music*. Illustrated by Charles Robinson. New York: Atheneum, Grades 5–8.

Cosgrove, Stephen. (1978). *Kartusch*. Minneapolis, Minnesota: Creative Education, Grades K–4.

Cunningham, Julia. (1980). *Burnish me bright*. New York: Dell, Grades K–6.

DeAngeli, Marguerite. (1949). *The door in the wall*. Garden City, New York: Doubleday, Grades 4–6.

Dengler, Marianna. (1979). *A pebble in Newcomb's Pond*. New York: Holt, Rinehart & Winston, Grades 4–6.

Dixon, Paige. (1979). *Skipper*. New York: Atheneum, Grades 5–10.

Fanshawe, Elizabeth. (1977). *Rachel*. Scarsdale, New York: Bradbury Press, Preschool–Grade 2.

Fine, Anne. (1979). *The summer-house loon*. New York: Thomas Y. Crowell, Grades 6 and up.

Fleischer, Leonore. (1979). *Blind Sunday*. New York: Scholastic Book Services, Grades 7–12.

Forbes, Esther. (1943). *Johnny Tremain*. Boston: Houghton Mifflin, Grades 6–8.

Fredericks, P. C. (1978). *Battle at the blue line*. Wheaton, Illinois: Victor Books, Grades 4–10.

Gage, Wilson. (1977). *Down in the boondocks*. Illustrated by Glen Rounds. New York: Greenwillow, Grades 1–4.

Garfield, James B. (1959). *Follow my leader*. Illustrated by Robert Greiner. New York: Viking, Grades 4–7.

Gerson, Corrine. (1980). *Passing through*. New York: Dial, Grades 7–12.

Gilson, Jamie. (1980). *Do bananas chew gum?* New York: Lothrop, Lee & Shepard, Grades 4–6.

Glazzard, Margaret H. (1978). *Meet Danny: Multiply handicapped*. Lawrence, Kansas: H & H Enterprises, Grades 4–6.

Green, Phyllis. (1978). *Walkie-walkie*. Reading, Massachusetts: Addison-Wesley Publishing. Grades K–2.

Greenfield, Eloise. (1980). *Darlene*. New York: Methuen, Grades K–3.

Grohskopf, Bernice. (1976). *Shadow in the sun*. New York: Atheneum, Grades 6 and up.

Hanlon, Emily. (1980). *It's too late for sorry*. New York: Dell, Grades 4–6.

Hanlon, Emily. (1979). *The swing*. Scarsdale, New York: Bradbury, Grades 4–6.

Haskins, James and Stifle, J. M. (1978). *The quiet revolution: The struggle for the rights of disabled Americans*. New York: J. B. Lippincott, Grades 7–12.

Heide, Florence P. (1978). *Secret dreamer, secret dreams*. New York: J. B. Lippincott, Grades 7–12.

Heide, Florence P. (1970). *Sound of sunshine, sound of rain*. Illustrated by Kenneth Longtemps. New York: Scholastic Book Services, Grades K–3.

Hichok, Lorena. (1958). *The story of Helen Keller.* New York: Grosset & Dunlap, Grades 5-7.

Honeyman, Arthur. (1980). *Sam and his cart.* Illustrated by Michael DeWaide. Saint Paul, Minnesota: EMC, Grades 2-6.

Hunter, Edith. (1963). *Child of the silent night: The story of Laura Bridgman.* Boston: Houghton Mifflin, Grades 4-6.

Johnston, Catherine D. (1977). *I hear the day.* Illustrated by Joseph Mark. South Waterford, Maine: Merrian-Eddy, Grades 2-3.

Kamien, Janet. (1979). *What if you couldn't . . . ? A book about special needs.* New York: Charles Scribner's Sons, Grades 4-6.

Keller, Helen. (1954). *Story of my life.* Garden City, New York: Doubleday, Grades 3-6.

Kent, Deborah. (1979). *Belonging.* New York: Grosset & Dunlap, Grades 5 and up.

Kingman, Lee. (1978). *Head over wheels.* Boston: Houghton Mifflin, Junior and senior high school.

Kipling, Rudyard. (1969). *Light that failed.* New York: Airmont, Grades 8 and up.

Lasker, Joe. (1980). *Nick joins in.* Illustrated by Joe Lasker. Chicago: Albert Whitman, Grades 1-3.

Lee, Robert C. (1972). *It's a mile from here to glory.* Boston: Little, Brown & Co., Grades 5 and up.

Litchfield, Ada B., (1976). *A button in her ear.* Illustrated by Eleanor Mill. Chicago: Albert Whitman, Grades 2-4.

Litchfield, Ada B. (1980). *Words in our hands.* Illustrated by Helen Cogancherry. Chicago: Albert Whitman, Grades 2-6.

Little, Jean. (1973). *From Anna.* Illustrated by Joan Sandin. New York: Harper & Row, Grades 4-6.

Little, Jean. (1962). *Mine for keeps.* Illustrated by Lewis Parker, Boston: Little, Brown & Co., Grades 4-6.

Long, Judy. (1976). *Volunteer spring.* New York: Dodd, Mead & Co., Grades 5-7.

MacLachlan, Patricia. (1980). *Through grandpa's eyes.* Illustrated by Deborah Ray. New York: Harper & Row, Grades 2-4.

Madsen, Jane M., et. al. (1980). *Please don't tease me.* Valley Forge, Pennsylvania: Judson Press, Grades 5-8.

Marcus, Rebecca. (1978). *Being blind.* New York: Hastings House, Grades 6-8.

Mayne, William. (1978). *Max's dream.* Illustrated by Laszlo Acts. New York: Greenwillow Books, Grades 5-9.

McDonnell, Lois E. (1962). *Stevie's other eyes.* New York: Friendship Press, Grades 1-3.

Mitchell, Joyce S. (1980). *See me more clearly.* New York: Harcourt, Brace Jovanovich, Grades 6–8.

Montgomery, Elizabeth R. (1978). *The mystery of the boy next door.* Illustrated by Ethel Gold. New Canaan, Connecticut: Garrard Publishing, Grades K–6.

Montgomery, Elizabeth R. (1979). *Seeing in the dark.* Illustrated by Troy Howell. New Canaan, Connecticut: Garrard Publishing, Grades 1–5.

Myers, Caroline C. & Barbe, Walter B. (Eds.). (1977). *Challenge of a handicap.* Honesdale, Pennsylvania: Highlights for Children, Grades 2–6.

Naylor, Phyllis. (1967). *Jennifer Jean, the cross-eyed queen.* Illustrated by Harold K. Lamson. Minneapolis, Minnesota: Lerner Publications, Grades K–5.

Parker, Mark. (1977). *Horses, airplanes & frogs.* Illustrated by Dan Siculan. Elgin, Illinois: Child's World, Preschool–Grade 3.

Peck, Robert N. (1979). *Clunie,* New York: Alfred A. Knopf, Grades 7–12.

Phelan, Terry W. (1979). *The S. S. Valentine.* Illustrated by Judy Glasser. New York: Scholastic Book Services, Grades 2–6.

Phipson, Joan. (1980). *A tide flowing.* New York: McElderry/Atheneum, Grades 7–12.

Pieper, Elizabeth. (1979). *A school for Tommy.* Illustrated by Dan Siculan. Elgin, Illinois: Child's World, Grades 1–4.

Potter, Marian. (1979). *The shared room.* New York: William Morrow & Co., Junior and senior high school.

Rabe, Bernice. (1980). *The balancing girl.* New York: E.P. Dutton, Grades K–3.

Radowsky, Colby. (1978). *P.S. write soon.* New York: Franklin Watts, Grades 7–12.

Reuter, Margaret. (1979). *My mother is blind.* Illustrated by Philip Lanier. Chicago: Childrens Press, Preschool–Grade 3.

Rhoads, Marie P. (1980). *Paul: The hunchback.* North Miami, Florida: IEM-HOTEP, Grades K–12.

Robinet, Harriette G. (1976). *Jay and the marigold.* Illustrated by Trudy Scott. Chicago: Childrens Press, Grades 2–4.

Robinet, Harriette G. (1980). *Ride the red cycle.* Boston: Houghton Mifflin, Grades K–3.

Rounds, Glen. (1980). *Blind outlaw.* New York: Holiday House, Grades 4–7.

Roy, Cal. (1974). *The painter of miracles.* Illustrated by Cal Roy. New York: Farrar, Straus & Giroux, Grades 7 and up.

Savitz, Harriet M. (1979). *Run, don't walk.* New York: Franklin Watts, Grades 7 and up.

Sesame Street. (1980). *Sesame street sign language fun.* New York: Random House, Grades K–3.

Simon, Norma. (1978). *We remember Philip.* Illustrated by Ruth Sanderson. Chicago: Albert Whitman, Grades 2–4.

Small, Mary. (1979). *And Alice did the walking.* New York: Oxford University Press, Grades 1–3.

Smith, Lucia B. (1979). *A special kind of sister.* New York: Holt, Rinehart & Winston, Grades K–3.

Smith, Vian. (1968). *Tall and proud.* Illustrated by Don Stivers. New York: Pocket Books, Grades 5–7.

Southall, Ivan. (1973). *Head in the clouds.* Illustrated by Richard Kennedy. New York: Macmillan, Grades 3–7.

Spencer, Zane & Leech, Jay. (1977). *Cry of the wolf.* Philadelphia: Westminster Press, Grades 6–9.

Spyri, Johanna. (1962). *Heidi.* Illustrated by Greta Elgaard. New York: Macmillan, Grades 5–6.

Sullivan, Mary B., et al. (1979). *Feeling free.* Reading, Massachusetts: Addison-Wesley, Grades 4–6.

Sullivan, Mary Beth & Bourke, Linda. (1980). *A show of hands, say it in sign language.* Reading, Massachusetts: Addison-Wesley, Grades 4–6.

Terr Harr, Jaap. (1977). *The world of Ben Lighthart.* Translated from Dutch by Martha Mearns. New York: Delacorte Press, Grades 5–9.

Thomas, William E. (1980). *The new boy is blind.* New York: Julian Messner, Grades 4–6.

Tunis, John R. (1940). *The kid from Tomkinsville.* New York: Harcourt Brace Jovanovich, Grades 7–9.

Vinson, Kathryn. (1965). *Run with the ring.* New York: Harcourt Brace Jovanovich, Grades 7 and up.

Wagoner, Jean B. (1944). *Jane Addams: Little lame girl.* Indianapolis, Indiana: Bobbs-Merrill Co., Grades 3–5.

Wahl, Jan. (1980). *Button eye's orange.* Illustrated by Wendy Watson. New York: Frederick Warne & Co., Grades K–3.

Wartski, Maureen C. (1980). *My brother is special.* Philadelphia: Westminster Press, Grades 4–8.

Wolf, Bernard. (1974). *Don't feel sorry for Paul.* New York: J. B. Lippincott, Grades 3–6.

Wosmek, Frances. (1976). *A bowl of sun.* Chicago: Childrens Press, Grades 3–6.

Yolen, Jane. (1977). *The seeing stick.* Illustrated by Remy Charlip and Demetra Maraslis. New York: Thomas Y. Crowell, Grades K–3.

Young, Helen. (1980). *What difference does it make, Danny?* Illustrated by Quentin Blake. New York: Andre Deutsch, Grades 4–6.

Zelonsky, Joy. (1980). *I can't always hear you.* Illustrated by Barbara Bejna and Shirlee Jensen. Milwaukee, Wisconsin: Raintree Children's Books, Grades K–5.

PERIODICALS

American Annals of the Deaf
    5034 Wisconsin Avenue, N.W.
    Washington, D.C. 20016

American Arts
    American Council for the Arts
    570 Seventh Avenue
    New York, New York 10018

AAESPH Review (Quarterly)
    American Association for the
        Education of the Severely/
        Profoundly Handicapped
    1600 West Armory Way
    Garden View Suite
    Seattle, Washington 98119

Art to Zoo
    News for Schools from the
        Smithsonian
    Office of Elementary and Sec-
        ondary Education
    Washington, D.C. 20560

The ALAN Review
    Assembly on Literature for
        Adolescents
    National Council of Teachers of
        English
    Department of Language
        Education
    125 Aderhold Hall
    College of Education
    University of Georgia
    Athens, Georgia 30602

Behavioral Disorders (Quarterly)
    Council for Children with Be-
        havior Disorders of the
        Council for Exceptional
        Children
    1920 Association Drive
    Reston, Virginia 22091

Behavior Therapy
    Academic Press for the Associa-
        tion for the Advancement
        of Behavior Therapy
    420 Lexington Avenue
    New York, New York 10017

Caption: The Closed Captioned Newsletter
    National Captioning Institute
    5203 Leesburg Pike
    Falls Church, Virginia 22041

Career Development for Exceptional
    Individuals
    Division of Career Development
    The Council for Exceptional
        Children
    1920 Association Drive
    Reston, Virginia 22091

Chicorel Index to Learning Disorders
    Chicorel Library Publishing
        Corporation
    275 Central Park West
    New York, New York 10024

DSH Abstracts
    Deafness, Speech and Hearing
        Publications, Inc.
    Gallaudet College, N.E.
    Washington, D.C. 20002

The Directive Teacher
    356 Arps Hall
    1945 North High Street
    The Ohio State University
    Columbus, Ohio 43210

Education and Training of the Men-
    tally Retarded
    The Council for Exceptional
        Children
    1920 Association Drive
    Reston, Virginia 22091

Education of the Visually Handicapped
    Association for Education of the
        Visually Handicapped, Inc.
    919 Walnut Street
    Philadelphia, Pennsylvania 19107

The English Journal
    National Council of Teachers of
        English
    Subscription Service
    1111 Kenyon Road
    Urbana, Illinois 61801

Exceptional Child Education Abstracts
The Council for Exceptional
Children
1920 Association Drive
Reston, Virginia 22091

Gifted Children Newsletter
Gifted and Talented Publica-
tions, Inc.
1255 Portland Place
P.O. Box 2581
Boulder, Colorado 80322

The Instructor
The Instructor Publications, Inc.
7 Bank Street
Dansville, New York 14437

*Journal for the Education of the
Gifted (Quarterly)*
Association for the Gifted of the
Council for Exceptional
Children
1920 Association Drive
Reston, Virginia 22091

Journal for Special Educators
American Association of Special
Educators
179 Sierra Vista Lane
Valley Cottage, New York 10989

Journal of Learning Disabilities
Professional Press, Inc.
101 East Ontario Street
Chicago, Illinois 60611

Journal of Reading
International Reading Association
800 Barksdale Road
P.O. Box 8139
Newark, Delaware 19711

Journal of Special Education
Grune and Stratton
Subsidiary of Harcourt Brace
Jovanovich Publishers
111 Fifth Avenue
New York, New York 10003

Journal of Speech and Hearing Disorders
American Speech and Hearing
Association
10801 Rockville Pike
Rockville, Maryland 20852

Journal of Speech and Hearing Research
American Speech and Hearing
Association
10801 Rockville Pike
Rockville, Maryland 20852

Language Arts
National Council of Teachers of
English
1111 Kenyon Road
Urbana, Illinois 61801

Learning
Education Today Company
530 University Avenue
Palo Alto, California 94301

Learning Disabilities Quarterly
Division for Children with Learning Disabilities of The Council for Exceptional Children
1920 Association Drive
Reston, Virginia 22091

Mental Retardation Abstracts
Superintendent of Documents
U.S. Government Printing Office
Washington, D.C. 20402

Newsletter
New York Branch of the Orton
Dyslexia Society
80 Fifth Avenue — Room 903
New York, New York 10011

Programs for the Handicapped
Office of Information and Re-
sources for the Handicapped
Clearinghouse for the Handi-
capped
Room 3106 — Switzer Building
Washington, D.C. 20202

Rehabilitation Literature
 National Easter Seal Society for
  Crippled Children and
  Adults
 800 Second Avenue
 New York, New York 10016

The Sight-Saving Review
 National Society for the Prevention of Blindness
 79 Madison Avenue
 New York, New York 10016

Teaching Exceptional Children
 The Council for Exceptional
  Children
 1920 Association Drive
 Reston, Virginia 22091

Volta Review
 Alexander Graham Bell Association for the Deaf
 3417 Volta Place, N.W.
 Washington, D.C. 20007

Yearbook of Special Education
 Marquis Academic Media
 Marquis Who's Who, Inc.
 200 East Ohio Street
 Chicago, Illinois 61611

ART-RELATED BOOKS FOR TEACHERS AND PARENTS
FOR MAINSTREAMED EVENTS

Alkerna, C. (1971). *Alkerna's complete guide to creative art for young people.* Columbus, Ohio: Sterling. (For all students.)

Allen, Roach Van & Allen, Claryce. (1974). *Language experiences in reading, teachers' resource book.* Chicago: Encyclopaedia Britannica Press. (For teachers and parents to use for enrichment and remediation activities.)

Anderson, N. & Laird, R.D. (1972). Teaching the deaf child to read. *Audio-visual Instruction.* 17. (Provides rich visual experiences through movies, slides, filmstrips and reading and signing of different types. Wyoming School for the Deaf Model of Instruction.)

Armelino, Barbara Ann. (1979). Developing critical skills through media analysis. *The English Journal,* 68, 56–58. (For teachers to be used with all youngsters.)

Arnheim, Rudolf. (1969). *Visual thinking.* Berkeley: University of California Press. See also *Art and visual perception,* (1964) and *Toward a psychology of art,* (1966). (For parents and teachers who may wish to understand the basic theory and research which shows that art is essential to learning.)

Bamman, H., Dawson, M. & Whitehead, R. (1971). *Oral interpretation of children's literature.* Dubuque, Iowa: William C. Brown Company. (Use of story telling, drama, oral reading and choral reading.)

Barron, F. (1969). *Creative person and creative process.* New York: Holt, Rinehart and Winston. (For the gifted and talented.)

Barzun, J. & Saunders, R.J. (n.d.). *Art in basic education.* Council for Basic Education. Washington, D.C. 20005. (For teachers and parents to be used with all youngsters.)

Behr, M., Baston Snyder, A. & Clopton, A. (1979). *Drama integrates basic skills: Lesson plans for the learning disabled.* Springfield, Illinois: Charles C. Thomas. (For teachers — especially those working in resource rooms.)

Berman, L.M. & Roderick, J.A. (Eds.) (1977). *Feeling, valuing and the art of growing: Insights into the affective.* Alexandria, Virginia. Yearbook of the Association for Supervision and Curriculum Development. (For teachers and parents.)

Bernstein, D. & Borkovec, T.D. (1973). *Progressive relaxation training: A manual for the helping professions.* Champaign, Illinois: Research Press. (For teachers and parents.)

Bettelheim, B. (1976). *The uses of enchantment: The meaning and use of fairy tales.* New York: Alfred A. Knopf. (The fairy tale with its imagery, fantasy, metamorphosis and monsters helps children and youth deal with their fears.)

Bills, R.E. (1959). Nondirective play therapy with retarded learners. *Journal of Consulting Psychology.* 14, 140–49. (For teachers and parents.)

Bloom, K., Eddy, J., Fowler, C., Remer, J. & Shuker, N. (1981). *An arts in education source book.* New York: American Council for the Arts. (For teachers and parents.)

Bogen, J.E. (1969). The other side of the brain II: An appositional mind. *Bulletin of the Los Angeles Neurological Society,* 34, 135–62. (Important basic research in the need for art to enhance learning for the "other" side of the brain.)

Britton, J., Burgess, T., Martin, N., McLeod, A. & Rosen, H. (1975). *The development of writing ability.* London: Macmillan Education. (For teachers.)

Broudy, H.S. (1970). On knowing. In H.S. Broudy (Ed.) *Proceedings of the philosophy of education society: Studies in philosophy and education.* Edwardsville, Illinois: Southern Illinois University, 89–103. (Important statement on humanistic learning and the arts.)

Broudy, H.S. (1972). *Enlightened cherishing: An essay on aesthetic education.* Urbana, Illinois: The University of Illinois Press. (For teachers to be used with all youngsters.)

Broudy, H.S. (1973). Research into imagic association and cognitive interpretation. *Research in the teaching of English.* 7, 240–59. (An important statement on arts and thinking.)

Broudy, H.S. (1979). Arts education: Necessary or just nice? *Phi Delta Kappan,* 60, 347–50. (For teachers and parents to be used with all youngsters.)

Butterworth, George (Ed.) (1977). *The child's representation of the world.* (Proceedings of the Annual Conference of the Developmental Section of the British Society, University of Surrey, England.) New York: Plenum Publishing Corporation. (Deals with art and meaning and the child's representation of the world for average, blind and autistic children.)

Cameron, J.R. & Platter, E.E. (1973). A photographic approach to poetry. *The English Journal,* 62, 60-63. (For teachers, parents and students in grades 4-8.)

Campbell, J. (1975). *Learning through art.* New York: Teaching Resources Corp.

Campbell, P.F. (1976). Literature review: *Research on children's comprehension of pictures.* (Technical Report #5, Tallahassee, Florida Project for the Mathematical Development of Children.) Tallahassee, Florida: Florida State University. (For teachers to be used for remediation activities.)

Caplan, F. & Caplan, T. (1973). *The power of play.* Garden City, New York: Anchor Press/Doubleday. (See especially Creativity through Play, in Chapter 5, 147-80.

Carroll, J.K. (1978). Simulation and instructional development: Partners in the educational process. *Journal of Instructional Media,* 5, 173-84. (For teachers.)

Chenfeld, M.B. (1973). *Teaching language arts creatively.* New York: Harcourt Brace Jovanovich. (For teachers.)

Cohen, D. (1968). The effects of literature on vocabulary and reading achievement. *Elementary English.* 45, 209-15. (For teachers and parents.)

Cohen, E. & Garner, R. (1976). *Art: Another language for learning.* New York: Citation Press. (For teachers, parents and students in grades 4-12.)

Cohen, M. (1974). Move him into reading with music. *Instructor.* 73, 15-17. (For teachers and parents.)

Combs, A.W., et al. (Eds.) (1978). *Humanistic education: Objectives and assessment.* Washington, D.C.: Association for Supervision and Curriculum Development. (See especially pp. 52-55 for important checklist for determining whether one has a humanistic school.)

Connell, D. (n.d.). *ITL (Integrated Total Language).* Novato, California: Academic Therapy Publications. (Multi sensory education for the learning disabled, blind, deaf, aphasic and motor impaired.)

Cowen, S.K. (1980). Assumptions, implications and consequences of the New York State Education Department validation of reading through art (RITA). Paper presented at the American Educational Research Association Annual Meeting, Boston, Massachusetts. (For teachers to be used in teaching reading activities.)

Cramer, R. (1978). *Children's writing and language growth.* Dubuque, Iowa: Charles E. Merrill Publishing Company. (For teachers and parents.)

Douglas, J.D. & Peel, B. (1979). The development of metaphor and proverb translations in children grades 1-7. *The Journal of Educational Research,* 73, 116-19. (For gifted and talented.)

Drake, C. (1964). Reading, writing and rhythm. *The Reading Teacher.* 18, 202-5. (For teachers of reading and music.)

Duke, C.R. (1974). *Creative dramatics and English teaching.* Urbana, Illinois: National Council of Teachers of English. (Pantomime, improvisation, role play, drama, filmography, characterization, sequencing, working with retarded and disturbed children.)

Edward, B. (1979). *Drawing on the right side of the brain.* Los Angeles: J.P. Tarcher, Inc. (A course in enhancing creativity and artistic confidence. Treats the non-verbal language of art, the shape of space, perspectives, proportion, seeing light, and drawing shade.)

Ehly, S.W. & Larsen, S.C. (1980). *Peer tutoring for individualized instruction.* Rockleigh, New Jersey: Longwood Division, Allyn and Bacon. (For teachers and parents.)

Eisner, E.W. (1972). *Educating artistic vision.* New York: Macmillan and Co., Inc. (For all teachers.)

Esposito, G. (n.d.). *Integrated arts: Project SEARCH.* Utica School District, 310 Bleecher Street, Utica, New York 13501. (The gifted and the arts.)

Feldman, E.B. (1970). *Becoming human through art.* Englewood Cliffs, New Jersey: Prentice-Hall, Inc. (For teachers, parents and students in grades 7-12.)

Flanigan, M. & Boone, R. (1977). *Using media in the language arts: A source book.* Itaska, Illinois: F.E. Peacock. (For students in grades 4-8.)

Fowler, J.S. (1981). *Movement education.* Philadelphia, Pennsylvania: Saunders College Publishing. (Drama, rhythms, music, children ages 3-12.)

Frey, H. (1980). Improving the performance of poor readers through autogenic relaxation training. *The Reading Teacher, 33,* 928-32. (For teachers.)

Gair, S.B. (1981). Teaching problem learners through the arts. *The Directive Teacher, 3,* 16-17. (For teachers and parents.)

Galaburda, A.M. (1978). Right-left asymmetries of the brain. *Science, 199,* 852-56. (For teachers and parents.)

Gatch, J. (1980). Why not start a speech choir? *Learning, 14,* 99-100. (For classroom and music teachers.)

Gerbrandt, G.L. (1974). *An idea book: For acting out and writing language K-8.* Urbana, Illinois: National Council for Teachers of English. (Small group methods tested by the author and his student teachers. Pantomime, charades, improvisation, unfinished sentences, scrambled sentences, in 700 examples by grade level, difficulty, and number of students needed.)

Getzels, J.W. & Jackson, P.W. (1962). *Creativity and intelligence.* New York: John Wiley. (For parents and teachers of the gifted.)

Getzels, J.W. & Csikszentmihalyi, M. (1976). *The creative vision: A longitudinal study of problem solving in art.* New York: John Wiley. (For parents and teachers of the gifted.)

Getzels, J.W. (1980). Problem finding and human thought. *The Educational Forum. 44,* 243-44. (For teachers.)

Gillespie, M.C. & Conner, J.W. (1975). *Creative growth through literature for children and adolescents.* Columbus, Ohio: Charles E. Merrill. (Includes book selection suggestions related to intellectual, social and physical development.)

Glazer, S.M. (1980). *Creating readers: A developmental approach.* Englewood Cliffs, New Jersey: Prentice-Hall, Inc. (For teachers.)

Guilford, J.P. (1967). Creativity: Yesterday, today, tomorrow. *Journal of creative behavior.* (A classic.)

Gumaer, J., et al. (1975). Affective education through role playing. *The Personnel and Guidance Journal.* 53, 604–8. (For teachers and parents.)

Hall, D. (1973). *Writing well.* Boston: Little, Brown and Co. (For teachers.)

Harley, R., Henderson, F. & Truan, N. (1979). *The teaching of braille reading.* Springfield, Illinois: Charles C. Thomas. (Use of psycholinguistic approaches of Goodman, Niles, Smith, Page.)

Harris, P. (Ed.) (1978). *Drama in education.* London: The Bodley Head Press. (For teachers and parents.)

Harrison, Jr., A. & Musial, D. (1978). *Other ways, other means: Altered awareness activities for receptive learning.* New York: Goodyear Publishing Company. (Includes relaxation activities, meditation, imagery, use of dreams, etc.)

Hennings, D.G. (1978). *Communication in action: Dynamic teaching of the language arts.* Chicago, Illinois: Rand McNally College Publishing Co. (Intermediate grades.)

Hensel, N.H. (1981). *Evaluating children's development in creativity and creative drama.* Palo Alto, California: R. and E. Associates, Inc. (At 936 Industrial Avenue, 94303.) (For teachers.)

Hochberg, J. & Brooks, V. (1962). Pictorial recognition as an unlearned ability: A study of one child's performance. *American Journal of Psychology.* 75, 624–28. (Art and visual thinking.)

Hochberg, J. (1980). Attention in perception and reading. In F.A. Young and D.B. Lindsley (Eds.) *Early experience and visual information processing in perceptual and reading disorders.* Washington, D.C.: National Academy of Sciences. (Related listening comprehension cues and the child's cognitive structure.)

Hoetker, James. (1975). *Theater games: One way into drama.* Urbana, Illinois: ERIC/ RCS and National Council of Teachers of English TRIP Series. (Of interest to elementary, secondary and college teachers and parents. Offers structured sequence of dramatic activities.)

Hollman, J. (1981). Games to promote creativity. *The English Journal,* 70, 83–85. (For teachers and parents.)

Hull, D. & Reuter, J. (1977). Development of charitable behavior in elementary school children. *Journal of Genetic Psychology.* 131, 147–53. (Use of role play.)

Hunkins, F.P. (1976). *Involving students in questioning.* Boston: Allyn and Bacon. (For teachers.)

Hurwitz, A. & Madeja, S.S. (1978). *A joyous vision: A source book for elementary art appreciation.* Englewood Cliffs, New Jersey: Prentice-Hall, Inc. (For teachers and all students.)

Jeffers, J. & Bailey, M. (1979). *Look, now hear this: Combined auditory training and speechreading instruction.* Springfield, Illinois: Charles C. Thomas. (For teachers and parents to be used in mainstreaming activities.)

Jipp, L.F. & Weinhold, M.W. (1979). Making walkabout a community reality. *Phi Delta Kappan,* 60, 725–27. (For teachers and parents of primary grade youngsters.)

Johnson, B. (1977). What can you do for the gifted on Monday morning? *Educational Leadership,* 35, 35–41. (For parents of the gifted.)

Jones, R.M. (1968). *Fantasy and feeling in education.* New York: New York University Press. (For parents and teachers — a focus on the affective domain.)

Jordan, D.C. (1979). R_x for Piaget's complaint: A science of education. *Journal of Teacher Education,* 30, 11–14. (Scientific approach to combining various symbol systems in teaching.)

Jung, C.G. (Ed.) (1964). *Man and his symbols.* Garden City, New York: A Windfall Book, Doubleday and Co., Inc. (A classic which shows man's symbols through art and literature.)

Kaplan, S.N. (1979). *Activities for gifted children.* Santa Monica, California: Goodyear. (For teachers, parents, and the gifted.)

Karel, L. (1975). *Avenues to the arts, second edition.* Kirksville, Missouri: Division of Fine Arts, Northeast Missouri State University. (Relating the arts to education.)

Kelly, E.Y. (1975). *The magic if: Stanislavski for children.* Hyattsville, Maryland: National Educational Consultants. (Drama, how to, grades 6–8.)

Khatena, J. (1978). *The creatively gifted child: Suggestions for parents and teachers.* New York: Vantage Press. (For teachers and parents for enrichment activities.)

Kiely, A. (1975). Lend me your ears . . . or at least draw me a picture. *Volta Review,* 77, 423–30. (Use of pictures and drawings to help develop speech and vocabulary.)

Klinger, E. (1971). *Structure and functions of fantasy.* New York: John Wiley and Sons. (The role of imagination and fantasy in learning.)

Knieter, G.L. & Stallings, J. (1979). *The teaching process and the arts and aesthetics.* St. Louis, Missouri: CEMREL, Inc. (For teachers for use with all youngsters.)

Koenke, K. (1980). Pictures and reading. *Journal of Reading,* 23, 650–53. (For teachers to use with remediation activities.)

Krone, A. (1978). *Art instruction for handicapped children.* Denver, Colorado: Love Publishing Company. (For teachers and parents in mainstreaming activities.)

Labuda, M. (1974). *Creative reading for gifted learners: A design for excellence.* Newark, Delaware: International Reading Association. (For teachers and parents for enrichment activities.)

Langer, S.K. (1964). Abstraction in art. *Journal of Aesthetics and Art Criticism.* 22, 379–92. (Use this work by Langer to obtain an insightful approach to aesthetics in education.)

Leese, S. & Packer, M. (1980). *Dance in schools.* Exeter, New Hampshire: Heinemann Educational Books, Inc. (For teachers.)

Ley, T.C. (1974). Getting kids into books: The importance of individualized reading. *Media and Methods.* 15, 22–24. (For teachers to be used for remedial and enrichment activities.)

Lieberman, J.N. (1977). *Playfulness: Its relationship to imagination and creativity.* New York: Academic Press. (For teachers and parents.)

Lowenfeld, Viktor & Brittain, W.L. (1975). *Creative and mental growth.* New York: Macmillan Company. (For teachers.)

Lundsteen, S.W. (1971). *Listening: Its impact on reading and the other language arts.* Urbana, Illinois: National Council of Teachers of English and ERIC. (Of interest to elementary, secondary and college teachers. Calls for articulation of the language arts.)

Lyon, Jr., H.C. (1971). *Learning to feel—feeling to learn.* Columbus, Ohio: Charles E. Merrill Publishing Company. (For teachers—especially useful in teaching affective objectives.)

Martin, L.Y. (1978). The role of play in the learning process. *The Educational Forum, 43*, 51–58. (For teachers and parents of primary grade youngsters.)

McCaleb, J.L. & Korman, D.L. (1978). Role-taking: A measure of communication development. *The English Journal, 67*, 41–45. (Use of role play and reference to an intended audience.)

McCarr, D. (1973). Individualized reading for junior and senior high school students. *American Annals for the Deaf, 118*, 488–95. (For teachers in remedial and enrichment activities.)

McCaslin, Nellie. (1974). *Creative dramatics in the classroom, second edition.* New York: Longman. (For teachers and parents.)

McDermott, E.F. (1971). Storytelling: A relaxed and natural path to lipreading, language and reading. *Volta Review, 73*, 54–57. (For teachers.)

Meccinate, J. & Phelps, S. (1980). Classroom drama from children's reading: From the page to the stage. *The Reading Teacher, 34*, 269–72. (For teachers.)

Moffett, J. & Wagner, B.J. (1976). *Student-centered language arts and reading, K–12: A handbook for teachers.* Boston: Houghton Mifflin. (May be used for remediation and enrichment.)

Moore, J.C., Jones, C.J. & Miller, D.C. (1980). What do we know after a decade of sustained silent reading? *The Reading Teacher, 33*, 445–50. (Use of silent reading coupled with meditation.)

Morrow, L.M. (1979). *Super tips for story telling.* New York: Instructor Publications. (For teachers and parents.)

Newby, R. (1974). Language and reading: A visual structure. *American Annals for the Deaf, 119*, 572–77. (Suggests use of illustrations, pictures, and drawings to teach meaning of abstract terms.)

Newsom, S. (1979). Can reading skills of teenagers in remedial classes be improved through the use of popular song lyrics? *Journal of Reading, 22*, 726–30. (Teenagers may enjoy this article.)

Paivio, A. & Csapo, K. (1969). Concrete image and verbal memory codes. *Journal of Experimental Psychology,* 80, 279–85. (A look at visual thinking from a research angle.)

Paivio, A. (1971). *Imagery and verbal processes.* New York: Holt, Rinehart and Winston. (Treatment of memory storage, images and imagery.)

Paivio, A. (1975). Imagery and long-term memory. In Alan Kennedy and Alan Wilkes (Eds.) *Studies in Long-term Memory,* New York: John Wiley and Sons. (Resource for empirical data or memory.)

Perelman, C. (1981). (Translated by William Kluback). *The realm of rhetoric.* Notre Dame, Indiana: University of Notre Dame Press. (Important book on writing for the gifted and talented.)

Piaget, J. (1951). *Play, dreams and imitation in childhood.* New York: Norton. (A classic.)

Piaget, J. (1960). *The child's conception of the world.* Patterson, New Jersey: Littlefield Adams. (A classic.)

Randhawa, B. & Coffman W.E. (1978). *Visual learning, thinking and communication.* New York: Academic Press. (Visual perception and learning. Mental mapping and naming. Visual simile and meaning. Pictorial comprehension. Mental images and original ideas.)

Relaxing for productive classroom learning. (1980). Six cassettes, for 5–18-year-old students. They are: Getting ready to listen; Calming down from playtime; Calming down from anger; Calming down from frustration; Turning sadness upside down; Learning from failure; Hyperactivity control; Tension vs. relaxation and Relaxing and slowing down. Ottawa, Illinois: Facilitation House.

Reynolds, A.G. & Flagg, P.W. (1977). *Cognitive psychology.* Cambridge, Massachusetts: Winthrop Publishing. (Suggests that there is a high correlation between the mental imagery of a word and its meaningfulness to a reader or hearer.)

Ritch, P.S. (1979). *Creative drama as a teaching strategy: Historical review and organizing framework.* Unpublished dissertation. *Dissertation Abstracts International,* 39, 4032A–33A.

Rockefeller, D. (1978). *Coming to our senses: The significance of the arts for American education.* New York: McGraw Hill Book Company, Inc. (A strong case for the arts in our schools.)

Ross, M. (1981). *The creative arts.* Exeter, New Hampshire: Heinemann Educational Books, Inc. (The nature of creativity. Relevant educational and psychological research in explaining the creative nature of human beings. Arts education curriculum.)

Ross, R.R. (1972). *Storyteller.* Columbus, Ohio: Charles E. Merrill. (Oral literature, choral reading, puppetry, singing, flannel board stories.)

Sarason, I.G. (1974). *Constructive classroom behavior: A teachers' guide to modeling and role playing techniques.* New York: Behavioral Publications. (May be used with students of all ages.)

Saunders, R.J. (1972). *Teaching through art.* New York: American Book Company. (Art print series.)

Saunders, R.J. (1977). *Relating art and humanities in the classroom.* Dubuque, Iowa: William C. Brown Company Publishers. (May be used in interdisciplinary teaching.)

Schlobin, R.C. (Ed.). (1982). *The aesthetics of fantasy literature and art.* Notre Dame, Indiana: University of Notre Dame Press. (For the gifted and talented. Topics include: the nature of fantasy, ethical fantasy for children: realms of literary fantasy; heroic fantasy and social reality; modern fantasy fiction.)

Schwartzman, H.B. (1978). *Transformations: The anthropology of children's play.* New York: Plenum Publishing Corporation. (Theoretical study of arts and meaning, drama, play, and anthropology.)

Sealey, L., Sealy, N. & Millmore, M. (1979). *Children's writing: An approach for the primary grades.* Newark, Delaware: International Reading Association. (For teachers and parents.)

Selfe, L. (1979). *Nadia: A case of extraordinary drawing ability in an autistic child.* New York: Harcourt, Brace, Jovanovich. (For teachers.)

Silver, R.A. (1981). *Developing cognitive and creative skills through art.* Bellevue, Washington: Edmark Associates. (For teachers.)

Sizer, Theodore R. (1973). *Places for learning, places for joy.* Cambridge, Massachusetts: Harvard University Press. (Necessity for general affect in school.)

Spiegel, D.L. (1981). *Reading for pleasure: Guidelines.* Newark, Delaware: International Reading Association. (Research on recreational reading; motivation of students; classroom library; grouping; widening student interests.)

Spolin, Viola. (1963). *Improvisation for the theater.* Evanston, Illinois: Northwestern University Press. (Should be in every teacher's library.)

Stanford, Gene. (Ed.) (1981). Classroom practices 1980–81: *Dealing with differences.* Urbana, Illinois: National Council for Teachers of English. (A must for teachers.)

Stark, B. (1976). A look at comic books at Illinois School for the Deaf, *American Annals for the Deaf,* 121, 470–77. (For teachers, parents and students.)

Stauffer, R. G. (1979). The language experience approach to reading instruction for deaf and hearing impaired children. *The Reading Teacher,* 33, 21–24. (For teachers.)

Strain, P.S. (Ed.) (1981). *The utilization of classroom peers as behavior change agents.* New York: Plenum Publishing Corporation. (For teachers.)

Swain, E.H. (1978). Using comic books to teach reading and language arts. *Journal of Reading,* 22, 253–58. (For teachers and parents.)

Swanson, H.L. & Reinert, H.R. (1979). *Teaching strategies for children in conflict.* St. Louis, Missouri: Mosby, Times Mirror. (Ideas for working with children who have emotional, behavioral problems.)

Swift, M.S. & Spivack, G. (1981). *Alternative teaching strategies.* Bellevue, Washington: Edmark Associates. (Offers wide repertoire of teaching approaches.)

Taylor, M.J. (1978). Using photos to teach comprehension skills. *Journal of Reading,* 21, 318 ff. (For teachers.)

Torrance, E.P. & Myers, R. (1970). *Creative learning and teaching.* New York: Dodd, Mead and Company. (Should be read by all teachers.)

Walkup, L.E. (1965). Creativity in science through visualization. *Perceptual and Motor Skills,* 21, 35–41. (For teachers.)

Ward, M. & McCormick, S. (1981). Reading instruction for blind and low vision children in the regular classroom. *The Reading Teacher,* 34, 434–44. (A good source for mainstreaming visually-impaired youngsters.)

Weinstein, G. & Fantini, M.D. (1971). *Toward humanistic education: A curriculum of affect.* New York: Praeger Publications for the Ford Foundation. (Another perspective to be considered in the classroom.)

Werner, P.H. & Burton, E. (1979). *Learning through movement: Teaching cognitive content through physical activities.* St. Louis, Missouri: Mosby, Times Mirror. (Good for mainstreaming.)

Witkin, R.W. (1974). *The intelligence of feeling.* Exeter, New Hampshire: Heinemann Educational Books, Inc. (For teachers and parents.)

Zinar, R. (1976). Reading language and reading music, is there a connection? *Music Educators' Journal,* 62, 70–76. (For teachers.)

SELECTED INSTRUCTIONAL MATERIALS

*indicates that the materials would be of special interest to the gifted and talented student.

*Abbs, Peter. (1971). *English broadsheets.* London: Heinemann Educational Books, Ltd. and New York: Silver Burdett. Writing ideas.

*Anderson, Yvonne. (1970). *Make your own animated movies.* Boston: Little, Brown and Co.

The artist's eye: Pictorial composition. Washington, D.C.: The National Gallery of Art Extension Program (Catalogue Number 010). Color slide program, 75 slides, 40 minute record, test.

Artyping, third edition. Baltimore, Maryland: Artistic Typing Headquarters, Teaching Aids Division, 3200 Southgreen Road 21207. (Use of fingers and eye control to devise artistic typing. Also included is Typewriter Art Filmstrip, 35mm., border designs, lettering, monograms, cross stitch designs, etc.)

*Ashby-Davis, Claire & Bonnici, Charles. (1976). *Hidden meanings.* Part of *PLAN reading in the content areas: English.* Oak Lawn, Illinois: Ideal. (How to read and write poems, plays, stories.)

Ashby-Davis, Claire. (1978). *Can of squirms, number 13: Secondary teacher education edition.* Downers Grove, Illinois: Contemporary Drama (Role play for teachers to be used in staff development. Stresses dilemmas in class and school which sample interactions between teachers and students, supervisors, other teachers, and parents.)

Blackwell, P.M., et al. (1978). *Sentences and other systems: A language and learning curriculum for hearing impaired children.* Washington, D.C.: Alexander Graham Bell Association for the Deaf. (Grades K–12, reading/writing/language development.)

Boiko, Claire. (1980). *Dramatized parodies of familiar stories.* Boston: Plays, Inc. (Simple plays.)

Boni, Margaret Bradford & Lloyd, Norman. (1947). *Fireside book of folk songs.* New York: Simon and Schuster. (Outstanding selections with colorful illustrations. Learning to read through memorization and attention to words in lyrics is suggested here.)

Books on tape. Catalogue available from Books on Tape, Department B, P.O. Box 7900, Newport Beach, California 92660. (Full length readings of best sellers on cassettes.)

Broudy, Harry. (1977). How basic is aesthetic education? Audiotape cassettes. Alexandria, Virginia: Association for Supervision and Curriculum Development. (For teachers and parents. 58 minutes.)

Brown-Azarowicz, Marjorie Frances. (1970). *A handbook of creative choral speaking.* Minneapolis: Burgess Publishing Co. (In a mainstreamed classroom, poor and good readers use these techniques to improve their flow of rendition and use of tone.)

Project C.A.I.R. (1975). Thompson, Connecticut: InterCulture Associates, (A kit containing an 11-day curriculum for grades 7–10. Free sample packet available. Cultures in the pupils' community are studied. Students act like anthropologists. Box 277, Thompson, Connecticut 06277.)

Classroom authors' kit. North Bellerica, Massachusetts: Curriculum Associates. (Grades 5–12. Students simulate being authors, agents, editors, publishers, bankers. Works are sold for publication.) Curriculum Associates, 5 Esquire Road, North Bellerica, Massachusetts 01862.

Classroom pairing reading tutorial starter set. (1973). Brooklyn, New York: Book Lab, Inc. (Pre-reading to 4.5 reading level. Pair tutoring is an excellent grouping for mainstreamed classes.)

Craft. Stevensville, Michigan: Educational Services, Inc., P.O. Box 219, 49127. (Offers students creative work in fossil prints, collage, burlap distortions, and op art.)

Create. Stevensville, Michigan: Educational Services, Inc., P.O. Box 219, 49127. (For the entire class. Photographs, diagrams, sponge prints, puppets, sand sculpture, weaving, 22 crayon activities.)

The creative classroom: Ideas for the intermediate grades. (1978). Stamford, Connecticut: Teachers Resources Library. (100 creative ideas by teachers. 77 Bedford Street, Stamford, Connecticut 06901.)

Davis, Maetta. (1980). *Typing keys for remediation of reading and spelling.* Novato, California: Academic Therapy Publications.

*De Kay, Ormonde (Trans.) (1980). *N'Heures souris rames.* (Nursery rhymes). New York: Clarkson N. Potter, Inc., (Word plays at a sophisticated level.)

The diagram group: Comparisons. (1980). New York: St. Martin's Press. (Development of visual perception. Visual comparison of animals, buildings, numbers, etc.)

*Dills, Lanie. (1976). *The official CB slanguage language dictionary.* Nashville, Tennessee: Lanie Dills. Distributed by Louis J. Martins and Associates, Inc., 95 Madison Avenue, New York, New York 10016.

**Domains in language and composition.* (1972). New York: Harcourt, Brace & Jovanovich, Inc. (24 paperbacks, grades 9–12, offering a wide variety of models, exercises and assignments.)

**Elaborative thinking: Intermediate.* North Bellerica, Massachusetts: Curriculum Associates, 5 Esquire Road, 01862. (Small group work in stretching the imagination. Reading and writing activities.)

Expression puppet. Incentives for Learning, Inc., 6000 West Van Buren Street, Chicago, Illinois 60607. (Velcro noses, eyes, mouths enable students to change expression on puppet to represent their own or others' feelings.)

Golick Margie. (1978). *Deal me in! The use of playing cards in teaching and learning.* New York: Jeffry Norton Publishers, Inc.

Got to be me. The Teachers Market Place, 16220 Orange Avenue, Paramount California 90723. (Elementary grades. Discussion cards. Workbooks. Role Playing. Mock interviews. Unfinished sentences.)

Gousett, James W. (1971). *Pantomimes 101.* Chicago, Illinois: The Dramatic Publishing Co. (Hearing impaired and deaf students can join hearing students in meaningful activities.)

Grady, Tom (Ed.) (n.d.). *Free stuff for kids: (The best of free and up to a dollar things kids can send for by mail).* Meadowbrook Press, Wayzata, Minnesota 55391. (Motivation for letter writing and follow-up discussion.)

HITS (High Interest Teaching Systems). Modu Learn, Inc., P.O. Box 3178, Mission Viejo, California 92690. (Cassettes of popular and rock songs, with related reading skills.)

Incentives for learning, parquetry plus. Incentives for Learning, Inc., 600 West Van Buren Street, Chicago, Illinois 60607. (Round, diamond, square shapes of different colors. Concepts taught are: whole to part, part to whole, designs, shapes to real structures.)

Kids' stuff books. Incentives Publications, Box 12552, Nashville, Tennessee 37212. (Activities book.)

Knight, G.C. *Building children's personality through creative dance.* (16 mm film. Color or b/w. Distributed by the Indiana University Film Library.)

Laye, Andrew. (1972). *Creative rubbings.* New York: Watson-Guptell Publications. (Use of fingers and arms — gross muscles. Seeing ordinary things in a new way.)

Walker plays for oral reading, grades 4–10. Curriculum Associates, 5 Esquire Road, North Bellerica, Massachusetts 01862. (Reading roles are at reading levels 3.1 to 5.5 for each play. Six copies of 12 titles in each set.)

Wittner, Joe & Myrick, Robert D. (1974). *Facilitating teaching: Theory and practice.* Pacific Palisades, California: Goodyear Publishing Co. (For the teacher, filled with more than 100 practical examples for facilitating questions, fantasy procedures, imagery procedures, classes in talking about feelings, and development of self-appraisal.)

Woodcock, Richard, Clark, C. & Oakes-Davis, Cornelius. (1979). *Peabody rebus reading program.* Circle Pines, Minnesota: American Guidance Service. (Teaches by use of the rebus, puts pictures into words.)

Writing through posters. Argus Communications, 7440 Natchez Avenue, Niles, Illinois. (Students use warm up, observation, analysis, interpretation skills, and a checklist for criteria evaluation of writing.)

Zubrowski, Bernie. (1979). *Children's museum activity books.* Boston: Little, Brown and Co. (For that field trip.)

RESOURCES

Alexander Graham Bell Association for the Deaf
    3417 Volta Place, N.W.
    Washington, D.C. 20007

American Association for the Advancement of Behavior Therapy
    420 Lexington Avenue
    New York, New York 10017

American Association for the Education of the Severely/Profoundly Handicapped
    1600 West Armory Way
    Garden View Suite
    Seattle, Washington 98119

American Association on Mental Deficiency
    5201 Connecticut Avenue, N.W.
    Washington, D.C. 20015

American Council for the Arts
    Publications/Catalogues
    570 Seventh Avenue
    New York, New York 10018

American Diabetes Association
    600 Fifth Avenue
    New York, New York 10020

American Foundation for the Blind
    15 West 16th Street
    New York, New York 10011

American Library Association
    50 East Huron Street
    Chicago, Illinois 60611

American Mensa
    1701 West 3rd Street
    Brooklyn, New York 11223
    (For those who score in top 2% on an intelligence test)

American Museum of Natural History
    Central Park West — 78th St.
    New York, New York 10024
    (Tours for special children and youth, for the visually impaired, and a sit-down discovery room.)

American Printing House for the Blind
    1839 Frankfort Avenue
    Louisville, Kentucky 40206
    (Braille, large print, records)

American Speech and Hearing Association
    10801 Rockville Pike
    Rockville, Maryland 20852

Association for Children with Learning Disabilities
    5225 Grace Street
    Pittsburgh, Pennsylvania 15236

Association for Children with Retarded Mental Development
    902 Broadway
    New York, New York 10010

Association for the Gifted of the Council for Exceptional Children
    1920 Association Drive
    Reston, Virginia 22091

The Children's Book Council, Inc.
    67 Irving Place
    New York, New York 10003

Children's Television Workshop
    (Activity Workbook)
    1 Lincoln Plaza
    New York, New York 10023

Council for Children with Behavior Disorders of The Council
    for Exceptional Children
    1920 Association Drive
    Reston, Virginia 22091

The Council for Exceptional Children
    1920 Association Drive
    Reston, Virginia 22091

Department of Specialized Educational Services
    Madison Metropolitan School District
    545 West Dayton Street
    Madison, Wisconsin 53703
    (Curriculum Guides)

Division for Children with Learning Disabilities of The Council
    for Exceptional Children
    1920 Association Drive
    Reston, Virginia 22091

The Division for Early Childhood
    The Council for Exceptional Children
    1920 Association Drive
    Reston, Virginia 22091

Division on Career Development
    The Council for Exceptional Children
    1920 Association Drive
    Reston, Virginia 22091

Division on Mental Retardation
    The Council for Exceptional Children
    1920 Association Drive
    Reston, Virginia 22091

EDMARC
    Educational Materials Review Center
    400 Maryland Avenue, S.W.
    Washington, D.C. 20202

Epilepsy Foundation of America
    1828 L Street, N.W.
    Washington, D.C. 20036

Gallaudet College
> 7th and Florida Avenue, N.E.
> Washington, D.C. 20002
> (Free book list of their collection of professional and popular literature about hearing
> > impairment)

Marc Gold and Associates
> P.O. Box 5100
> Austin, Texas 78763
> (Task analysis of instructional strategies for severely handicapped persons for daily living
> > and vocational skills.)

International Committee Against Mental Illness
> 40 East 69th Street
> New York, New York 10028

Jewish Braille Institute of America
> 110 East 30 Street
> New York, New York 10016

Media Services and Captioned Films Branch
> Bureau of Education for the Handicapped
> 7th and D Streets, S.W.
> Washington, D.C. 20202
> (Free loan of captioned films and other media to schools and organizations which serve
> > hearing impaired persons. Catalogue available.)

Muscular Dystrophy Association of America
> 810 7th Avenue
> New York, New York 10019

National Association for Retarded Citizens
> 2709 Avenue E East
> Arlington, Texas 76011

National Association for Visually Handicapped
> 305 East 24th Street
> New York, New York 10010

National Association of the Deaf
> 814 Thayer Avenue
> Silver Spring, Maryland 20910

National Captioning Institute, Inc.
> 5203 Leesburg Pike
> Falls Church, Virginia 22041

National Easter Seal Society for Crippled Children and Adults
    800 Second Avenue
    New York, New York 10016

National Federation of the Blind
    218 Randolph Hotel Building
    Des Moines, Iowa 50309

National Multiple Sclerosis Society
    257 Park Avenue South
    New York, New York 10010

National Society for the Prevention of Blindness
    79 Madison Avenue
    New York, New York 10016

Office of the Gifted and Talented
    U.S. Office of Education
    Washington, D.C. 20202

The Orton Dyslexia Society
    80 Fifth Avenue — Room 903
    New York, New York 10011

Recording for the Blind, Inc.
    215 East 58th Street
    New York, New York 10022

John Tracy Clinic
    806 West Adams Blvd.
    Los Angeles, California 90007
    (Free correspondence courses for parents of young deaf and deaf-blind children.)

DIRECTORIES OF INTEREST

Directory of Agencies Serving the Visually Handicapped in the United States
    American Foundation of the Blind
    15 West 16th Street
    New York, New York 10011

Directory of Catholic Special Facilities and Programs in the United States for Handicapped Children and Adults, Sixth Edition.
    National Catholic Educational Association
    One Dupont Circle, Suite 350
    Washington, D.C. 20036